About this book

Heather McClelland, BA, Dip Ed, Dip PS, Dip Social Health is a qualified body-focused narrative therapist who has worked in clinical practice for thirty years. Her case load has always included a high proportion of people living with the many devastating life ramifications of developmental trauma.

In '*The Magic Loom*' Heather invites adults who survived trauma in their childhood to become more aware of their sensations. She helps them interweave the narratives and wisdom of both body and mind as they safely explore and make meaning of the past and put it behind them. This is a text for therapists primarily, teaching with metaphor and case-study. Therapists will discover why and how weaving the body and mind together in interpersonal narrative style conversations meets the needs that contemporary scientific research is clarifying.

It is the author's hope that survivors themselves may find they can identify with the stories of trauma recovery as they unfold and engage with '*The Magic Loom's*' conversational style and translation of the languages of therapy and of science.

Praise for The Magic Loom

In this beautifully crafted book Heather McClelland illustrates tending to the body's expressions of distress within a therapeutic conversation. Stories of practice provide powerful and moving examples of how she respectfully weaves a body focus into narrative therapy conversations. This inspiring book will be of interest to practitioners working in any context where the body's voice needs to be heard and responded to.

Sasha McAllum Pilkington, narrative therapist, specialty palliative care

I was so taken with this book that I kept wanting to read ahead. Each time I read further I found myself being moved by its depth. This is the first clinical work to make the connection between narrative therapy and somatic approaches in such a practical and clear manner. The author reminds us that the body does remember the forgotten stories that are often held in it. Narrative approaches combine well with principles of somatic therapy providing many ways for the client to re-author the stories. This work is an excellent clinical tool for therapists wanting to work in more of a body-connected and body-knowing postmodern therapy which honors such connections.

Rafis Nin, LCSW, EMDR Trauma Psychotherapist and Narrative practitioner

Heather McClelland's The Magic Loom *will be of particular interest to counsellors and psychotherapists wanting to integrate narrative and somatic approaches utilizing state-of-the-art findings from neuropsychology. Heather's combination of theory with case examples make for a great teaching text, whilst her clear exposition will also be of interest to the general public. Recommended.*

Robert Quinlan B.A., B.SW., Dip. S.O. Hyp., M.A.A.S.W. (acc), Mental Health Practitioner (Medicare acc.), university lecturer, national and international workshop facilitator and senior counsellor in fields such as addiction recovery, palliative care, chronic illness, hypnotherapy.

The Magic Loom *provides a very readable concise integration of therapeutic modalities supported with client story, practical interventions and post the event client feedback. There is throughout the text a brilliantly nuanced use of therapeutic metaphor. As the role of metaphor is foundational in both Narrative and Body Psychotherapies reading this text becomes a teaching tool in itself. I look forward to using it as a text for courses in Psychotherapy making full use of its comprehensive yet concise summary of theory and its close association with practice.*

Doug Sotheren B.A., M.Th., Dip. R.E., CCA., counsellor/clinical supervisor/group trainer in the fields of Relationship Counselling, Clinical Supervision and Somatic approaches to counselling practice.

The Magic Loom's *deeply human and inspiring, yet humbling case-studies and snippets, deftly interwoven with the author's perspective on narrative therapy and body therapy, stretch the reader to think freshly about both modalities in a most hopeful and multi-dimensional way. The clarity of her prose gives the reader a glimpse into otherwise complex ideas and processes, making what is obscure accessible to general readers as well as to those engaged in the therapy field. Heather describes a process, a craft, an enquiry ... to unlock, invite, give voice to the hidden wisdom of the body in a profoundly respectful, collegial manner while ensuring that safety and equality are paramount.*

Eva Canning, MAPS B.A., B.Ed. (Counselling), senior counsellor and supervisor

I was greatly impressed with The Magic Loom. *The way the author weaves her personal experience and growth of knowledge into the book gives a very gentle feel to the text, unlike most text books. It's as if she is conversing with the reader, teaching quietly, rather than baldly stating facts and conclusions. I read through tears at many times and ultimately I'm left feeling immensely grateful for what the author is advocating. I believe this will be a very valuable book. The choice to use 'she' as the generic pronoun gave me a kick of enjoyable satisfaction every time I saw it. I'm not sure I've ever read a 'textbook' before that uses 'she' as the generic.*

Robyn Phillips, Lawyer BA(Hons) LLB(Hons) and Social Development Consultant MSD

The Magic Loom *provided me with an engaging, insightful reading experience and it gives me hope that early childhood trauma can be addressed more commonly with this gentle, compassionate therapy that trusts and works with the body's own wisdom. I loved the author's kind, respectful approach to both the subject and her clients. Many times I was moved by the interaction between client and therapist. I gained a lot of personal understanding while witnessing the contributor's stories and processes. I feel this is an important book that bridges the understanding of the neuroscience of early trauma with tools for healing at a really core level.*

Sue Collins, educational administrator

This book is dedicated to the people who lived its stories.

Published by:
Heather Jean McClelland
Uki, NSW, Australia
hmcclelland66@gmail.com

 A catalogue record for this book is available from the National Library of Australia

Text copyright Heather McClelland

First published in Australia in 2018

All rights reserved. No part of this publication may be reproduced, stored in a retrieval system or transmitted in any form or by any means, electronic, mechanical, photocopying, recording or otherwise, without the prior written permission of the publisher unless it is to be used for educational and/or therapeutic purposes.

ISBN 978 0 646 99018 7

Editor: Julie O'Brien

Designer: Tina Wilson

Cover page image: Susan Kinneally

The Magic Loom

Weaving body and mind in narrative therapy conversations with survivors of early trauma.

Heather McClelland

Note: The female singular personal pronoun is used throughout this book except when a male is being referred to.

Acknowledgements

It is often said that an author is changed by the process of writing. This has certainly been true for me. Many of my faltering suppositions and experiments have been validated and given greater weight. I continue to be excited by the way the model works in practice as I encounter others whose lived experience and responses to a body-focused narrative approach reverberate with what I have learned from others before them and found to be backed up by the weight of research evidence.

I would like to again thank all the people who so willingly contributed their narratives and at a later stage helped me to refine and authenticate the documentation of our shared conversations. In many ways each of you has become a co-author with me of this new therapy model. I'm very grateful for the unique ways you have each given it your commendation. It is because of your collegial support that The Magic Loom has been written into existence.

Extra special thanks go to my mentor Jonathan McClelland. Without his understanding of narrative approaches, his gifts of curiosity, validation, honest critique and amazing patience, this book-writing task may have foundered.

It goes without saying that I am indebted to the array of researchers, lecturers and writers whose treasure I have mined in order to make greater sense of what I was encountering in my work.

I am indebted beyond words to former psychotherapist, now editor, Julie O'Brien, who has thrown her professional support behind this therapy model and its metaphor and has helped to ensure that the manuscript is worthy of its message.

My thanks go out to artist and friend Susan Kinneally whose support for the book is evident in the work she has put into the book's beautifully composed cover.

Tina Wilson is the person who has both designed this book and mentored me through the intricate publishing process. As a result of her knowledge, flexibility and wisdom, The Magic Loom can be accessed in the hard copy, print-on-demand and electronic book categories. She is quite simply, a wonderful person with whom to work.

I am grateful to a number of readers from the narrative therapy community world-wide who have written in praise of The Magic Loom as well as colleagues, friends and family members who have also read, advised and written their praise. Particular thanks go to Poh Lin Lee who wrote the book's foreword in France in the midst of an incredibly intense family and professional schedule.

To my husband Bryan go my heartfelt thanks for accompanying and encouraging me through every stage of the book project's long gestation.

Heather McClelland

Foreword

Poh Lin Lee, B.Soc Work, M. Narrative Therapy and Community Work, currently works as a Therapy Trainer, Supervisor, Counsellor and Consultant at Narrative Imaginings, France and is part of the international Teaching Faculty of the Dulwich Centre, Adelaide, Australia. She has worked in a wide range of countries particularly with displaced people who have a history of torture and trauma.

In this current western context, going slow, listening to the body and engaging in a relationship with our bodies with an ethic of care, is not just a therapeutic approach, it is a political act. An act that protests and resists the ways in which harm is inflicted upon our bodies, trespassed by others and controlled by discourses of body image, militant practices of exercise/wellness and coerced to keep up the frantic pace of what is expected of us.

The body, for people seeking asylum and held in mandatory detention is significant in its relationship to our ability to protest and enact agency when human rights and status are withheld. In my context as a narrative therapist responding to people displaced by persecution, state-inflicted violence and seeking asylum, the idea of trauma is interchangeable with acts of social injustice.

Trauma or social injustice seeks to disconnect us from our sense of self, our identities, our bodies, our loved ones, our communities, our hopes and intentions. The trauma or injustice towards one serves to benefit another. We cannot be discussing therapeutic responses to trauma without considering power at all times; to engage in therapy is to engage in social and political action.

On first glance the idea of considering our relationship to our body may look like an individual, exercise. However with a narrative therapy lens we start to deconstruct how our relationship to our body is constructed by multiple stories shaped by the diversity of the world we are immersed in - family, culture, community, society, history, legacy, discourse, politics… and then we start to arrive at the complexity of these stories in action in our very bodies down to the cellular level - and there we are left humbled by how much we have to learn through these conversations with our body.

Heather proposes, through this account of her shared conversations and thinking behind her practice, an invitation to us to consider how multiple bodies of knowledge can be brought together to offer a multifaceted response to trauma. In this artful weaving of the magic loom Heather avoids the different approaches merging into a knotted mess and demonstrates a steady hand in maintaining the integrity of each approach in its focus and intention, recognisable from one another whilst complementary and attuned.

It is impressive that, despite the practices originating from diverse and at times seemingly contradictory theoretical positions, Heather takes time to build a shared ground that supports partnership rather than competitiveness between the different approaches. This shared ground is reflected through a foundation of ethical practice and therapeutic posture that is consistently carried throughout both the explanations of theory and the richly told stories of practice.

Heather invites those of us, who are practitioners responding to trauma in diverse contexts, to consider a more inclusive approach in our work in response to people and the trauma that overshadows in the most powerful way – one that is holistic and embodied from the wider context down to the stories that reside within our bodies.

Poh Lin Lee.

B.Soc Work, M. Narrative Therapy and Community Work

Contents

Introduction 1

    Narrative foundations of this model.. 2

    Over-reactivity - a potent trauma signal 3

    Development of a new approach.. 7

    How the book is organised 8

PART ONE - The Theory and the Model 9

Chapter 1 - Narrative Therapy 11

    Narrative approaches to therapy 12

    A personal journey..19

    Narrative history and philosophy...21

    Narrative work with trauma 23

    An intersubjective creation of meaning...26

    Conclusion 27

Chapter 2 - Contemporary Somatic Therapy..29

    Western cultural assumptions about the body..30

    The history of body therapy..31

    The transformative practice of body therapy...33

    How Pearl's body told its story..38

    Resonance and intersubjectivity 40

    Ethical considerations..42

    Conclusion 44

Chapter 3 - Trauma and Trauma Therapy 47

    Complex developmental trauma...48

    Triggering and sensations...52

    Memories of trauma 58

    Trauma therapy requires embodied relational processes......................61

    Conclusion..63

Chapter 4 - The Magic Loom 65

    The body as the first responder to trauma..65

    A three-phased body scaffold approach..68

    Using body strategies to calm arousal...71

    The Magic Loom 77

THE MAGIC LOOM

PART TWO - The Practice 81

Chapter 5 - Hannah's Experiential Journey 83
Complex developmental trauma and trust 87
Therapeutic rocking 93
Hannah has the last word 95

Chapter 6 - Making Theoretical Meaning of Hannah's Experience 99
Intense sensations and neural firing patterns 99
Raising awareness of the body leads to cognitive change 100
Attachment and regulation 100
Prolonged stress and trauma on a continuum 101
The rocking experiment 101
Awakening maternal templates to improve regulation 102
Early manifestations of shame and terror 102
Changing disturbed physical action patterns 103
Optimising the therapy relationship 103
Conclusion 106

Chapter 7 - Body-focused Narrative Conversations Featuring Isolation 107
Mindy attains her own resilience 107
The Magic Loom at work with Mindy 114
Tim discovers a new way of relating 115
The Magic Loom at work with Tim 120
Rick increases his emotional cohesion 120
The Magic Loom at work with Rick 123

Chapter 8 - Body-focused Narrative Approach to Transforming Emotions 125
Kerry takes hesitant steps towards self-compassion 125
The Magic Loom at work with Kerry 128
Pearl moves into a new relationship with her anger 128
The Magic Loom at work with Pearl 131
Gerry finds new self-definition 132
The Magic Loom at work with Gerry 134

Chapter 9 - Weaving Body-based Issues into Narrative Conversations 135
Anton reconnects to his roots 135
The Magic Loom at work with Anton 141
Kerry finds a new sense of agency 142
The Magic Loom at work with Kerry 145
Hannah chooses passion over procrastination 145
The Magic Loom at work with Hannah 147

CONTENTS

Chapter 10 - Rocking as a Body-focused Narrative Therapy Strategy....................149

Simeon acknowledges his own inner wisdom..149

The Magic Loom at work with Simeon...152

Simeon's experience of rocking..153

The Magic Loom at work with Simeon...154

Samantha finds new confidence in re-authoring her narrative.....................154

Samantha's experience of rocking...158

The Magic Loom at work with Samantha...161

Chapter 11 - Body-focused Narrative Therapy with Couples 163

Linda discovers an intergenerational understanding of her early trauma 163

The Magic Loom at work with Linda and Rick..168

Clem weaves a path to liberation..169

The Magic Loom at work with Clem 171

Angela deepens her understanding of over-reactivity.................................171

The Magic Loom at work with Angela 172

Angela and Clem become newly aware of each other................................172

Anthony and Elizabeth make sense of their relational conflict....................174

The Magic Loom at work with Anthony and Elizabeth..................................179

Chapter 12 - Body-focused Narrative Therapy with Children, Adolescents and Families.....181

Amy builds her own safe boundaries...181

The Magic Loom at work with Amy..185

Heidi writes her own counter-document...185

The Magic Loom at work with Heidi 187

Mindy provides holistic support for her children 187

The Magic Loom at work with Mindy, Larry and Becky................................190

Owen finds empowerment and connection..190

The Magic Loom at work with Owen 195

Carly discovers a sense of significance and equality...................................196

The Magic Loom at work with Carly and her family.....................................199

Conclusion..201

Features of the model..201

Philip advocates for the model..209

References..211

Epigraph Sources...217

About the Author...218

xiii

Introduction

The human organism ... interacts with the environment as an ensemble.
Antonio Damasio

In this book, I introduce a new approach to narrative therapy, for use in particular, when working with people who have experienced early trauma. It explicitly includes the body and the body's narratives alongside those of the mind. In this approach, help is given to the therapy participant at the appropriate stage in the therapeutic conversation to become aware of her body and begin to listen to it. The aim is to give body processes the same space and freedom to express themselves as the mind is afforded when standard narrative approaches are pursued. As a person's awareness is raised, she begins to discover her body's narratives and inherent wisdom. This enables a level of healing that cannot be reached through the mind alone.

This approach emerged out of my ongoing professional development, which opened me up to new theoretical models, as well from my clinical experience, in which I noticed that engaging a person's body experience in the therapeutic conversation opened avenues for healing that we could not reach using cognitive processes alone.

My clinical work began in the 1980s, when adult survivors of child sexual abuse were just beginning to speak up about what they had experienced. The complicated impacts of such trauma had not been fully researched nor understood at that time. Survivors have continued to be highly represented among my clientele throughout thirty years as a therapist – probably not surprising when the incidence of developmental trauma is considered. To work more effectively with this cohort, I built on my arts degree and post-graduate diploma in pastoral counselling by undertaking successive postgraduate studies in somatic and narrative approaches to therapy.

The narrative refusal to take a top-down approach to therapy, and its emphasis on the creation of respectful and collegial approaches, struck me from the first as particularly well suited to trauma-related work. Its ways of externalising problems and seeking out alternative narratives to live by seemed extremely relevant approaches for those whose lives had been, and continued to be, subjugated by the impacts of early trauma.

As I grew experientially in my understanding of somatic psychotherapy, I also began to consider some of the evidence about traumatic impacts that researchers in neuroscience and other psychotherapeutic fields were amassing.

I began to embed the narrative and somatic therapy approaches in to my practice, and I worked, sometimes intuitively and creatively, sometimes analytically, to find ways to integrate them more effectively. At the same time, I wanted to guard against losing what is uniquely beneficial in the philosophy and practice of each.

A workshop conducted by internationally renowned trauma therapist Babette Rothschild, not long after I completed my postgraduate studies, inspired me. Not only did her respectful, client-centred and collegial therapy have a lot in common with narrative approaches, she also demonstrated many ways of engaging the body as well as the mind to support recovery. I was particularly attracted by her use of accessible body strategies to resource people so that they could lower their somatic sensory arousal. Hers became an influential therapy model for me of body-mind integration.

In 2016, I attended an international conference on child trauma. Hearing from a range of neuroscience-informed research scientists and therapists, who demonstrated their science- informed therapy work, also had an influence on me. I was affected by the respectful and gentle ways they engaged and connected with young traumatised children, as well as with adult survivors continuing to struggle with the trauma that had occurred in their childhoods.

Collaboration is central to narrative practice. The therapist is always learning from and alongside the client, and she too is changed by the encounter. The term 'intersubjectivity' (the sharing of subjective states by two or more people), to which I'd been first introduced during my somatic apprenticeship, is applicable to narrative practice. The interactive and de-centred therapy conversation and relationship ensures this experience (Duval & Béres, 2011), as there is always an equal meeting between two subjects. The client is the expert on her own life. As I expanded my theoretical and scientific knowledge, my trust in both narrative and somatic approaches to therapy strengthened. However, my clients, with their lived experience of the impacts of early trauma, contributed most to my education.

Narrative foundations of this model

Using an interpersonal and collegial approach, the narrative therapist helps a person to reflect on her life experiences and begin to look at them differently (White, 2007). It is hoped that through an explorative conversational process, the participant will discover a more life-affirming narrative.

The therapist joins with the person as she brings problems into the conversation, and does her best to listen and to understand the issues that are restraining the person's life. In the collaborative conversation, effort is made to generate preferred ways of living, which can then be embodied or acted on. The narratives themselves form the bridge between the person and the therapist. The more narrative therapy is studied, the more it becomes clear how complex the bridging is between the person with intimate knowledge of their experience and the listening therapist (Freedman & Combs, 2002).

It is self-evident that, like all approaches to therapy, narrative therapy is an embodied practice. The body is implicitly (usually unconsciously) present, and it exerts continuous personal and interpersonal influence, even when it is not explicitly mentioned or explored.

The narrative practitioner believes that it is not enough to merely generate ideas for preferred ways of living. These must be enacted or lived out. In fact, a re-authoring process that changes a person's life narrative does so by its becoming embodied. The person lives out their transformation. My thesis is that the more narrative therapy is understood, the more embodiment is also understood to be *sine qua non*.

The body has been described as new territory for the narrative practitioner (Shachar, 2010). The body-focused narrative therapist sets out to intentionally and explicitly expand the territory of enquiry. She does this in much the same embodied, interpersonal and collegial way as she does to highlight other little-explored territories of a person's life.

White (2007) makes the point that there can be gaps in the storylines of a person's life. Sometimes, he suggests, these gaps are so large that they exhaust a person's meaning-making resources. My proposal is that when early trauma is continuing to bring the past into the present in a person's life, disempowering gaps can be filled effectively by allowing her body to speak. The person who is consulting the narrative therapist may have long been experiencing the continuing repercussions of trauma in her life. Many of these affect her body. However, they have never been noticed or named. She is presenting for therapy because her own resources have been exhausted, and she is finding it difficult to come to terms with her present life challenges, let alone to resolve the past.

I don't recall the first time I asked someone about her body sensations. I'm not sure what prompted my curiosity in that direction. Perhaps my own body unconsciously felt the tension in the other person, and an intuition led me to make sensation the focus of my enquiry. However, one of those clients who helped me to understand the need to allow the body to speak was Tim.

Over-reactivity – a potent trauma signal

I commonly experienced people seeking help for their over-reactivity. They often described it as a sense of being emotionally overwhelmed or of feeling that life was out of control. I found myself speculating about the role early trauma might be playing in these people's lives.

Tim is an example of someone brought to therapy by the intensity of his emotional reactivity. A beloved pet had died, and Tim couldn't understand why his grief was so intense. He felt overwhelmed. His out-of-control feelings pointed me in the direction of his body. I asked Tim to give his attention to the sensations he had been feeling in his body when his grief was at its most intense.

In asking Tim this question, I was attempting to give his body its metaphorical voice. I was a colleague standing therapeutically alongside him. As I started to use words to express my curiosity about the impacts of triggering on his sensations, I was naturally making use of the investigative language routinely used to scaffold any narrative therapy conversation. However, I was intentionally using my words and engaging my curiosity in the service of Tim's body.

I was hoping that the curiosity I expressed would become infectious. If I could be consistent in connecting to Tim by means of body-awareness-raising questions, I hoped that he might be gradually bridged into a new relationship with the resource of his body, an ever-present and vital part of his identity.

It is my observation now that this practice immediately opens the door to new possibilities. By focusing on the somatic, and specifically on the sensations of the body that have been experienced in the midst of turmoil, the person can quickly move forward into beneficial mindful reflection.

I wasn't aware that Tim had given any thought to the bodily sensations that were underlying his emotional rollercoaster, but when asked to do so, he was able to be present to himself in this way without any difficulty. He described a tightness and a sense of pressure in his chest.

I encouraged him to keep his awareness on the pressure in his chest, and the next instant Tim was telling this story:

> When he was about eight he set out enthusiastically one day to try his hand at fishing in a dam not far from home. He was quite alone. He felt a bit clumsy with the unfamiliar task of casting the fishing line. It took him by surprise when, having got his line into the water, there was a sharp tug on the line. Then came a moment of intense horror. A small, spreadeagled frog flew through the air as he reeled in his line. It was all bloody and mutilated, caught in its jaw by the hook he had baited only a few moments before. In a huge panic, he lowered his catch to the ground, picked up a nearby rock and dashed the little frog to death.

Tim was surprised. He and I shared a sense of awe at his telling. Over time, I began to name stories that emerged out of a person's awareness of body sensations as 'body narratives'.

I found myself turning to the narrative practice of externalising. As I did this, I was not asking Tim to externalise his body, but to experiment with externalising the self-sabotaging state of frenzy that was so troubling to him. I asked him if there was a name for the emotional state he had recently experienced. He called it "the overwrought state". Its effects were many.

Over many years the overwrought state had interfered with his life repeatedly. He was a vet, but he couldn't handle the sickness and death of animals in his care. His life had often seemed to fall apart. The over-emotionality was such a problem that he was finally forced to give up his livelihood. He could no longer work as a veterinary professional.

When Tim was spelling out the effects of the overwrought state on his life, the heaviness of this somatic (body-based) problem narrative showed itself in his demeanour, his furrowed brow and slumping shoulders. This was reflected in his mind, as he spoke of his life as "spoiled".

I empathised with this heaviness and asked him to continue his reflection. I was particularly curious about what the arrival of the frog memory meant to him. I noticed that he immediately sparked up.

Tim expressed amazement that this small event had been remembered in his body. It had seemingly pursued him for years. The trauma of it had had very serious and far-reaching impacts on his life.

He was marvelling at his body's truth and was in the grip of a moving realisation. He was doing his own noticing. The totally new experience became a jumping off point (pivotal). He wanted to understand more.

I reflected that the memory was of an event that had been traumatising for the eight-year-old he had been. The details of this small story formed the storyline (White, 2007) of the little explored territory of his body. An experience from the back of the library of his experiences had been found and dusted off, simply by shining the light on his body. Gaps in Tim's life narrative had been filled. His body was resourcing him and now he could begin to make meaning.

There was an almost immediate and new sense of agency. As the conversation continued, Tim began to ask his own curious questions. There was no re-traumatisation. Perhaps becoming aware of his body was providing a greater sense of internal safety. His body was playing a crucial role in his making meaning of his experience.

As Tim's co-authoring therapist, my role was to stay alert and to orient myself in Tim's direction. White (2011) expands traditional narrative approaches when he notes the way a person in therapy can pick up a feeling of resonance when the therapist responds respectfully to her words, ideas and values. Such resonance promotes healing.

My implicit responses to Tim's body language were being augmented by an explicit exploration of the somatically-cued narrative material to which I also brought my collegial commitment. I could tune in to Tim both implicitly and explicitly with my responses, and orient myself to his body language and his body narrative as well as to his words, his discoveries and his values.

Tim was already weaving the past and the present together. I sought more details so that his storylines and their meanings might be thickened, or increase in a richer complexity.

Killing the frog with that rock was something for which Tim, now a man in his early forties, had never been able to forgive himself. He told about all the shame and guilt and the intense self-blame that he had gone on carrying.

As I stayed empathically with him, he started to enlarge on how easily the frog's life could have been saved.

The hook could've been removed. Anyone could see that the frog would have recovered.

He repeated these sentiments a couple of times. Then he modified his stance.

I suppose that's hindsight, isn't it? It's the view of a scientist or anyone really, with an adult's experience of life! But I was only eight years old. I guess it was panic that made me do it.

There was silence. Tim's story had prompted not just further body awareness but dual awareness (Rothschild, 2000). He was noticing his childhood experience and beginning to empathise with his more vulnerable self from his adult vantage point. Rothschild's naming of the healing benefit of this dual awareness is similar to White's (2006) recognition that when a person can explore different parts of her history and find consistency over time, the internal resonances that arise can be life-giving.

As the conversation continued, I turned myself in the direction of Tim's values, and asked him to talk about what had been precious to him as a child.

He began to share how much he had always valued the life of animals, how much he loved them, how he had never been the sort of kid who would be cruel to small creatures and that he would never intentionally do anything to harm them.

Now he was getting clarity about his real motivation for the way he responded. Yes, he could see that he had panicked and he went on to speak what was true for him:

I didn't want the frog to suffer! That's why I picked up that rock. I didn't want it to be in pain!

As Tim articulated how precious the life of animals had always been to him in childhood, he was recognising for the first time that his killing of the frog had been an act of compassion. His compassion was implicit in his behaviour in a way he hadn't recognised before. Previously he had remembered his panic somatically and that panic had kept repeating itself in his adult experience. Narrative exploration now joined his mind and his body to develop self-understanding and the meanings inherent in his earlier responses.

The cued body narrative had helped him explore the second story of trauma (White, 2006), the story of his own responses. When a focus on the body cues a narrative, it means that some responses previously hidden are brought into view. There may be other vital information in those responses that speak of what was and what still is precious and important for the person's life. In Tim's case, his love of animals had never changed. In adulthood his values were consistent with those of his childhood.

This began to change Tim's long-standing shame. He started seeing events in a different light as he confirmed his own values and intentions. The way this event had blighted his life was unchanged. However, he was beginning to construct a narrative about it that was new. His body had produced an accurate memory, and Tim was exploring it in company with someone who, with open and respectful curiosity, was keeping his interests central. As I attended and drew attention to Tim's body, a co-authoring project was underway.

Development of a new approach

I have experimented over several years with ways of coming alongside a person, such as Tim, to raise awareness of the body's struggle. I have been privileged to become the 'near-at-hand witness', as narrative practitioners describe it, as person after person has begun to take fruitful notice of what her body is telling her.

This book is case-study heavy. I have drawn from conversations with everyday adult individuals and couples in country New South Wales, Australia. I've also had the privilege of working with adolescents and children, sometimes individually and sometimes together with their families. I'm grateful that some of these people have permitted the inclusion of their conversations with me.

As a narrative therapist, I recognise that exploring the details of a person's contexts is vital if meanings are to be fully understood. Some of the case studies are protracted so that the reader can also understand these contexts.

As I have worked with these survivors of trauma, I have noticed a repeated theme. Each contributor has sought help because of what she (or a parent) has described variously as an experience of over-emotionality, over-reactivity, excessive anxiety or out-of-control anger. Sometimes the person has talked about an underlying (and longstanding) burden of distress or despair. At times it's been an invading and repeated loss of functionality that has arrived with little warning. In the case of those with partners or spouses, reactive conflict has been spoiling the relationship.

In researching the three approaches of narrative therapy, contemporary somatic therapy and trauma therapy, I was struck by the fact that the language used in different modalities may suggest that they are at odds with each other. Sometimes articulations by therapy practitioners have a different emphasis to those from a neuroscience background. However, I came to understand that, as far as early trauma is concerned, narrative and somatic practitioners and neuroscience researchers are actually describing different sides of the same coin, or different parts of the proverbial elephant.

As I began to document the lived evidence of the early trauma in the lives of the people consulting me, I recognised the many points of connection between the experiential and the theoretical evidence I was encountering. The prolonged impacts of early trauma had themes common to many lives. Soon this documenting project became more, as I amalgamated ideas into a therapy model that began writing itself into existence. As it progressed, it was deriving a solid empirical foundation.

The hope that first motivated me to develop my ideas arose out of my experiences in the therapy room where my conversational collaborators who had experienced early trauma were educating me. There was always the experience of intense sensations that just seemed to sit there waiting to be raised to awareness. I became intrigued by how quickly a person moved forward to take up an alternative narrative as she became aware of her body. As early-trauma researcher and writer Peter Levine (1997) explained it, by attending to the ongoing impacts of early trauma on a person's body as well as on her mind, the survivor can be helped to leave behind the impacts that have been haunting or sabotaging her life.

A body focus can and has been added to many types of therapy. My passion became to research the specific efficacy of teaming a body focus with the many narrative approaches to therapy already in use, and its application in a trauma context. I named this 'body-focused narrative therapy'.

While it will have special significance for narrative practitioners, the book's format, with its mix of experiential learning, theoretical viewpoint and multifaceted case studies, is intended for all therapists who wish to learn about and/or to utilise a body-focused approach. It therefore has been written in a way that makes the body-focused narrative approach accessible to practitioners who are not trained in the narrative approach.

How the book is organised

The first part of the book is more theoretical and sets up a context for the body-focused narrative therapy model by introducing narrative therapy, contemporary somatic therapy and trauma therapy in the first three chapters respectively. Chapter 4 acts as a pivot between the theory and the lived experience of those for whose benefit the book is intended. It introduces body-focused narrative therapy using the metaphor of the Magic Loom.

In the second part of the book, the voices of those who have the lived experience of trauma are privileged. They tell their stories. This section also showcases the body-focused narrative approach in practice, aided by the Magic Loom metaphor, and substantiated by the research of neuroscience and the theoretical underpinning of the three approaches introduced earlier.

In the case-study documentation, I have used the exact words spoken whenever these were recorded in my case notes. However, many of the therapy questions and some of the client responses have had to be reconstructed. I am extremely grateful for the later collaboration of each contributor. Some provided reflective comment. One person who goes by the name of Simeon in this book, documented not only what he remembered from our therapy conversations, but some of what occupied his mind along the way (his stream of consciousness). I couldn't have otherwise captured this in the record.

The names and some details in the stories have been changed in order to preserve anonymity.

I want to thank the contributors for their willingness to share their personal and often intimate stories and conversations with others. I hope that many people who have suffered into adulthood as a result of early complex developmental trauma might become beneficiaries of the gathered narratives, as well as of this holistic therapy approach.

PART ONE
The Theory and the Model

Chapter 1
Narrative Therapy

Narrative approaches seek out and use counter plots ... to countermand the dominant stories of sickness and abnormality. Stephen Madigan

Narrative therapy provides a way of helping a person sift some of her life stories in order to choose the narratives she wishes to live by in a more intentional and conscious way. It uses the metaphor of life as a library of experiences. According to the library metaphor, expanded for my purpose here, a truckload of books of experience arrives at each person's door every day of her life, and a sorting process, mainly unconscious, ensues. Some of the books are immediately set to work in service of certain accepted identity conclusions. Narratives about these are constructed and shared and often repeated. They are placed on display right at the front door of the library. Others are scarcely noticed and/or quickly disregarded. Some are so intense that they can't be processed easily. These may become dominant, associated as they are with traumatically troublesome and intractable ongoing problems. They can impact a person's internal world and self-talk, while failing to see the light of day. Undiscussed, these books may remain intensely influential but gather cobwebs in the backblocks of the library.

The work of the narrative therapist is to take up a metaphorical torch and to walk alongside a person as she explores not only the showpieces, but some of the other narratives that have been assigned into those deeper reaches of the library. The work involves cleaning the cobwebs off the past so that helpful exploration can take place. It provides the person with opportunity to reflect on the skills, competencies, beliefs and values that come into view. She can be helped to explore a past that is well known to her, but also to resurrect experience never before noticed and named.

Narrative approaches to therapy

Narrative approaches are concerned about meaning-making. People tell stories to themselves and others, about their lives and relationships. Alice Morgan (2000) says that:

> *Narrative therapists are interested in joining with people to explore the stories they have, their effects, their meanings and the contexts in which they have been formed or authored (p. 10).*

All narrative conversations enable a person to consider the meanings of the events and experiences in her life. The plots and counterplots, when explored, provide the particularities that enable the storylines to come to life. Details and aspects of language, such as image and metaphor, enrich the exploration. The narratives make more sense as they are intentionally organised into a cohesive whole. They are said to 'grow thicker' as their complexities are considered, and the person moves herself away from simplistic or black and white interpretations of events or experiences (Morgan, 2000). As she engages in the therapy conversation, the person often gains insight into her own preferences for living.

Understanding that stories don't just reflect life but shape it, during these explorations the therapist can help a person change her relationship with the problems in her life. The aim is to increase her sense of personal agency.

Michael White (2004) explains it in this way:

> *Re-authoring conversations invite people to continue to develop and tell stories about their lives, but they also help people to include some of the more neglected but potentially significant events and experiences that are "out of phase" with their dominant storylines. These events and experiences can be considered "unique outcomes" or "exceptions" (p. 61).*

The concept of 'exceptions' is important in narrative thought. The search is for storylines that run counter to the other more dominant themes. It is fruitful to examine in as much detail as possible these different storylines when they are alluded to.

Re-authoring

Every re-authoring conversation is unique. It is the person who has come into the therapy relationship who is the primary author while she is encouraged to consider aspects of her own life previously unexamined. The therapist makes space for the narrator's voice. What meaning does she find in the events about which she chooses to speak? How does she interpret the links between these events and the themes of her life? What are her deductions and what do these say about what is important to her? What conclusions is she coming to about her own identity and the identity of others (White, 2007)? As she sets a framework of open enquiry, the therapist becomes a co-author alongside the narrator.

Pearl began to examine her life through the reality and the metaphor of dance. In one conversation she described her childhood life in the world of ballet as a "closed experience". She felt herself narrowed into a world of competition by the expectations and judgments of others. She came to feel little sense of herself outside that world.

> *The word 'closed' became a pivot in the conversation. Pearl began to talk of the open nature of the new kind of dance with which she was experimenting. She described feeling visible and free. She was creating alongside others. She had discovered that living wasn't just about pleasing someone else. She was reflecting on the source of her intense jealousy and rage. Enjoying her own creativity, she was finding that she now wanted only good for the lives of others. It wasn't just the dancing. Every aspect of her life was feeling different.*

When I reflected later on Pearl's sense of agency, I recalled the words of body therapist, Stanley Keleman (1975). He is a somatic practitioner, but here he was describing an important aspect of narrative therapy.

> *The uniqueness of us human animals is that we are open-ended. Our lifetimes continually offer us fresh possibilities for forming unprecedented relationships with others and with our surroundings. Our open-endedness is intrinsic to our human unfolding (p. 73).*

The narrative scaffold of questions is always open-ended. Narrative style curious questions helped Pearl to gradually form and thicken a new narrative. She was experiencing the contrast of the exception she had found, as she considered its details and grasped its meanings.

Deconstructing the role and influence of the competitive world she had inhabited as a child and adolescent helped her shape a new narrative. The problem she had begun to step away from belonged in a wider social context. It wasn't hers alone. The emotional intensity of the problem's effects on her seemed to decline as she began to take the bigger picture into account.

Asking about her values helped Pearl to specify some of her new identity understandings. There were changes both in her sense of herself and in the way she saw herself relating to others.

How narrative conversations are constructed

The foundation for building narrative-focused generative conversations is a language-based scaffold or framework. It is made up of curious or investigative questions to which the therapist herself does not have the answers. She brings a genuine spirit of enquiry. The conversational participant's lived experience is constantly being brought into the foreground and mined for its treasures. Questions asked by the therapist often emerge from what the person consulting her has just said. The latter is the expert on her own life.

The therapist, on the other hand, takes responsibility for choosing the questions that help highlight exceptions and give direction to the collaborative conversational exploration. In this way, the scaffolding project aims at complexity and helps a person move towards it in a step-by-step learning process (White, 2004). The ideas of the Russian educationalist Vygotsky (1986) have had a strong influence on narrative thought and practice. He articulated the importance of scaffolded enquiry for any learning experience. Teachers scaffold learning tasks from the simple and concrete towards the more complex and abstract. The scaffolding of questions in a narrative therapy conversation takes it back and forth between therapist and client. The aim is always to help the person move away from negative controlling narratives towards those that are more generative, to move from thin conclusions to thicker ones, to explore the meanings of events (White, 2004) and to gradually build and embody alternative, life-affirming narratives.

A de-centred approach

The therapist wants to stay empathetically with the person who is sharing her narratives. She takes her cue from the narrator and orients her enquiry towards the storylines, themes and values being unearthed. Prioritising the voice of the storyteller like this, along with values of respect and non-blame, produces a de-centred approach to therapy. The practitioner hopes the storyteller will not only feel seen and heard, but that she will gain the freedom to make her own discoveries and to directly experience 'sparkling moments', a term often used in narrative discourse to describe moments of newness and transformation. The therapist supports the expertise of the person in therapy by using a tentative voice, inviting her to experience openness and the available freedom with which to constitute herself. In this way, the practitioner helps the person who is exploring her life to construct her own narratives as she herself evaluates the significance of her explorations and notices her own unique outcomes. She is the one who makes her own choices and names her preferences.

In contrast to being experienced as a top-down expert, the therapist wants to be perceived as a colleague walking alongside the person. To this end, she does her best to offer transparency about her own position and to be clear about her own biases. The narrative therapist is willing to share some of her own vulnerability and human-ness with her client.

Quiet co-authoring

As Morgan (2000) suggests, therapists need to be good at keeping themselves out of the way. There is an absolute need for people to constitute themselves. The therapist has the privilege of being a quiet co-author.

The narrative metaphor guides the therapist to become aware of the subtle ways she can be seduced into top-down practice. The tendency to exert one's own biases or one's own expert knowledge is common and often unconscious. I remember my shock and my instant desire to argue when a homeless man with whom I was working told me that his preference was to remain a victim. I had to bite my tongue not to leap into pontification and advice-giving.

I was surprised when the client in question returned the following week and told me a story that was at odds with the stand he had articulated the week before. I came to see that having the space to choose victimhood had given him a platform from which to push away in his own good time.

Dogmatism and pontification close enquiry down. On the other hand, a narrative therapy conversation has the opposite impact. Many aspects of a person's life can be explored. Maintaining the de-centred nature of the conversation, while also noticing and naming the knowledges and inner wisdom that someone like Pearl may never have explored, helps the therapist ensure that the process of re-authoring a life narrative is a genuinely collaborative enterprise.

Externalising

Helping people change their relationship with the problems in their lives is another central narrative practice. It is usually achieved by the practice called 'externalising', which can quickly initiate a change process. As the therapist helps a person to name 'the problem' she is facing, the therapist begins to use a personalising form of language in reference to it. The nature and impacts of the problem's influences are opened to view. Once the problem is given a name or a nickname, preferably by the person herself, then questions about the context, the history, the effects and the tactics of the problem can advance the exploration. The problem, under its new name, may even be interviewed by the therapist. In these ways, emotional distance from the problem is provided. The person feels less defined by it and the idea of taking a stand in response to the problem can often be entertained as a direct result.

Gerry was quick to externalise a bullying tendency that he decided to call the 'Captain'.

> He described how he often "swelled and strutted and muscled in on the scene" with his wife. When we explored the history of the Captain together, Gerry remembered how problematic he had once been at work. It was by talking things over with his boss that he came to appreciate the usefulness of workplace protocols. He decided to put peacefulness at the centre of his dealings and to imaginatively "pull down a trap door" on the Captain's tactic of focusing on the failings of his colleagues.

The history of this trapdoor intervention revealed a skill of the imagination and of stand-taking that Gerry hadn't known was his. He realised that he had relied on this skill of his to shut out the abuse of those on the sidelines of his son's soccer matches when he was referee.

When the conversation turned to the home context, Gerry was quick to recognise that the self-respect and respect of his work colleagues he had gained was not present in his view of himself at home or in how his wife viewed him. He began to wonder whether there was real masculine strength on show with the Captain going on the rampage or was he more of a true man when the Captain was kept under wraps?

White (2007) says:

> As people reconstruct the stories of their lives, it quickly becomes apparent that they are drawing from a stock of maps relevant to journeys already taken, and that they know a lot about map-making. There are always occasions in a person's life when they have succeeded in escaping a problem's influence (p. 76).

As well as exploring the two landscapes of action, the workplace and the home, when Gerry was asked about what was precious to him, landscapes of his identity also came into view. He put a value on his own integrity in both arenas. White (2007) points out that once exploration begins, people find out that "they know more than they think they know" (p. 76).

In my role as therapist, I was able to help Gerry move bit by bit from the immediacy of his own lived experience in the workplace to forge links between what he had achieved there and what was possible for him to achieve on his home ground as well. Through the way I asked the questions (the conversational scaffolding), Gerry could gradually move from familiar ground into the realm of what was possible elsewhere. Vygotsky (2007) calls this the movement towards "the zone of proximal development" (p. 272).

The word 'respect' harboured emotional significance for Gerry and provided an opening in the conversation. Mining this word for its meanings moved him forward in his thinking and in his sense of agency. During the social collaboration of the externalising therapy conversation, he was discovering ways he could influence his actions and shape the course of events in his own life. Through processes of reflection he was considering his values and discovering the stands he wanted to take.

Deconstructing normalised beliefs

Once an externalising process like this has helped a person feel more separate from a problem, it often helps if she can take a second look at the problem from a wider perspective. In Gerry's case, enquiry about social attitudes to masculinity and the history of his own beliefs about what it means to be a man in society today might become a line of enquiry. It could relate to the self and others, individually and in community. Helping a person to see the pervasive nature of social assumptions and to understand how this normalising relates to the problem being grappled with, can move her even further away from attributing to herself a 'spoiled identity' as this experience is termed by narrative practitioners.

When Rick began one therapy conversation, his immediate concern was with his assertiveness. He felt that his lack of it was affecting his home-based business. I reminded Rick about how he and his wife had explored their beliefs about "modern corporate culture" in a previous conversation. I'd noted down some of their perceptions and the stand they had taken well before coming for therapy. They had become clear about its hidden powers and they had moved away from what they saw as a kind of slavery. The couple had also listed a range of qualities that had made the change possible. They had actively turned their own passivity and discontent into assertiveness.

Naming and detailing this deconstruction of some social assumptions was therapeutic. It helped Rick to challenge his present predicament. Assertiveness had been his ally before and he knew how to befriend it again.

This episode fleshes out White's description (2007) of the therapy task as "casting people as active mediators and negotiators of life's meanings and predicaments both individually and in collaboration with others" (p. 103).

David Newman (2010) describes how he collects "living documents" (p. 27) as faithful as possible to people's own phrases and their local language, and offered by them to share with others who may be struggling with similar concerns. He picked up the understanding from David Epston (2000) that finding ways to link people around an ever-expanding archive of local knowledges and themes using the written word is an important task for narrative workers.

A therapeutic document

Powerful influences had led Henry to internalise a sense of a spoiled identity. Shame and self-hatred may have been internalised as a result of trauma's impacts, and a context of isolation may have entrenched a pattern of self-blame.

Depression and alcohol abuse were the problems Henry was facing. In one conversation, he discussed the influence on his life of his grandmother. I wrote down as many of his words as I could.

> *I always feel the stabilising influence of my grandmother. She opens her arms and offers a big hug when I arrive at her place. And she gives me her time as if she has all the time in the world! Looking back, I remember that when I was younger I always got the feeling she was interested in me. She's been there for me from the beginning. She's unchanging, her reactions are always reliable, and she's given me the gift of feeling connected.*

> *My gran is earthy and solid. Thinking about my history with her, I see how, in a very fragmented childhood, there's developed a pull for me towards the place where she lives. Even now the landscape there feels solid and reliable, stable and loving. I long for and imagine this landscape even when I am far away from it. This might even have affected my choice of a career. I work in land care and horticulture and it makes me feel worthwhile.*

> *I see too that I'm a person who has the same ability to connect as my gran has. I can always be supportively present with my own kids. Even when we have extended times apart, I've been able to retain a depth of relationship with them.*

Inviting a person to bring into the conversation significant witnesses to his life is an important narrative approach. Exploring his connection with his grandmother (with my interactive but minimal prompts) turned out to have meaning in more than one area of Henry's life. A new self-story was beginning to form.

I noticed how holistic this enquiry turned out to be. Henry's response to his grandmother's physical welcome and her earthy connection to her geographical environment played an implicit role that he had made explicit as we talked.

Jeffrey Bogdan (1986) says that:

> like most social groups, families rather than being unitary in nature are made up of many minds, each with its own perspective on the world, communicating with and adapting to one another over time … an ecology of ideas (p. 36).

This concept of an ecology of ideas adds to the richness and interconnected nature of the web that narrative therapists are interested in exploring. Family-of-origin exploration is never unitary. For Henry, exploring the significance of his grandmother in the ecological web of his family provided meanings that he had never before considered.

Re-membering conversations and the relational web

'Re-membering' conversations are conversations that arise out of the exploration of a person's relational web. The comparative influence of others on a person's identity can be weighed. It is often a surprise to reflect on ways in which significant others have conveyed their interest. It can be even more remarkable for a person to explore the influence of her own life on the lives of others. After this kind of reflection takes place, decisions can then be made about whether to curb the influence of a former relationship and/or to promote another into a more influential position. Within narrative conversations, former identity conclusions often come up for review.

As already mentioned, opportunities for choice-making and agency tend to expand when a person has the chance to reflect on the aspects of life she deems precious. She may also take time to consider which of her associations and the influences they represent line up well with the cherished values which she has made her own.

Identity founded upon an association of life

White (2007) says that the "association of life has a membership composed of the significant figures and identities of a person's past, present and projected future whose voices are influential with regard to the construction of a person's identity" (p. 129). In narrative thought, this understanding of identity starts with the recognition that an infant's development relies on her relationships with others. Initially it is a relationship with her primary carer. As a person's associations change with her life stages, so too does her sense of self or her identity. When new storylines are discovered in new relational contexts, the discovery may immediately contribute to change, perhaps to an expansion of identity or self-view.

A narrative approach takes seriously the fact that expert opinion is often expected and familiar to a person. It can play a subjugating role in her life. Parents, always expert in a child's eyes, may set up a trend in her thinking towards passive dependency. There are patterns in the way that power is used in the wider society that can also be influential. A person may unconsciously place others into positions of authority in her life, for example, taking for granted that a doctor's expertise is to be accepted without question. As a result of such assumptions, a person's agency is reduced, and negative identity beliefs reinforced. Life can easily become framed by a negatively dominant narrative.

Outsider witness groups

The practice of inviting 'outsider witness groups' in the flesh to respond to the narrator in the therapy room is a practice unique to narrative practice. The witnesses, who may be a group of therapists, other people seeking therapy, or friends of the narrator, first take a turn at listening to the person's stories. They often listen from behind a screen. They move out from behind the screen in order to re-tell what they have heard, particularly mentioning aspects of the story that have chimed in for them or that might in some specific way have potential to move them forward in their own lives. Morgan (2000) says that these witnesses "re-tell what they have heard in ways that contribute to rich description of alternative stories of people's lives and identities" (p. 126).

Known as 'definitional ceremonies' (after the work of Barbara Myerhoff, 1986), these helpfully structured patterns of speaking and listening provide a real sense of immediacy for the one who, often for the first time, may be able to perceive the profound way her own life has the power to impact the lives of others. She is an actor on the stage of life.

A personal journey

I began my own journey with narrative approaches during mature-age postgraduate studies. I found that experimenting with its principles immediately began to energise the work I was engaged in at that time, both as a therapist to homeless men and as a community worker among street sex-workers and residents of a low-income housing estate.

I was particularly attracted by the invitation to explore the way power is used in relationships and in society. I was eager to better understand the ingredients of an intentionally respectful approach both to therapy and to community work. How did the relationship between therapist and narrator remain equal and collegial?

Though no philosopher myself, I became inspired by the work of Michel Foucault, a historian of systems of thought, and I was impressed by his idea that 'normalising judgment' is a mechanism of social control (Foucault, 1980).

Normalising judgment and its antidotes

I didn't have to look far to see the stigmatisation of the homeless people I worked with and to notice how rarely any street sex-worker was treated respectfully as a person. My attention was drawn to the idea that in our society some people are divided off from the rest of society and assigned a spoiled identity (White, 2007). Many of the people I knew who were living with mental illness were objectified in this way and treated as if the illness was a summation of their identity.

I was understanding how labelling not only affects how a person sees herself but that it also influences those who make the judgments and attach the labels. The judgments are so pervasive in society that over time they become normative or taken for granted. When this happens, little awareness remains of other ways of thinking. This of course is even more true in early childhood when a person's own experiences are the only ones she can take into account. The dogmatic pronouncements and behaviours of early caretakers are experienced as the norm and they tend to influence every early taste of life.

I found myself beginning to deconstruct some of my own embedded assumptions, many of which had arisen out of dogmatic expert parental opinion and the un-critiqued religious givens that I had grown up with. I was embarking on my own awakening journey.

Thin and thick conclusions

A small example of this was when I discovered that I needed to leave behind an entrenched belief that I had derived that to be gay was to be unfruitful because only a heterosexual bond produces children. Simply being challenged to think about whether there were other ways for a person's life to be fruitful forced me to consider alternative ideas. This process of my own clarified the way a narrowing and dogmatic idea or judgment can devalue people and reduce relationships into an invisible power struggle. I came to see my erstwhile belief as an example of what in narrative thought is named a 'thin' conclusion. As thin (often black and white) conclusions about life and identity are explored and normalisations are questioned, such simplicity can be replaced with 'thicker conclusions', which are more nuanced, complex and realistic.

I first heard the story of The Prince and the Peasant from one of my university lecturers. The allegory has stayed with me as I've continued to learn about some of the ways normalising power can be effectively challenged.

The Prince came riding by and all the peasants in the field stopped their tilling. Doffing their hats, they bowed low. One peasant joined the others, but as the prince continued on his way, he turned his back on the prince, and bowing low, he let out a loud fart!

Foucault's ideas about power are different to both traditional and, in the above case, feudal models, where it operated as raw coercion. The peasant in the story had no doubt about the power that was operating against him.

In *Truth and Power* (1980b) Foucault articulates a positive understanding of power, which has been influential in laying the foundations of the narrative endeavour.

> *What makes power hold good, what makes it accepted, is simply the fact that it doesn't only weigh on us as a force that says no, but that it traverses and produces things, it induces pleasure, forms knowledge, produces discourse. It needs to be considered as a productive network which runs through the whole social body, much more than as a negative instance whose function is repression (p. 119).*

Narrative approaches work to develop the equality and inclusivity that helps every individual find her own ways of being part of such a productive network of power. In contrast, as he researched modern social systems, Foucault discovered and named the 'dividing practices' I was seeing in my work and he found them common in Western culture as far back as the mid-seventeenth century (White, 2007).

As societies have developed and become more complex, the subtle power over people exercised by social institutions has often left them unaware. This contrasts with the situation for the peasant in my story. The figures of power in the life of a feudal peasant used direct, often crude methods of engendering fear and compliance. Nowadays, authority figures and institutions favour subtle pontification and dogma and lean on position, training, social standing and expert knowledge to increase a sense of superiority and power. Authoritarian individuals, positions, ideas, figures and institutions today can exercise a normalising influence over time, which is at once indirect yet quite pervasive in its effects on a person or a whole group. Inequality often becomes entrenched and systemic.

This is illustrated, for example, by the way that attitudes about patriarchy, including a passive approach to the domination of men and to the inequality and even the submission of women, continue to be passed down the generations by people of both genders. A person can be quite blind to the sense of entitlement that underlies a great deal of top-down behaviour maintaining the status quo.

In Foucault's words, "People become accomplices to a system of social control in which they exercise and act upon judgments about life according to established norms about life and identity" (quoted in White, 2007, p. 103).

Narrative history and philosophy

Two therapists and thinkers, Michael White and David Epston from Australia and New Zealand respectively, were the first to begin to articulate the principles of narrative approaches and to apply them to therapy. Over time, both principles and practice evolved as a result of the further leadership of these two men, although they welcomed contributions by many other researchers and practitioners. The narrative endeavour is marked by its openness to innovation, and a therapist is encouraged to test new ideas in collaboration with each client with whom she works. As already mentioned, the main aim is to help the latter gain greater agency in her life by discovering narratives that are alternatives to those that have been negatively dominant.

Leaning on post-modern and post-structuralist ideas, the founders of a narrative pathway to therapy and to community work were explicitly differentiating its underpinnings from ways of thinking characterised as modern. This belief system was normalised during the nineteenth and twentieth centuries, and was based on concepts of absolute truth and/or on mechanistic scientific enquiry. In therapy with experts influenced by Freudian theories, the search for a person's true self, true essence or one real identity was commonplace. At the same time, as with Descartes, the aim was to gather facts and scientific observations, using the classification of disease groups and symptoms known as empiricism or positivism. Stratified approaches formed the foundation of modern psychiatry and behaviourism.

White (2007) called the outcome of such approaches "internalised state conclusions" (p. 120). He suggested that such classifying systems tend to lock a person into a practice of self-labelling, such as in the statement "I am an anorexic". The whole of a society reduces a person to a label or a simplified diagnosis. Stereotypes become set in nature and lead to an internalising process that narrows a person's sense of self and identity. The person unconsciously takes on the prevailing and normalising thinking as her own.

Narrative therapists instead help the person to become curious, explorative and reflective. As her awareness of normalising influences grows, the client is set free to make her decisions more intentionally. When she comes to understand the taken-for-granted influences that have made up her personal context and affected her sense of identity and the ways she has met life challenges, she is freed to make the decisions she prefers. Internalising processes give way to intentional ones. Narrative philosophy sees the importance of helping a person choose her own preferences about her identity and her way of living freely rather than being bound by the choices made for her by others or by the system. This approach is known as a constructivist philosophy of knowledge.

Newman (2010) tells of receiving in a personal communication in October 2009 the following words, really a plea, from David Epston:

> Can those who suffer and those who care for them be conceived of as not merely 'passive recipients' of our knowledges, but as creators and users of their own 'knowledges'? (p. 26).

A person's life and identity are influenced relationally. Exploring the context of her life and its history helps make the social influences on her life more apparent. Opening up narratives to historic and contextual exploration enables her to actively explore her old identity conclusions, to discover alternative and fresh ways of thinking about her narratives, and to consider and choose those she prefers. White (1997) notes that narrative therapists don't speak of the truth of a person's identity but help them to consider "accounts that reflect who we are as multi-desired, as multi-motivated and as multi-intentioned in life as our lives are multi-storied" (p. 231).

The peasant described earlier was agentive, acting on his own behalf to subvert the powers. He also had the inner wisdom to refrain from taking on the powers directly. I can see him regaling his friends around the fire with the narrative of his humorous act. He could keep his spirit alive by using his own power in an effectively subversive way!

Small acts of resistance

Narrative therapists call his kind of action a small act of resistance. Even today, normalising power can be dangerous as, for example, in situations of abuse and domestic violence or other forms of institutionalised power. It can cause multiple harms to a subjugated person who, unlike the peasant, may be confused by the subtlety and pervasive nature of the way power or influence is affecting her. Beliefs and ideas that have pervaded the childhood context have often been closed to critical thinking. Dogmatism is a means of keeping another generation or a total population under control. It perhaps wards off parental insecurity or fear of social chaos. Often it is the fear such use of power engenders, sometimes traumatic, which keeps the child, adult, or group of people trapped and passive.

Narrative approaches to therapy open up enquiry so that, through a wide process of exploration, a person can gain enough agency to take up small acts of resistance and contemplate stands she wants to take so that power is equalised.

Narrative work with trauma

Narrative systems of thought and practice have contributed some unique ways to help survivors of trauma move forward in their lives. Many of these are described in *Trauma, Narrative Responses to Traumatic Experience,* a collection of writings edited by David Denborough (2006). As a result of trauma that occurs in a child's early life stages, that child may develop a negative fear-based dominant narrative. I have extended the library of books' metaphor to suggest that she may have buried degrading experiences in the back of the library. When she has not been able to make sense of what has happened in her past, this lack of resolution is powerfully influential. She may have formed a belief that the world is not responsive to her. A strong sense of self may be elusive, and feelings of isolation and victimhood may prevail. When the trauma involved the child's earliest relationships, her capacity to trust is likely to have been deeply affected. Fear may haunt her every life experience.

The benefits of the de-centred conversation for trauma

The respectful approaches of narrative practice are particularly effective for a person who is struggling with this complexity. Positioning a person who suffered trauma as a child as the expert on her own life and at the centre of a collaborative conversation can immediately begin to positively influence self-definition. Experiencing this kind of de-centred conversation can in fact begin a process of re-integration. It can help a person to feel visible and known. Her wisdom is given significance. Her life matters.

White (2011) notes that people accord certain aspects of life great value and express this in their daily lives. Even when life is "experienced through the thrall of dissociated traumatic memories, even at this time, there is some principle operating in the selection of memories" (p. 25).

Focusing on the second story of trauma

When Kerry was only thirteen years old, her mother died as a result of alcohol abuse. Kerry remembered an incident.

She was lying in bed one night conscious of her parents fighting. She heard a loud crash and cries of distress and when she rushed into the living room she saw blood all over her mother's face. Kerry grabbed a towel and rushed over to staunch the blood.

As I put the focus of our explorative conversation on Kerry's responses, she became pleased and surprised that in such an emergency she had taken the initiative. She had only been eight years old when it happened. She was always determined to do her best. When the frightening nature of the noise, the yelling and the crashing and the sight of the blood were acknowledged, she recognised her courage. Even though the drinking and the family violence were causing havoc in her life, her response had been compassionate. Her heart had gone out to her mother.

This aspect of her identity was thickened as Kerry talked about the gentle way she took care of her treasured pet cat as a child and described the same gentle self in her way with her children. She was realising that she had fostered this way of being and that other people, especially her friends, noticed it. Nonetheless, it was totally unexpected for her to see that she must have already chosen to be a compassionate person as a very young child and under such traumatic circumstances.

Double listening

Focusing on a person's responses to trauma like this can bring balance to the way trauma is perceived. Pat Ogden (2015), a well-known sensory-somatic therapist, reinforces this point by saying that when attention is drawn to the response a person like Kerry once made to trauma, she can then make a more positive association with the memory. Neurologically, this positive association can alter the way the memory is stored in the brain. As a person like Kerry is helped by appropriate questions to focus on her own actions and responses she is turned in the direction of agency and away from that sense of being overpowered. The destructive power of the trauma shrinks.

White uses the term 'double listening' (2006). Stories of trauma can be the focus of a person's life and sometimes of a therapy process. However, narrative practitioners intentionally elevate the importance of the second narrative, which describes the person's responses to the trauma. It may never before have been noticed or named.

Bringing these responses to light often provides people with accounts similar to Kerry's of inner wisdom and courage, of values and commitments. What may have been unknown or only thinly acknowledged can then be recognised as multi-layered and significant.

White also points out (2006,) that often the values people have chosen for their lives implicitly demonstrate what may never have been spoken. Having a person reflect on how her values were expressed at the time of the trauma brings impetus for far-reaching change. He says, "it is what people deem precious which speaks most clearly of their own intention not to allow the trauma to have the last word" (p. 29).

The therapy focus on trauma's second story can decrease the risk of re-traumatisation, which sometimes occurs if people re-engage too closely with blow-by-blow accounts of traumatic events from the past. Russell Meares (2016) suggests that when traumata have been multiple and cumulative, the twentieth century practice of isolating and detoxifying the malignant effects of traumatic experience can be "inappropriate, ineffective, or worse" (p. 21). It can actually enlarge rather than shrink the impacts.

On the other hand, applying medicalised Band-Aids to symptoms such as anxiety or depression may be at the expense of addressing important psychic issues, such as a person's negative identity conclusions. For the narrative therapist, putting the focus on the second story of trauma immediately expands a person's sense of agency and concurrently leads them to address the central issue of identity.

Resonance on the inside

Kerry conveyed that she was experiencing reverberations between the compassion and gentleness she saw in her childhood self and the same qualities in herself as an adult. She was discovering an inner consistency in her values and ways of responding, which can be described as resonance on the inside. For her, the effect of this consistency squared with White's words that it "gives rise to new feelings of well-being and pleasure or agency" (2011, p. 127).

Kerry was in the box seat (noticing her earlier experience as a vulnerable child) as she recognised that she had refused to let trauma take away the compassion that had already become so important to her. Her chaotic and neglectful childhood couldn't extinguish what she had chosen. Her very commitment to her own values offered her a tangible tribute.

In the category of 'absent but implicit', White (2006) suggests that even a person's ongoing psychological pain and emotional distress may signify how greatly the trauma was at odds with the person's own ideas of what life is meant to be. There can be "beliefs about acceptance, justice and fairness, treasured hopes and dreams, moral visions of how the world might be better, or significant pledges, vows and commitments" (p. 154).

In her narrative, as she considered her response to alcoholism and violence, Kerry was becoming my co-theorist, demonstrating to me that even very young children can make important promises to themselves about how they wish to be in the world. They can do this even in the face of great trauma (White, 2011).

White (2011) raises the importance of relational resonance for those who have been through early trauma. I remember a conversation with Linton that shows the importance of such resonance.

In exploring his friendship with his mate Jeremy, he recalled that Jeremy's warm tone of affirmation and interest in the practical details of his life moved him to mutuality and to make the discovery that he was "not just a machine". Linton decided that in his relationship

> *with his wife he didn't need to go straight into fix it mode when anything went wrong. He was a really relational person. He had evidence of that with his kids. Walking in Jeremy's shoes with his wife would mean really being present rather than merely solving problems or reacting explosively.*

The concept of walking in someone else's shoes comes from White (2004). The resonance that Linton experienced as a result of how his friend Jeremy related to him helped him consider societal assumptions about masculinity and to reach out beyond the narrow Mr Fixit persona that society had handed down to him. Here was an exception to his usual sense of himself. It was enough to have him considering taking a conscious stand. Reflecting on a resonating friendship was moving or transporting him in his sense of himself.

Resonance within the therapy conversation

When genuine resonance is picked up in a therapy conversation, this can play a part in healing the emptiness, which is often the way people like Linton describe a dominant story characterised by a scarcity of early emotional connection. In the therapy conversations with Linton, the attempt was being made to provide respectful and genuinely de-centred therapeutic space and to pose scaffolding questions in order, in White's words (2011):

> *to identify 'the aspects of life' which had been accorded value and then to respond in ways which heighten curiosity, scaffold preferred meanings and load aspects of the person's life with significance (p. 127).*

The particularities and contexts of each person's life are explored in some detail. I noted that Linton was beginning to talk about himself in ways that seemed more alive and self-empowering. White draws attention to the fact that early developmental trauma can impact the language of inner life associated with the memory system called 'the stream of consciousness' (2006). When resonance is experienced, it has, in his view, the power to revitalise this language and to help a person begin to recognise themselves more easily and, as was the case with Linton with Jeremy, to see, hear and acknowledge, perhaps for the first time, something very different about themselves.

An intersubjective creation of meaning

When very early trauma has damaged an infant's sense of safety in the world, and her ability to bond and to self-regulate, the therapeutic relationship itself needs to be a trustworthy and an equal one. Duval and Béres (2011), researchers and teachers of narrative approaches in the United States, name the generativity that can result from "an intersubjective creation of meaning" (p. 10). Two people as equal subjects in the therapy room are working and conversing in a collaborative way.

Through observing therapeutic interactions with large cohorts of narrative therapists, in their research work, these researchers concluded that "it appears as though it is the combination of 'decentering the therapist and centering the person requesting assistance,' which contributes to the co-construction of meaning" (p. 10).

They describe the ability of the therapist to be present and to reflect in the moment, as critical. The nature of intersubjectivity means that it is not just the client whose life is being transformed. They suggest that "more often the [client responses] represent a sense of transport for the therapist" (p. 10).

This notion of intersubjectivity fits with what White (2007) also describes as a common outcome for outsider witness ceremonies. The latter are considered 'definitional ceremonies' because they acknowledge and 'regrade' people's lives instead of judging and degrading them (p. 104). Equality and collegiality in therapy relationships can make the difference. Respecting 'the other' means that the therapist helps the person consulting her to reflect on the stories she brings, which have always been created in particular social and cultural contexts, sometimes traumatising ones. The focus on context is an important narrative contribution since every trauma situation is different. Meanings cannot be generalised.

Conclusion

In introducing narrative approaches to therapy, I have explored aspects of its history, philosophy and practice. Narrative therapy takes power seriously. It is always going to be helpful for survivors of early developmental trauma and abuse to engage with a therapist who not only understands how power is misused, but who is committed to being accountable herself about her own practice and committed to the expansion of shared operational power in the lives of individuals and communities.

The narrative therapist makes use of a conversational practice that keeps the person who is consulting the therapist at the centre of the enquiry, setting her up to be able to investigate, explore and reflect. By scaffolding a conversation with a raft of curious questions that she orients towards her conversational partner, the therapist helps her begin to effectively re-author the narratives of her life. This co-authoring practice differentiates itself quite starkly from many therapies where it is the expertise of the therapist that is uppermost. In contrast, for narrative practitioners, it is the person consulting the therapist who is the expert on her own life.

Narrative practice works to pry apart negative dominant stories, helping the person discover new meanings by exploring her own history and taking past contexts seriously. When a person is helped to externalise the problems she brings, it becomes clear how exactly these problems have had the power to oppress and demonise. The approach that sees problems as themselves, 'the problem', and understands the corollary that the person is not the problem, can set a person free from a belief that her identity is spoiled or damaged by what she has suffered.

Narrative's unique way of deconstructing the normalising beliefs that can subjugate whole populations by robbing them of personal agency can mobilise a person's own reflective and choice-making capacities. Acts of resistance and stand-taking help the person move away from the past and turn in an alternative direction.

Narrative practice is not interested in a search for some deep essential truth that lies within the self. Instead collegiality and human connection are brought into view, so that relational influences, both historical and in the present, can be assessed. The idea that identity is socially constructed and that a person's sense of self is open to change throughout the life cycle brings hope for recovery from trauma.

Narrative practitioners strive to take a person's contexts and her own responses into account and they are always interested in expanding a person's sense of agency in the world. The narrative therapist takes up a metaphorical torch and helps a person discover and then explore some of the neglected narratives in her library of books of experience, including traumatic ones.

Chapter 2
Contemporary Somatic Therapy

Our body is not only a temple for the soul, it is also the sage within the temple.
Clyde Ford

Contemporary somatic therapy is holistic and integrative of body and mind. The cultural and philosophical context of the West has long mitigated against somatic therapy. Body psychotherapy is now often described as contemporary somatic therapy. 'Somatic' is considered a more accurate term than 'body' because it contains the idea of the total person as an embodied whole. The name comes from the Greek word *soma* which has a complex history of meanings, the simplest being 'person'. Despite this, I intend to use the terms 'body' and 'soma' interchangeably.

In his introductory notes to the experiential course *Adding a body focus to counselling practice* (2002), which provided my early training in somatic therapy, Doug Sotheren wrote:

This course begins from the assumption that all of life is embodied life, and that the initial point of contact between human beings is always a body contact (p. 8).

Our language is expressive of our body-inclusive life. Metaphors contained in images such as 'he has a backbone', 'she is stiff necked', 'he fell in a heap', and in phrases such as 'the news weighed me down', 'I felt as if the mat had been pulled out from underneath me', and 'she nearly jumped out of her skin', reveal that we understand that we are embodied beings.

Our bodies have a language of their own (body language), which scientists and communication specialists suggest make up from sixty to eighty per cent of all interpersonal communication. No relationship can take place without a body connection. The journey begins in utero. From first to last, our experience of life is as embodied beings.

The area of prosody, the rhythm and tone of communication, is one example of the amount and complexity of information being made available whenever one person communicates with another. Russell Meares (2016) describes an audience that was able to correctly link fifty different emotional nuances to the phrase 'this evening', when it was spoken in varying tonalities (p. 35). He points out that misunderstandings often arise because we are unable to 'hear' the particular emotion behind the words being spoken to us. The study of prosody he is referring to illustrates how just one aspect of the body can influence how meaning is communicated. All the other senses increase this complexity.

Western cultural assumptions about the body

The cultural context of the West has not been particularly hospitable to the facts and influence of our embodiment. In this culture, the intellect continues to be most often given prominence for problem-solving and is routinely turned to as the source of healing. Our education systems tend to teach us to think our way out of our difficulties. Despite the fact that most people know cognitively that we are more than an intellect, in reality many of us have learned to habitually treat our bodies as if they don't exist. Perhaps when we are physically ill or injured, we give our bodies some attention, but often when we are unwell, we unconsciously set ourselves against our bodies attitudinally, as if they are letting us down. This seems to apply even more so when trauma's bodily impacts are intense. The signals a person's body provides are ignored and rarely considered useful or even open for exploration to aid her recovery. Indeed, the body, with its uncomfortable symptoms tends to be ignored or negatively judged, criticised and shunned. The result of this is that the person who experiences bodily reactivity often develops an extremely judgmental way of talking to her inner self.

As I was writing this, I found myself wondering whether factors like these are what make our population so vulnerable to a voracious pharmacological industry. Psychosomatic symptoms, which implicate our sensations and emotions, are not easily recognised as such. We move from one pill to another in order to fix the problem. In the medical or therapeutic world, attending to one's body signals isn't usually part of the treatment plan.

It is not automatic or necessarily easy to raise awareness of our body or what it is communicating. Embarking on a journey to notice our body's sensations or signals, let alone to discover the stories that are written into our bodies, may seem like foreign territory to many. The misunderstandings around land tenure and land ownership for Australia's first people provide a similar difficulty. It is hard for Westerners to comprehend the knowledge of our indigenous sisters and brothers that their stories are 'written into the land'. Their sense of identity is closely linked to the place, the specific area of land where they were born or nurtured or where their ancestors lived. Identity can be threatened if and when this sacred ownership or connection is not acknowledged.

When therapy ignores the territory of the body, it can also run the risk of privileging forms of meaning-making that are logo-centric, male dominated and Euro-centric. This is a power issue, but it is also a practical one. If therapy originates primarily from academic, word-based understandings, we run the risk of missing a wealth of crucial information.

The seventeenth century thinker Descartes, who famously proclaimed "I think, therefore I am", formed a link in a long chain in Western thought from its Greco-Roman roots. The term 'logos', with its connection to male logic, was considered a more evolved or civilised approach to discourse than the embodied (feminine) 'sophia' or wisdom. The influence of such ways of thinking has been pervasive. Researcher and therapist Allan Schore (2003) says that:

> the separation of the operations of the mind from the structure and operation of the biological organism, the body is the result of the fact that this dualism (often named 'Descartes error') has been carried forward into the present day psychological and medical sciences (p. 111).

The history of body therapy

Body psychotherapy has worked against this dualism. It finds its roots in the early twentieth century with the work of Wilhelm Reich, who practised at the same time as Freud. He contended that society inscribes itself not only on the psyche but also on and in the body. He called his approach 'a vegetative' one. He attempted to show ways in which a person's bodily expression corresponded with her mental attitude. A particular body shape might come to attract a label such as 'stoical', for example (Heller, 2012). Reich's therapy could be described as largely a character analysis in the realm of the body, and some of his ideas and interventions attracted controversy.

Since Reich's death, the entry into the Western world of the non-dualistic teachings of Eastern philosophies has combined with post-modern and post-structural ideas in contributing to a greater evolution of somatic approaches. The Australian College of Contemporary Somatic Therapy (2017) describes how different schools of thought have influenced today's understanding. Each person's life and sense of herself are now understood to be influenced by a complex mix of the biological, social, cultural and ecological worlds we inhabit.

For the somatic practitioner in the West, there has been a need to scrutinise dominant cultural narratives about the superiority of Western culture and outlooks and to actively challenge them. The practitioner has needed to break down and to examine many taken-for-granted assumptions commonly entrenched around race, gender and religion, for example. Misused power and dogmatic belief systems have been examined and, as a result, body-focused therapists have replaced any thought of absolutism as a guide to behaviour, with a commitment to greater personal freedom and agency. There has needed to be a willingness to carefully consider ways in which power is used and misused, including in therapeutic settings.

Early feminists highlighted the significance of the body in the process of redefining the meanings of gender and of power relations. They demonstrated that gender itself is socially constructed, and articulated how the body is often used as a text of culture and a site of social control.

Scientific research has contributed to the understandings that counter a mind-body dualism. Imagine the following scenario.

You have no awareness that your heart rate is accelerating or of a nauseous sensation in your stomach. You can't tell whether you are sad or angry. When you are interviewed you find it difficult to make rational decisions or statements.

This scenario describes the lived experience of a cohort of brain-injured people who agreed to be part of a neurological study in the last decade of the twentieth century. Learning from the neuroanatomical studies of Hanna Damasio, who studied the brain lesions of this group, her husband, Anton Damasio (1994), was able to engage the group in extensive follow-up interviews and to make important links. This early neuroscientist hypothesised that the lack of rationality was connected with the deficits in body-awareness and emotion, which was the common experience of the group members. He came to the tentative conclusion that sensation and emotion are necessary to rational thought. Further he concluded that just projecting a cognitive judgment is not enough; it is the feel of it that counts.

As he did further neuroscience research, he expanded these findings. He observed that biochemical traces become inscribed in a person's body in ways that correlate with her past experiences, both pleasant and unpleasant. He invented a way of talking about these inscriptions, naming them 'somatic markers'. He was able to demonstrate that, behind conscious awareness, these markers guide in the making of decisions (Rothschild, 2010). He deduced that subtle but intense sensations help a person weigh up consequences, decide direction or identify preferences. He demonstrated also that emotions and their accompanying sensations provide cues to memory. Damasio (1994) began to use the name 'the neural self', clarifying in a broad way that neurological processes play a role in the development of identity or sense of self.

A clinical faculty member of the school of medicine at the University of California and experienced psychotherapist, Alan Schore (2003) has integrated a host of research from different disciplines, particularly about issues of attachment, regulation and the impacts of early trauma.

He noted that neuroimaging researchers have continued to throw even greater light on Damasio's findings (Schore, 2003). It is now more accepted that a person's biology is an influence that needs to be taken into account when the sense of self is explored. Unlike the assumptions that influenced Descartes, we thus now understand from scientific research that the body, its sensations and emotions, underlie all a person's rational processes.

Somatic therapists who include a body focus in therapy do so with the aim of giving due weight to all a client's contexts and influences. They recognise that a person implicitly or unconsciously constructs a sense of self within her own uniquely embodied relational orbits. They understand that she grows and develops within the dynamic interplay of her biology, her history and her culture.

As a result of early trauma, a person's body may be offering her signals which could be of use, but which are often uncomfortable, not noticed or constantly suppressed. The somatic therapist regularly follows a practice of raising a person's awareness of her body and its sensations. This may include exploration of aspects such as her bodily impulses and patterns of gesture and movement, shifts in bodily alignment, and in colour, temperature or breath. It may include changes in tone, muscle contraction and subtle repositioning.

The transformative practice of body therapy

I remember the breakthrough it was for me personally when I became aware of the slight slump that made up the body configuration of the chronic melancholic mood with which I had long struggled. Being encouraged in therapy to experiment with my posture led me to the discovery that a tiny re-structure of the way I often hold my chest and my facial muscles, could help move me out of a low mood. As I began to practise this body strategy, I repeatedly experienced a leap in agency and greater relational freedom. With reflection I could understand the way my body had learned to habitually slump in response to a disregarding adult dominance in childhood. This mindful exploration of my small body movements became a means of transformation. I could engage a new bodily configuration at will. The relief of a brighter mood motivated beneficial change. Every time the melancholy mood arrived, I needed to firstly become aware of it and then to practise making the small changes in my bodily configuration. My cognitive understanding then got behind my body process. There were important gains. I noticed a new willingness within myself to branch out relationally. On reflection I realised that I had never experienced anything like the same sense of empowerment through verbal therapy on its own or as a result of years of effort to gain mental insight into my chronic tendency towards depression.

The plasticity of the brain makes it possible for us to build new neural pathways (Doidge, 2015). None of us can change what happened to us historically, but evidence now suggests that growth in body awareness can help us change the impacts of past harms and enable us to seize the present. The willingness and ability to reflect and then the repetition of the relevant strategies are crucial. For me there was no lack of motivation, but of course I had to practice.

Pat Ogden (2015) describes how she helps a person explore changing her habitual posture and physical action patterns. She shows how these changes, as I discovered, in turn influence all aspects of a life. In her video, she shows a person choosing to change her tendency to pull back when meeting someone and instead taking the risk to make a small move forward. She related how making even a minimal change in a somatic pattern like this can alter how the person finds herself relating to others. It can lead to greater self-confidence, the development of better internal resonance and in turn improve a person's cognitive ability.

As I watched Pat Ogden's video evidence, I observed her de-centred approach. She respected each person as she helped one after another to become more aware of how she was holding her body or avoiding eye contact. She introduced safe options for experimentation, often joining the person to experiment with a more expanded mode of walking or a more aligned way of holding her body. In back-and-forth conversational exchanges, each person was given space to voice how she herself was perceiving the changes she was making.

Practitioners and trainers in more body-focused methodologies use means such as the videoing of casework, and even the use of spectacles that provide feedback on the therapist's body language, to clarify, develop and even measure therapy skills. They are evolving ways in which body-based interventions can be more easily recognised as evidence-based.

Bio-energetics, another longstanding model of somatic therapy, also seeks to attend to non-verbal body-based implicit processes rather than put sole reliance on explicit and verbal processes as the primary means of healing. Like Ogden, bio-energetics spokesperson Virginia Schroeter (2016) believes that when a person is aided to explore what her body is showing her, some of the findings of the polyvagal theory developed by Porges and colleagues (2011) are borne out. This theory attempts to elucidate the language of the body from the point of view of the nervous system. It is thought that including the body in therapy is likely to activate the social engagement system of the autonomic nervous system (Schroeter, 2016). This sophisticated system enables a person to calm and soothe herself, in contrast to being over-mobilised or shut down as a result of the more primitive fight, flight or freeze nervous system activations. This will be discussed further in the next chapter.

Earliest regulation

Like every mother, it's not hard for me to remember the euphoric sensations and the tenderness that flooded me when I set eyes on each of my newborns for the first time. How precious it was to feel his or her fresh-minted gaze, to engage in skin-to-skin contact, to hold, to talk, to rock, to feed and to marvel at this tiny being who was at once so dependent on me, and who quickly learned my face and responded to my voice so intently. He or she was soon initiating contact with me and bringing me great joy.

Schore (2003) helps us understand more of the fascinating story of infant development. He believes that the self of the infant begins its formation as a result of sensory experience in the womb. He names this a 'body self'. After birth, what's known as the dance of attachment between mother and child continues to involve all the senses. Schore contends that it is in the emotionally available relationship with the primary carer, that the infant learns how to bond closely and then how to be parted. Over a period of time and given a consistency of experience she learns how to establish healthy boundaries between 'the self' and 'the other' (pp. 54–59).

Schore (2003) is interested in important nuances of attachment theory, particularly the understanding of its originator, John Bowlby, that the infant's attachment to the mother develops out of her distressed states.

I have a piercing memory of one of my babies becoming intensely distressed by a sudden loud noise, perhaps it was a siren. He had never been so upset. I remember how vital it was to be able to quickly

CHAPTER 2 CONTEMPORARY SOMATIC THERAPY

calm and settle him. It was my job to be what Schore (2003) calls "the regulator of my baby's negative state" (p. 44). I needed to do this again and again, whenever any upset or stress occurred.

Schore (2003) explains that it is through the messages of the body, experienced within a close relationship, that the infant gradually learns to self-regulate in response to life's stresses. Because of the importance of this, he developed regulation theory. From the beginning, an infant's body and its sensations are being met by crucial embodied and relational responses, which guide her towards increasing self-regulation.

Daniel Siegel (2010), in his quest to better understand the complex development of the human mind, reinforces that this is inextricably linked to the earliest influence on the child of both her own body and the bodies of those who relate to her. It seems to him that the infant comes into the world ready to make connections, and her earliest intimate relationships together with the early neural shaping of her brain, nervous system and body over all, become the foundation of a secure sense of herself, which in turn contributes to the formation of mind.

Through facial expression, tone of voice, gesture and posture, she comes to attune herself to or to resonate with the other, and to experience a palpable sense of intimate connection. Throughout her lifetime, her survival, her vitality and her wellbeing continue to depend on a meeting of minds that takes place within deep emotional, body-based relationships.

When trauma is repeatedly blocking a person's life, and early dysregulation becomes endemic, the person's body is always responding. It stands to reason that its messages should be taken into account in therapeutic work. The person's body can be thought of as a treasure trove to be mined, as is her thinking. The quest is to help the person gain the self-regulation and the resilience that may have been stopped in its tracks by trauma and a lack of caring support.

Body awareness and state dependent recall

Rothschild (2000) draws attention to an everyday experience common to us all. When we return intentionally to a postural state we were in earlier this can aid or trigger memory recall.

> You were just in your living room and wanted something. You came into the kitchen and ...
> 'What was it I came in here for?' You scratch your head. You swear. You can't remember. You
> wrack your brain. You go back to the spot where the intention originated, assuming the same
> sitting posture you were in at that moment – BINGO! 'Now I remember!' (p. 54).

This describes the state-dependent recall first recognised by Damasio (1994). The sensations of which you were not conscious when you were sitting act as somatic markers if you return yourself to that same sitting posture. They successfully and accurately cue your memory.

Clyde Ford (1975) reports the following small therapy vignette to illustrate how body-awareness can be raised during a therapy session, and can bring along with it healing information in the form of cued memories.

As Carmen told her story, her head and eyes were down, her shoulders were rotated forward, and her arms were slumped over her legs. I asked her to close her eyes for a moment and to be aware of how she was holding herself.

"What's that like?" I asked after several minutes. Carmen started to cry.

"This is how I held my body as a young child of three or four," she replied. "I'd listen to my drunken father yell and scream at my mother, while staying in a corner just like this, ashamed and afraid to look at them" (p. 109).

Integrative intent

Body psychotherapy never denies the importance of verbal systems of therapy. It never claims to be a standalone approach. While there are always at least two bodies in the room, and the body is implicit in every therapy exchange, for the contemporary somatic therapist, aspects of body and of mind are understood to be complementary. Verbal therapies are essential if a person is to reflect on what her body is telling her and to give mindful attention towards it. It is through the workings of her mind that a person is able to go on to explore many other aspects of experience, such as history and culture, metaphor and meaning.

Like Damasio (1994), Rothschild, (2000), Ogden, (2016) and Porges (2011), I have had the privilege to observe the integrative thrust that occurs when a person's body is included therapeutically. Somatic arousal or freezing seems to lessen, internal fragmentation to heal and cognitive processing to yield clarity. Relationships also seem to improve almost as if by magic.

Somatic experiencing

Ford (1975) did some integrating work with John who was one of several sexual abuse survivors seeking somatic help as an alternative to talking therapy. John was dissatisfied with what traditional verbal therapy had provided.

He was experiencing fierce and ongoing pain in his shoulder. Ford's notes tell of a simple body-focused intervention he offered to help John heighten his awareness of the sensations of pain. He asked him not to speak at first but to act out what was happening in his painful shoulder. Here is what he observed.

John stood in silence for several minutes. Then like an actor in a black and white silent movie, his body began to speak. He started by facing me then slowly turning away. As he swivelled away his body began to crumple: He dropped his head, let his knees buckle, bent his arms and drew them into his chest.

John remained in that collapsed standing position for several minutes before sitting down. He was emotionally spent and managed only a single word, "shame", he uttered, "shame".

Eventually John's voice got stronger. "Shame! I've been walking around with the shame of my abuse locked in this shoulder" (p. 115).

The sensations in John's shoulder had cued his intense emotional sense of shame. It was as if this emotion had lodged in his body and had been causing pain until it was noticed. As John reflected on the overwhelming shame that had dogged his life, he began to describe his sense that he was "getting his shoulder back". It was as if it no longer had to be constricted by unexpressed trauma-induced emotion. His pain was released, and he could work on understanding and digesting the disabling emotion of shame.

Self-experience of split-off emotion

Self-stories of emotions dissociated in the body as John's were may seem far-fetched. However, his experience struck a strong chord with me, because I too have experienced psychosomatic pain in my shoulder. For me it was a different emotion to which I had been numbed. In response to an incident of bullying in my workplace, I failed to experience my anger at all. It was as if early fear had taught me to freeze anger out. My shoulder became inflamed. I sought medical help and physiotherapy, but weeks passed, and nothing alleviated the pain.

It was in body psychotherapy, when my trusted somatic psychotherapist provided a rhythmic type of massage, that my anger was cued. By experiencing the anger in a bodily expressive way (by lying face down on my bed, kicking and pummelling), I was better able to digest the recent bullying experience. In doing so, I was bringing my body and my mind together. I could give space to the anger my body had somehow stored early in my life and which had been triggered by the bullying episode. I was able to understand, metabolise and digest my experience better.

The fierce inflammation in my shoulder quickly disappeared after the experimental anger work. Pain in my shoulder thereafter became a useful signal. Any twinge of pain in my shoulder was recognised, not for its discomfort but for its usefulness as a signal to which I could respond. I became much better at recognising that I was angry (or afraid). Over time, I learnt not only to know my own angry emotion but to be able to deal with it. I learnt to express it with integrity so that my body didn't have to over-contain it. When adequately expressed, my anger was able to perform its normal protective function. Anger is sometimes needed for safety. It can be used productively and creatively to set things right. For me, early dysregulating trauma had robbed me of this. I had been split off from my anger and instead learned a fearful kind of passivity. I had been stripped of the agency I needed to be able to stand up for myself in the workaday world of adulthood.

Body stories

Contemporary somatic psychotherapists are interested in the forgotten stories that are often held in the body, as they were for Carmen and John. In most of the case vignettes in this book, memories that may have been lost cognitively but which have been held and remembered in the body are described as they become available to the protagonist by a simple process of awareness-raising.

When the body is intentionally engaged in this way, it seems that its discourses, however small, carry great significance. The incorporation of the body and a person's accompanying growth in somatic awareness expands her consciousness and, as has already been mentioned, this opens the way for cognitive change.

The body is sometimes described as a kind of bridge between emotions and cognition. It can also be described as a place or a platform from which a person can notice impulses and make associations. It is my experience that the body is the arena in which the person can easily recognise arousal, intensity or freeze in her autonomic nervous system, and then find useful body-based ways to soothe, contain and digest it (Carrol, 2002).

Somatic experiencing is the name for a person's subjective recognition of the phenomenon we can also call organismic knowing. This kind of knowing is very different from the rational knowing we most often rely on. As a person increases her awareness of her body, she comes to trust what her body organism already knows.

How Pearl's body told its story

Pearl had first sought therapy because she was tired of her over-reactive angry outbursts during conflicts with her husband and children. She felt that her own instantaneous and seemingly automatic behaviour was her biggest problem.

When I enquired about the sensations she had felt in her body during the latest outburst, Pearl talked about a burning sensation in her gut. She was happy to give it her mindful attention for a few moments.

Pearl immediately began describing an event that occurred when she was three or four.

> *I can see myself crouching in the bathroom. I'm with my mum. Now I remember! Mum and dad had been fighting and throwing things at one another. I know that I was terrified!*

It turned out that Pearl had been a helpless witness of family violence on many occasions. She expressed her astonishment that her body had been able to take her back to this frightening childhood reality. She began to reflect on how the problem of her angry reactivity with her kids in the present was linking her to her own childhood. Her body accurately remembered traumatic dynamics from the past. This legacy was still impacting her life.

The sensation-based memory provided a window of insight for Pearl into her early experiences and emotions. Her new awareness of her body allowed her to better understand her childhood experience. She could begin to be on her own side instead of against herself. Was it the noisiness of her present family conflicts or the powerlessness they ignited in Pearl? Was it some or several aspects of the relationship dynamics she was immersed in that instantly awakened her brain to the alarm reactions of long ago? Certainly, the intense sensations acting as somatic markers awakened a significant memory (Damasio, 1994). Neuroscientists (e.g., Perry, 2006) confirm that dysregulating trauma experiences tend to be repeatedly recycled, as was occurring for Pearl.

CHAPTER 2 CONTEMPORARY SOMATIC THERAPY

Awareness of her body took Pearl on a somatic journey. She learnt to manage her over-reactivity using body-based strategies. Gradually she learned to accept rather than to shun her body's messages and to quickly modulate the arousal of her body's alarm systems and the repeated triggering of her childhood experience.

Pearl and her organismic knowing

In a later session, Pearl began to take the conversational lead, which as her therapist I could follow with my own attentive bodily presence and empathy. As she explained the flexibility and openness of the aerial dancing she was enjoying, she talked about a felt sense of pleasurable excitement. When her body was well aligned and her posture strong, she grew in confidence. Being in her body was bringing her a sense of healing. Relationally, she was also experiencing the resonance of an appreciative crowd. She noticed too that when her friends invited her to participate in something new she was no longer holding back. Her fear seemed to be evaporating. There was a new sense of agency. By trusting in her organismic knowing Pearl was literally expanding herself.

I reflected that, for her, there seemed to be a thrust towards integration and healing. Discovering the enjoyable sensations of her bodily movement was helping Pearl to digest and manage her fearful emotions and to make changes in her thinking processes and patterns of behaviour.

I wondered if this meant that she had engaged her social engagement system effectively, because the evidence was that she had a new ability to trust herself and others (Porges, 2011).

The Cambridge Body Psychotherapy Centre (n. d.) makes the following observation:

> The release of tension gives the person a sense of more relaxation and space inside the body. Counselees report that they begin to experience more choice and flexibility in their daily lives. Sometimes the work with muscle tension or breath is accompanied by memories, images or emotion connected with past events. Often just recognising the source of these emotions or being able to name or express the related emotions, brings relief and a sense of coming home.

Release of bodily tension

Experiential training in adding a body focus to the work of therapy was of great benefit for me. During an experiment in pairs, I recall lying on my back on a mattress. My body was somewhat tense, although this was such a familiar state that I didn't recognise it. I can see now that it was as if I couldn't really trust the ground to hold me. My partner asked me where I was feeling tension. I became conscious of tightness in my neck. She moved herself to simply support my neck with her arm. That small act of encouragement and bodily support somehow gave me permission to let my body come down.

Tension was released. In that moment I experienced what I can only describe as a kind of spontaneous unwinding. This wouldn't have been dramatic to an onlooker, but I felt a rhythmic movement in my body as if a giant screw inside me was unravelling itself.

This experience of interpersonal bodily support allowed my body to complete a healing movement. The embodied empathy of my fellow trainee had provided the bridge I needed to be able to trust my own body.

Unexpectedly, in the days and weeks following this event, I experienced a release of constriction in my gastrointestinal tract, which has been maintained ever since. I perceived a new sense of emotional freedom and I now resonate with the idea that there is an organismic knowing within the soma of each person and the felt sense is an important inner sense that can be fostered.

Resonance and intersubjectivity

During my course in 2002, the term 'intersubjective field' was being used to describe the relational space that can open up between a therapist and her client. When the conversation is personally respectful the two people can become attuned to each other and there is room for the exploration of bonding and separating that Schore (2003) describes. Intersubjectivity, the responsive relationship between two subjects, sits alongside the theories of attachment and regulation. It always begins with two bodies coming into relationship and the experience of empathetic support such as I myself had experienced with my fellow trainee.

Decades earlier, when considering social influences on the sense of self, Ford (1975) drew attention to the work of Condon (1975). This researcher, like many others since, micro-analysed the way interactions take place between people. He observed that we resonate somatically with each other, our bodies moving and changing subtly, moment to moment. He described this as being not unlike the way striking a tuning fork and bringing it close to another tuning fork causes the second one to vibrate.

Schore (2003) refers to some of his earlier work (Schore, 1994) when he draws a direct parallel between the empathic processes of the intuitively attuned mother and her infant and the similarly intuitively empathic therapist who psycho-biologically attunes to and resonates with the trauma survivor's shifting affective states, thereby co-creating with her a context in which the therapist can act as a regulator of the patient's physiology.

Stolorow and Atwood (1982) emphasise how the therapist can work in tandem with the person whose body sensations also help her grow in self-regulation.

> The self-reflective empathic therapist has an opportunity to act as an interactive affect regulator of the patient's dysregulated states … and over time it facilitates the 'evolution of affects' from their early form in which they are experienced as body sensations, into subjective states that can gradually be verbally articulated (p. 42).

Stolorow and Atwood are suggesting that the therapist needs to be operating from a well-regulated self-reflective place herself. She needs to be able to read body language and to be aware of her own body. There may be other life arenas, such as her friendships or her roles as a partner or as a parent, where she develops the skills of tuning in to others.

Body language and the matching of biological states

Schore (2003) highlights the importance of the nonverbal exchange in the therapeutic process in practical terms. Tone of voice, body posture and facial expression are vital relationally. He collects together a wide range of research that suggests the right brain hemisphere specialises in nonverbal communication and nonconscious operations. It is thought to be the part of the brain that mediates empathy.

Schore's opinion is that the right brain-to-right brain attunement possible in an intersubjective counselling dyad provides the best opportunity for the newness of relational experience, which can help a person improve her self-regulation.

In Stuebe's (2009) account of Schore's presentation in Australia, which had taken place the same year, she reported that a significant surprise of the seminar to her was that Schore was now espousing body-based intersubjectivity as his key theoretical stance. Earlier he had emphasised psychoanalytic theory, particularly object relations and self-psychology, for their contributions to effective therapy and, in particular, for trauma resolution. These theories suggest that the way people relate to others and to situations in their adult lives is shaped by the relationship they had with their mother or first caretaker who is defined as the first 'object'. The work of the therapist is to provide the consistent mirroring that the child did not receive and with deep empathy to offer the client the experience of a good (supportive) object.

Perhaps intersubjectivity is a less hierarchical model than object relations and marks the shift between modern and more post-modern approaches to therapy. It features a bottom-up approach, which is de-centred and where equality and respect are paramount. The body is clearly honoured.

Returning to memories of my own newborns, I recall the mouth-moving games I played with them in the early months of life, and the fascination I felt as my baby mimicked the movement of my tongue or my lips. Attunement and the ability to resonate with the feelings of others or to empathise are now thought to rely on mirror neurones, as described by a team of Italian neuroscientists, including Vittorio Gallese (2007). This team proposed that it is through the use of mirror neurons that a tiny baby not only mimics her mother, but that gradually a person develops the ability to sense what is going on in the mind of the other (Siegel, 2010).

Body-based biological attunement allows us to experience resonance, and this experience connects us humans together. Body-to-body experience paves the way for the resonancing of language and ideas. In espousing intersubjectivity, Schore (2003) was not abandoning the wisdom of earlier theories, but he was drawing attention to the way that the therapist tunes her body in with the body language of the client.

The skill of pacing, or following the client's body language, is taught in training courses for most therapy approaches. The empathy Schore is calling for goes beyond the outreaching of the mind and even the emotions. It amounts to a matching of biological states. The therapist responds not only to the words spoken, but may find herself responding somatically, her own body resonating with the soma of the client.

Ethical considerations

An important responsibility of care rests on the shoulders of the body therapist. Once there is an initial rapport with the client, a relationship of trust needs to be developed over time.

We probably all know the vulnerability we feel with regard to how other people view our bodies. I remember my own reaction on one occasion when a physiotherapist, who was a stranger to me, made the instant observation that I had "a lot of old tension in my neck like a set of heavy iron cables". I remember reacting inwardly to those words with a familiar sense of despair and shame. It felt judgmental. It was as if I had been caught out and there was something deeply wrong with me.

Unless clients come specifically to consult a body practitioner, a process that asks them to include their body in the exploration may feel quite confronting or strange at the very least.

The training for body therapy often emphasises the importance of accurate observation on the practitioner's part. She is sometimes taught to describe her observations to the client.

During my own training, Sotheren (2005) repeatedly called on his students to "mistrust all theory and all ideas that may demand that the therapist should know better than the client" (p. 12).

As I developed my confidence as a body therapist, I realised that if I failed to deliberately pay attention to this principle, there was a risk of slippage in terms of my respectfulness. Accurate observation is no doubt important. However, I was seeing that speaking your observations to the client can quickly trap a therapist into a one up, one down power dynamic.

I like the way Ford asked Carmen earlier what she herself observed and felt about her body reactions. While she considered her answer, he was able to stay present with her. When the client is given the respect and space to initiate and describe her sensations and images, and the therapist is responsive to this, this paves the way for the client to feel a resonance that is her own.

The Cambridge Body Psychotherapy Centre (n.d.) describes a therapeutic attitude of gentle curiosity, and mindfulness as an attitude of kind attention which can be encouraged so that the person comes gently to a raised awareness of parts of her body that may be tense or restrictive. When this happens, practitioners are likely to observe what I myself learnt through experience, namely that "simply bringing awareness to tensions and holding patterns without forcing something to happen or change, is enough to bring about a release of restrictions".

Touch as a healing strategy

Schore (2003) draws attention to touch in his description of regulation theory. He recognises touch as the earliest experience of every infant and thus beneficial for healing.

Many somatic therapists use touch intentionally as a healing strategy. A careful consideration of the ethics of touch, especially in relation to sexual abuse survivors, is an appropriate part of any training regime for safe practice. Both safe touch protocols and safe space protocols are put in place. These put the person who has come for therapy into the driving seat, so she can decide what is acceptable for her.

Ford (1975) describes an example of this.

> *First, I asked Jennifer to find an area of her body where she felt safe about being touched. She identified that area as the back of her right hand. Then I asked her to give me permission to touch her right hand when she was ready. With permission granted I touched the back of her hand and instructed her to ask me to stop touching her when she was ready (p. 113).*

This protocol of complete respect for the other illustrates what is at the heart of an ethical approach to somatic therapy. Tension can ease as a result of simple touch, and such an exchange can be transformative. Ford (1975) speaks about a second-order benefit of this kind of respect as well. Using the above protocol, he describes the way Jennifer began to reassert the right of choice that had been damaged within early overpowering relationships.

Ford (1975) also points out some of the dangers inherent in the use of touch interventions. They must always be carefully negotiated within the therapy relationship. However, sometimes empathy is not enough. He considers that advanced levels of skill and experience are required if touch is to be used helpfully. He illustrates this point with an example of an abuse survivor who was experiencing difficulty with her boundaries. "There are times in therapy where such a person, might crave and push for the kind of touch which can lead to unhelpful emotional flooding" (p. 114).

Sometimes a therapist needs to take a step back and to follow a path of caution. While often it can be deeply healing, touch also has the potential to trigger traumatic memories and the arousal of emotions that can feel overwhelming. In Ford's view, it is easy for an inexperienced therapist to inadvertently cause the harm of re-traumatisation. This can be a major problem for trauma work.

Since Ford's time, unethical practices, both verbal and somatic, have caused variety of harms. Leading a person by subtle suggestion or manipulation can even lead to the fabrication of false memories of abuse, which are extremely damaging both to the person in therapy and to the purported perpetrator (Rothschild, 2000).

Working with the body does not require touch

So long as proper attention is given to matters of power and consent, Rothschild (2000) believes that judicious touch can be useful. However, the body strategies she most often uses, and those utilised in this book's therapy model, are non-touch strategies.

Using a meditative body-based exploration from Fisher (2001), I included the body without touch in my work with Angela and Clem.

This couple were able to see in their mind's eye an image of themselves during a recent conflict, as if it had been captured by a sculptural artist. Then they could embody what they had imagined. I remember Clem taking up a slumped position on the couch while Angela stood at some distance looking at him somewhat haughtily from above. It was Angela's vision they were putting into effect.

> Clem began to talk about how hard he found it to be around Angela's family because of what he described as their "cold eye contact". He always seemed to be found wanting. Even their welcoming words seemed calculating. Angela had never thought about eye contact before, but she immediately concurred with Clem's assessment of her family. Was this why she had always felt left out as a child?

On hearing her response Clem was able to share with Angela that when she got angry her eyes became hard and cold like the rest of her family. It was this coldness that triggered him. He told her that at these times he felt like "a waste of space" and "the little boy who was unwanted by his father".

When I asked her about other contrasting relational experiences, Angela was surprised to be able to bring to mind examples of softer eye contact.

> She began to talk about a close friend and how the warmth of this friend's gaze drew her in and emotionally connected her. Then she articulated a new awareness. Her habitual way of making eye contact when uncertain, unhappy or angry must have been contributing to the flare-ups between her and Clem and adding the emotional intensity that neither had been able to understand.

The feeling was of mutual understanding and the couple were able to go on and explore their own relationship in terms of softer eye contact and a more receptive atmosphere. As they enacted this alternative reality they talked of a palpably different feeling in their bodies that would be easy to remember. They were co-theorists teaching me about the power of the felt sense and a way in which our bodies can affect each other.

Conclusion

In this chapter, I have described how contemporary somatic therapy has evolved within a context in the West that has been largely antagonistic towards or unaware of the body. Since the seventeenth century, the mind and reason have been elevated to a place of superiority over the body and its sensations and emotions. Attitudes arising from this kind of dualistic philosophy continue to be quite pervasive in Western society today. They have invaded therapy where cognitive approaches are still often considered the only approaches that are evidence-based, measurable and therefore worthy.

However, neuroscience has demonstrated that the body is not only important to the healing of traumatic impacts, but that its sensations underlie all rational thought and decision making. The self, while it is relationally-influenced, also has biological and neural aspects to it.

This chapter also explored the body's implicit role in attachment and regulation at the beginning of an infant's life. Dysregulating and traumatizing events and relationship patterns at this early stage can deeply affect both the body and the mind of a survivor. These impacts need to be addressed in therapy. The next chapter explores both the effects of trauma in more detail, and the approach to working with this taken by trauma therapists.

Chapter 3
Trauma and Trauma Therapy

Traumatic memories come back as emotional and sensory states with little verbal representation. Bessel van der Kolk

The magnitude of the problem of developmental trauma for human societies is obvious to those who work at the coalface with suffering children and adolescents. When we take into account the impacts of early trauma that continue to disrupt a person's life into adulthood, the magnitude is even greater. It is my work with adults that has prompted this book and is its major focus.

In the preface to *Life story therapy with traumatized children: A model for practice* (2005), Richard Rose wrote:

> *Fully one third of adults experience multiple forms of significant adverse childhood events – often traumatic in nature. And we now know these adverse and traumatic experiences change us in all ways – our bodies and our minds, our hearts and souls are seared and then twist and change to help us survive (p.13).*

Trauma can be defined as the experience of a real or perceived threat that invokes fear and helplessness, confusion, pain and loss of control. It causes states of high arousal and the associated responses of fight, flight or freeze, resulting in immobilisation when trauma can't be escaped. It tends to overwhelm the normal coping mechanisms of social engagement. The way the brain and the nervous system react with long-term repercussions to this kind of sensory somatic overload is central in this chapter.

Complex developmental trauma

Australian GP Cathy Kezelman, who has acted as the national president of Adults Surviving Child Abuse (ASCA, now known as Blue Knot Foundation), and who is herself a survivor of childhood sexual abuse, believes that trauma and its treatment is still not well understood, and that medical protocols are often not appropriate (Kezelman & Stavropoulos, 2012). She points out that most developmental trauma finds its origin within early relationship dynamics, and warns that this type of complex trauma can tip lives over into extremes of dysfunction and the appearance of mental illness. Misdiagnosis is common and medical treatments can proliferate and complicate.

Bessel van der Kolk (2017), professor of psychiatry at Boston University, suggests something similar. He believes that there is a serious public health emergency arising out of an over-diagnosis of bipolar disorder in children who are actually struggling with the dysregulating impacts of complex trauma.

An integrated mind and body system

In *Descartes Error* (1994), neurologist Antonio Damasio explored the big picture for human beings. He set out to challenge the promotion of rational thinking above the experience of the body and above other forms of knowing. He noted that:

> *Surprising as it may sound, the mind exists in and for an integrated organism; our minds would not be the way they are if it were not for the interplay of body and brain during evolution, during individual development, and at the current moment (p. xv).*

As described in Chapter 2, years of research convinced Damasio that when a person is feeling and acting as if she is being repeatedly traumatised, cerebral insight and understanding are not enough. The body also needs to be brought into the picture.

Van der Kolk (2006) is referring specifically to the context of early trauma when he comments that:

> *the rational executive brain, the mind, the part that needs to be functional in order to engage in the process of psychotherapy, has very limited capacity to squelch sensations, control emotional arousal or change fixed action patterns (p. 3).*

Dr Peter Levine (1997) is a psychologist and researcher who has studied stress and trauma over forty years. He translated Damasio's holistic ideas into the realm of therapy by creating a theoretical construct that synthesises the many aspects of a person's experience that are affected by stress and trauma. In the acronym he uses to explain this, SIBAM, 'S' stands for sensation, 'I' for images, 'B' for behaviours/gestures/action patterns, 'A' for affects/emotional responses and 'M' for meanings/cognitive understandings. Levine has shown that when all these aspects are holistically explored during the therapy conversation, a person is enabled to gradually integrate the physical, the emotional and the cognitive impacts of her traumatic experience.

Pat Ogden and Kekuni Minton (2000) make a plea for putting the body first in such exploration:

CHAPTER 3 TRAUMA AND TRAUMA THERAPY

By using the body (rather than cognition or emotion) as the primary entry point in processing trauma, sensorimotor psychotherapists directly treat the effects of trauma on the body which in turn facilitates emotional and cognitive processing (p. 149).

Trauma activates different parts of the nervous system

Peggy Mason, a lecturer in neuroscience at Chicago University, explains that for a person to gain clear understanding of any overstimulating event, linkages must be made between parts of the peripheral nervous system and the central nervous system, which is made up of the brain and the spinal column (Mason, 2014). Neurons, much more varied and complex than other cell types, use both electrical and chemical energy to communicate (send signals) from and between all the parts of the central and the peripheral systems. The following diagram shows the complex signalling that is involved. The start arrow leads the reader to make sense of the diagram using the numbered prompts.

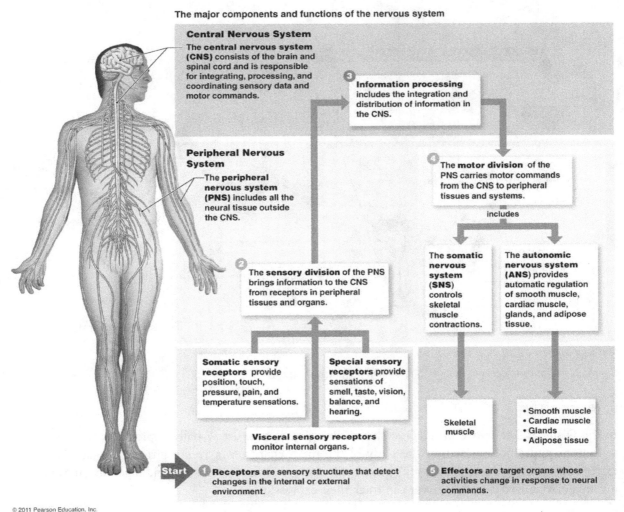

Figure 1. The major components and functions of the nervous system. Source: Pearson Education, 2011.

49

Primitive brain and neural systems overreact to alarm and threat

The brain's rapid response to threatening signals, for example, that leads us to quickly withdraw a finger from a hot stovetop or experience a startle response to a sudden loud noise nearby, alerts us to possible danger and is familiar to us all. Bruce Perry, therapist and researcher, explains that while the brain's alarm signals keep us safe from danger, the primitive brain tends to overreact to threat (1999). Early alarm experiences set up the brain to repeatedly initiate patterned neural activity in the primitive areas, the brainstem and the diencephalon. Once the lower brain is mobilised, it, in turn, connects to the mid-brain's limbic or survival centre, and a release of hormones, such as cortisol, leads to what a survivor experiences as an arousal, which, in turn, interferes with the processes that link to the sense-making (cognitive) processes of the neocortex.

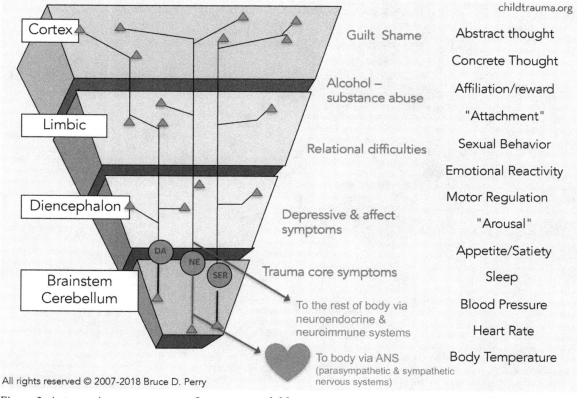

Figure 2. Autonomic nervous system. Source: www.childtrauma.org.

Over-reactivity and distorted interpretations

In the Disney Pixar movie *Inside Out*, stimuli bringing change are visually depicted as they elicit sensations and emotions within the body of the main character, a young girl. At eleven, she is experiencing the stress of her family's geographical move. The emotions of fear, anger, disgust and joy are personalised, and the viewer can track their expression.

Because her usually supportive parents are preoccupied, the little girl's period of stress is extended. Negative emotions overwhelm her familiar experience of joy. Her interpretation of a new school and a teacher's overtures of welcome are distorted into messages of exclusion, and viewers can see the emotional arousal of her nervous system. Her prowess in ice hockey is upended by fear-driven anger. She strikes the ball aggressively and muscles other players aside. Her behaviours (action patterns) and even some of her core memories are vulnerable.

The movie succeeds in visually introducing us to the way past experiences, imagination and expectation all affect how this young girl interprets the present. Her brain is misleading her as she tries to interpret and make sense of an unfamiliar environment.

The movie's message is that even a well-supported child can be vulnerable to the impacts of stress, which occur without conscious volition and which quickly develop a life of their own. Due to feelings of isolation and the prolonged duration of her stress, this child regresses into primitive (brainstem-related) ways of responding. Once supported, however, she is quickly helped to calm herself and in time to resolve her situation.

Stimuli either from inside or from outside the body always leads to change (Mason, 2014). If the stimulus is reasonably strong it produces a sensation (although this is not always sensed consciously, as, for example, when extra hormones enter the bloodstream). We don't necessarily interpret the magnitude of a stimulus accurately, especially in childhood.

This difficulty with interpretation is part of the problem for any person who has experienced trauma early in life as Perry (2006) and many other researchers make plain. Her first experiences of trauma influence a child's later interpretations. Meanings she may take from the worst of what happened to her, or from stress she experienced chronically or in a prolonged way, set up her unconscious (implicit) expectations regarding the future. An early traumatic set of circumstances, if left unresolved, can continue to influence her ongoing interpretation of circumstances, of others and of the world in general.

Perry in Goodwin and Attias (1999) discusses his research into how memories of fear work in the lives of the at-risk children with whom he has been closely connected throughout his career. This research shows that the brain keeps on associating the past with the present. Its neurones repeat patterns like those activated by fear earlier in such children's lives and, as a result, their behaviour tends to become hyper-reactive.

Mason (2014) makes the point that, for adults who were traumatised as children, the fear engendered by early traumatic events tends to be recycled many times. Every time the earliest dynamics are unconsciously recalled, the trauma memories are consolidated. A history of trauma or abuse can weaken a person's capacity to function at the levels she would attain to if she felt safe. If her brain is telling her that she needs to be constantly alert to danger, she spends a lot of time in trauma states.

Triggering and sensations

Damasio (1994) developed the theory of somatic markers, making a significant contribution to the ability to explore the ongoing effect of traumatic events. He demonstrated that later stressful dynamics in the life of someone who has experienced childhood trauma impact the person's somatic markers, and often cue implicit (unconscious) memories of earlier or original impacts. Like van der Kolk (2002), Damasio stated that triggered trauma memories return without coherence and in the form of flashbacks and sensory-somatic over-reactivity.

Damasio (1994) commented that "feelings, [sensations] along with the emotions they come from, are not a luxury. They serve as internal guides" (p. xv).

Although narrative therapy has not usually put an explicit focus on the body, White (2006) echoes Damasio's findings when he describes specific cues that trigger memory.

> Traumatic memory is invariably triggered by a general stress, by specific circumstances of duress and/or by specific cues. These cues mirror some aspect of the original trauma and they may be internal, as in specific emotional and sensory experience, or external as in specific circumstances or relational events (p. 73).

The polyvagal perspective

After decades of research into the evolutionary development of the autonomic nervous system, neuroscientist Dr Stephen Porges and his team from the Brain and Body Centre of the University of Illinois in Chicago came up with a new perspective that links autonomic function to behaviour (2011). The team challenged the long-held belief that the autonomic nervous system is a dual system, and identified a third aspect of the system. Previously, the autonomic nervous system had been understood to respond to stress in hyper- and hypo-active ways, which function rather like the arms of a see-saw (Mason, 2014). The new finding was that while humans share the first two parts, the parasympathetic and the sympathetic nervous systems, with, respectively, reptiles (the lizard brain) and other mammals (the mouse brain), the third more highly evolved branch of the autonomic nervous system is specific to more sophisticated animals, especially primates, in the survival value it enables. Healthy newborn humans, in particular, exhibit what Porges and his team (2011) call 'social engagement capability'.

Humans come into the world with advanced and complex skills to communicate our needs, since we are dependent on caretaking longer than other animals. Parents also need sophisticated skills to keep their infants safe. The anatomy of voice, hearing, touch, visual contact and facial expression induce pleasurable sensations in both baby and mother. Proximity is maximised for safety and bonding. Emotions of love help us survive right from the start (Chitty, 2013; Porges, 2011).

Under non-stress conditions, each part of the autonomic nervous system plays its role: the parasympathetic nervous system is normally responsible for rest, relaxation, digestion and immobilisation without fear, while the sympathetic nervous system is the energised state we need when we are working, exercising or learning in an alert and engaged manner (Porges, 2011). The social engagement system is activated by social warmth, a friendly animated face, the prosody of the voice (its pitch and tones, its undulations of welcome and interest). A person engages socially by listening, interacting, bonding, communicating, thinking and feeling in an integrated way. This social engagement biology is now understood by many researchers to be at the heart of attachment biology.

Porges' theory focuses on the physiology of nerve structures, starting within the ears and the face as the baby hears a soothing voice and learns to rely on the calmness of the mother's face. (Vagus nerves are cranial ones extending through the neck into the thorax and upper abdomen. On the abdominal side of the body they're described as ventral vagal nerves and at the back as dorsal). The theory demonstrates that when a person can make use of the recently evolved ventral vagal brake, her sophisticated social engagement system is able to act as a controller over the sympathetic nervous system and help her calm her alarm systems readily. Porges describes physiological 'portals' that somatic touch practitioners may be able to use to help a person access this kind of brake. Rather than staying with the crude sympathetic nervous system instincts of fight or flight, or moving into parasympathetic nervous system shutdown (or freeze), a trauma survivor may be helped to access the more nuanced calming of the social engagement system, while at the same time improving the regulation of her internal organs (Porges, 2011; Schroeter, 2016).

In this polyvagal theory, Porges suggests that under intense or prolonged stress the infant or young child will first use the inborn social and relational tactics of her social engagement system. If these become exhausted, her fight or flight and active (conscious) freeze sympathetic nervous system reactions will be activated. If again this does not help her feel supported, her brain will automatically move her into the immobility and shutdown of parasympathetic nervous system activation. Gillet and Franz (2013) and body psychotherapist Vincentia Schroeter (2016) refer to Jackson's mechanistic theory of dissolution which states that whenever higher nervous system arrangements are suddenly rendered functionless, lower or more primitive systems are activated. These authors consider that the capacity for using the more evolved strategies can be eroded by abuse and prolonged stress, and, consequently, the more primitive defences are likely to become habituated (Australian Childhood Foundation, 2011; Porges, 2011).

An infant justifiably interprets neglect or abusive parental behaviour as life-threatening, that is, traumatic (Chitty, 2013). This interpretation often only happens at an implicit, non-verbal level (Beebe, Knoblauch, Rustin, & Sorter, 2005).

In the following (slightly abridged) report, childhood stress/trauma and its causal stimuli are described in the light of the polyvagal perspective by Schroeter (2016).

> *A five-year-old client told his mother he was going to "jump out the window and kill myself".*
> *The Mom was distressed because she had not expected him to become behaviourally unsettled*

even though she and his father were going through divorce. She thought he would continue to be "her happy little boy". She sought professional help and early in the consultation I brought out a box with wooden balls that had to be hammered vigorously with a wooden mallet to make them go into available holes ... The child hammered those balls for 40 minutes! Afterwards his Mom reported that he could now verbalize "I'm mad that you sent Dad away". When his mother validated his anger, she reported that he came out with the words, "I love you" (p. 21).

Angry and aroused and not feeling the parental support that he needed, this child was temporarily unable to access his calming social engagement system, and his sympathetic nervous system was instead activated. His mobilising behaviour (misbehaviour) communicated the stress he couldn't put into words. When he experienced no escape from the traumatising stimuli of his parent's divorce, he began to display the shock and shutdown associated with the activation of his parasympathetic nervous system.

Polyvagal theorists suggest that any input that improves a person's ability to orient into the present and to communicate can inhibit the use of the more primitive stress responses (Schroeter, 2016). In this account, the child was helped to orient into the present by hitting brightly coloured wooden balls (a body-movement psychotherapeutic approach). As the child activated his arms and hands to pound the wooden balls and moved into an extended period of energised activity, he was using the capacity of his mobilising sympathetic nervous system. (This might also be conceptualised as constructive anger work.) Perhaps counterintuitively, this activity, rather than further arousing the child, lifted him out of the immobilising shut-down feelings associated with the parasympathetic nervous system.

He then moved via his mobilised sympathetic nervous system back into his social engagement system experience, and demonstrated enough of a sense of calm to be able to give voice to his feelings of anger. The encouraging tones of the therapist's voice, also body-related, may have contributed to helping him to begin to make use of his social engagement system. Voice prosody is crucial to social engagement (Porges, 2011). The nerves in his middle ear could by now better pick up the soothing sounds of his mother's voice and he could begin to draw a sense of calm as a consequence of her right-brained empathy (Schore, 2003). Her availability (close physical and emotional connection) brought him out of his isolation and he could accurately interpret the fact that she was present to him in his distress.

Encouraging a client of any age to find ways of shifting into the use of her social engagement system allows her to make use of its flexibly calming coping style, which is much more nuanced than the fight, flight or freeze options of the more primitive parts of the autonomic nervous system. Shifts can occur at an implicit level, which is below conscious awareness, but they can also take place intentionally (with conscious volition) as the person becomes aware and can forge links with her neocortex. When a person's heart rate, for example, increases as an involuntary response to stimuli, she can choose to use deep breathing (an example of a body strategy) or meditation (an activity of the mind that affects her physiological experience) to help her lower it.

The polyvagal theory (Porges, 2011) also seems to confirm what earlier might have been dismissed as quasi-mystical connections between the brain, the organs and the affective structures of the body. The mid-brain amygdala, which is central to a person's mood, feelings and attitudes, belongs in the limbic region of the brain, and when a traumatic incident occurs, it signals the ANS almost instantaneously. All the parts of the nervous system communicate (via signalling neurons) back and forth. Messages from peripheral parts of the body via the senses are sent to the neocortex and they influence our cognition and how we respond to the world (Damasio, 1994; Schroeter, 2016). Understanding the reality of bi-directional communication of the organs to the brain, as well as the brain to the body, is a revolutionary concept.

Somatic practitioners, such as Ogden and Minton (2000), have for a long time promoted the idea that there is a wisdom within the body and its most cellular aspects, as was described in Chapter 2. This 'bodily knowing', long intuited, taught and relied on in the therapy room, can be accessed as a person raises her awareness of her body. She can develop her felt sense by giving her body her mindful attention (Schroeter, 2016; Siegel, 2010).

Porges' theory of the impacts of fear

Porges (2011) coined the term 'neuroception' to define the automatic and unconscious capacity by which we humans detect safety or danger. A person might, for example, see what looks like a snake on the road. She immediately freezes in an alert state. She does not go closer until she assesses whether it is just a stick or is in fact a snake. The automaticity (ability to act without the mind being slowed down by all the required low-level details of the response) is evolutionarily adaptive for the quick action that may be needed to survive danger (Schroeter, 2016).

Early trauma can distort this neuroceptive capacity. A person's brain may instead make associations with her fear. As a result of the distortion caused by early trauma, she may unconsciously begin to sense danger everywhere. This kind of distortion can take root within the activations of the autonomic nervous system because it occurs almost entirely below the level of cognitive awareness (Porges, 2011). Known as a faulty neuroception, the tendency to feel afraid is an implicit factor that can continue to disrupt a person's life even as an adult.

The result of an unmitigated early trauma response is a spiral of autonomic and emotional dysregulation that produces progressive damage if it is not reversed. The main long-term effects are perpetrated through exaggerated swings between the sympathetic fight or flight system of the sympathetic nervous system, and what is now described as the dorsal (back) vagal immobilisation system of the parasympathetic nervous system. The safety blanket of the social engagement system can be described as becoming thin and frayed. Over time, due to lack of use, the brain prunes the neuronal branches so much that the social engagement system is weakened (Schroeter, 2016).

Polyvagal perspectives, however, provide good news. Porges' belief is that a person of any age can reignite her social engagement physiology and rediscover its unique way of promoting calm. She can be helped to gradually move beyond conditioned and habitual fear and into a better-regulated state (Porges, 2011; Schore, 2003; Schroeter, 2016).

The phenomenon of dissociation

Dissociation is thought to be part of a normal implicit (unconscious) continuum that includes day dreaming and the ability to focus on a task or to zone out while there is noise happening all around. Disabling dissociation is at the intense end of the spectrum and is commonly conceptualised as the freeze response to trauma (Schore, 2003).

Some researchers believe that the parasympathetic nervous system dissociated or freeze response is at the heart of every post-trauma difficulty (van der Kolk, 2002, 2006). Siegel (2010) believes that each time a person experiences flashbacks, for example this more deeply ingrains a disintegrated state.

Schore (2003) provides the following widely accepted definition of dissociation:

> *a very early appearing survival mechanism for coping with traumatic effects. It can be described as the mind's attempt to flee when the active coping of flight or flight is unavailable. It can amount to an evacuation of the self (p. 62).*

In early infancy, two response patterns to abuse and neglect are postulated regarding the autonomic nervous system. First, frantic screaming signals distress. The autonomic nervous system is aroused or hyper-aroused via the sympathetic nervous system. Second, when the infant's extreme agitation fails to attract supportive intervention, a dissociative response (through the parasympathetic nervous system) may take its place as she falls into a state of protest, despair and immobility. There is a withdrawal of effort or a numbed avoidance (Schore, 2003). Depression and flat affect or the phenomenon of flashbacks can signal dissociation, which may have become a person's patterned response whenever memory of old trauma is triggered.

If we think about the theorised third part of the autonomic nervous system, the social engagement system, in the context of this description, it is often the lack of interpersonal support that is the traumatising factor. Because the child's attempts to remain calm using the resources of her own social engagement system are not supported, her brain is likely to fall back on the activation of the primitive brain's mobilising and immobilising processes.

Every young child needs to survive emotionally as well as physically. A colleague of mine referred to the opinion of some researchers that the brain dissociates in order to flee from its own knowledge. Immobility provides a safe space that would otherwise be filled with intolerable emotions and the sense or the thought that "this person who is hurting me is my loved one who is supposed to protect me".

Dissociation can be described as disrupting normal continuity across consciousness (Siegel, 2010). Researcher, lecturer and therapist Dr Robert Scaer (2014) describes the mechanism of dissociation in slightly different terms. He conceptualises a 'dissociation crucible' and suggests that a whole range of bodily impacts, remembered somatically, become dissociated elements, which may later be re-experienced or felt (repeatedly) in a person's sensations and emotions. These sensations go on causing trouble from underground, as it were, until the traumatic memories are made more explicit and can be properly understood and connected into the person's wider body experience.

Whatever the mechanisms behind dissociation, its results in a person's life are likely to be distressing. The person who has learned early to dissociate often finds it difficult to be fully present to herself, to others and to her life's experiences. Whenever a situation becomes intense or stressful it may look, to a companion, as if she has disappeared into another zone (van der Kolk, 2006).

Siegel (2010) reminds us that a variety of "self-states" are a part of every person's life, and that the key to health is "collaboration between these states" (p. 197). When dissociation causes a person's experience of herself to be split or fragmented, collaboration on the inside is difficult. This difficulty with collaborating tends to generalise to her external experience and be applied to the relationships that would normally draw her safely outside herself.

Scaer (2014) describes the primitive fight, flight or freeze responses of the autonomic nervous system as a host of somato-sensory impacts affecting the heart as much as the hands, the gut as much as the muscles. Various sensations match the emotions of terror, rage and humiliation. The person might describe her body as severely constricted because of shame, and it can feel de-personalised by terror. Another may describe the sensation of feeling as if she is outside her own body or alienated from it. There can also be sensations of bizarre distortion or craziness, which Scaer attributes to the large release of endorphins into the body whenever the old trauma is reactivated. Such a range of sensations can, in his view, have a narrowing, interrupting and corrupting effect on the present moment. He speculates that the body-based effects of trauma can combine to cause both the dissociative and the fragmenting effects on the self that recycle in a repetitively confusing way in the life of the survivor.

Findings from research undertaken with cohorts of adults living with PTSD underline both the powerful influence of the emotion of fearfulness and its multiple sensory (body-based) components that are stored and retrieved across many brain areas. Scaer (2014) cites common articulations of survivors who have experienced trauma, such as, "Life will never be the same again", "My life has stopped in its tracks" and "My life feels fragmented". The person's autobiographical memory may be affected, and it's as if her sense of self has become stuck in the traumatising moment (p. 13).

Schore (2003) has drawn the conclusion that attachment trauma prevents an infant from being adequately resourced with the internal certainty that she can effectively soothe and calm herself. He says that:

> *Traumatic attachments occurring in critical period of organisation of the right brain will create an enduring vulnerability to dysfunction during stress and a predisposition to post traumatic stress disorder (p. 238–239).*

He considers that the intersubjective closeness of a right brain to right brain therapy relationship is crucial for trauma therapy. For people traumatised as infants, implicit (perhaps right-brain) repair, is central.

Memories of trauma

Over the past two decades, study of typical and atypical brains has increased our understanding of memory systems and how early trauma affects them. Memory is a set of dynamic integrated systems. Multiple sensory components are stored and retrieved over many brain areas. During a child's developmental stages, different kinds of memory, namely, the cognitive, the motor and the emotional, are in the process of being organised and regulated (Fivush, 2011).

The limbic system of traumatised children can become increasingly responsive to relatively minor triggers (Perry, 1997). Sometimes nicknamed 'the emotional brain', the limbic part of the central nervous system is made up of two parts, the amygdala and the hippocampus. The limbic system instantly activates the peripheral autonomic nervous system and it initiates the fight, flight or freeze responses to threat. When it perceives danger, the amygdala sets in motion a release of hormones, such as cortisol and adrenaline. When children are under threat, the fast tracks of the limbic system are activated before the slower prefrontal cortex has a chance to evaluate the stimuli (Streeck-Fisher & van der Kolk, 2000). There is increased emotional (limbic system and amygdala) sensitivity and impulsiveness, and under these conditions learning and problem solving are impacted negatively. The amygdala may continue to sound an alarm inappropriately, so that memories also come to be encoded, stored and retrieved inappropriately.

The hippocampus is the part of the limbic system that normally helps a person to process information in rational and objective ways. This structure lends time and spatial context to memories and events, and it seems to some researchers (Bower & Sivers, 1998) that it acts as a critical structure for bringing together sensory parts of a person's experience and binding them to the cortically-based 'experiencing self'. If the hippocampus is not functioning effectively, the sensory repercussions of trauma may be stored in isolation. Somatically stored memories are thus split off from the activations of the neocortex (the thinking and reflecting processes). To the trauma survivor, the memories that are triggered later in life usually feel fragmented and/or nonsensical because they only arrive in a somatic form (sensation and emotion).

Pre-clinical and clinical studies (Damasio, 1994) bear out the finding that trauma can cause alterations in the memory function of the hippocampus in children. It is thought that the cascade of hormones through the brain in response to trauma may suppress the activation of the hippocampal system. As a consequence, the laying down of explicit cognitive and autobiographical memory may be affected. The person can remember accurately, but only in an intense and confusingly somatic way. Memory theorists underline that emotion is the main facilitator of memory formation and that memories are made primarily about events that have an emotional tone to them (Kihlstrom, 2005; Mason, 2014). While any old memory can be cued years later if similar emotional stimuli turns up, the experience of trauma is said by some researchers to dramatically affect how the memories are shaped (Scaer, 2014).

The role of autobiographical memory

A range of research interlinks selfhood with memory (Watson & Berntsen, 2015). There is a well-established view that autobiographical memories are organised hierarchically and at different levels of abstraction. Research with children shows that, by about five years, a child can make links over time, make and explain predictions and understand causal connection and temporality. A child of this age can think about the past and has knowledge about prior experience, thinking and emotion (Lagattuta & Wellman, 2002). Memory of life periods, general events and specific episodes all contain important information about the self. Appraisals about one's self can be projected back to the past and forward into the future. Autobiographical memory is defined by Fivush (2011) as:

> *The ability to represent oneself as an experience-er of events, as a continuous being with a past, a present and a future that links specific episodic representations into a meaningful sequence of events that define a person and a life (p. 561).*

Representations of key events in a person's autobiography include sensations such as "the tingling of the face in joy, the heart-pounding adrenaline rush of scoring a winning goal or the clenching of the gut in grief'" (Scaer, 2014, p. 4). The body's involvement is at the centre of experience. It is implicated in relation to a person's memory of past sensations as well as to her sensory experience in the present moment (Scaer, 2014). This resonates with Damasio's (1997) idea that the self may, in essence, be thought of as 'the embodied mind'. Self-identity is being created and repeatedly accessed as remembered information. Over time, this is developed into reasonably settled self-schemas.

Early trauma may promote a sense in a child's memory that "bad things will always happen to me". The negative beliefs tend to become overgeneralised in the brain. As well as implicitly recycling in the person's sensations and emotions, the sense that threat is always current (faulty neuroception) can lead to unhelpful patterns of avoidance, which negatively cramp a person's life (Watson & Berntsen, 2015). The Australian psychiatrist Dr Russell Meares (2016) explains that trauma means injury or damage, and that with trauma, there is a loss of continuity and cohesion. The diversity-in-unity of selfhood can be lost and, as automatic thoughts are forced on a person, the ownership of her own personal reality, her sense of agency in the world can fade.

Stream of consciousness

Dorothy Berntsen (2009) links newer discoveries about memory and the self with the stream of consciousness conceptualisation first described by William James in 1890. James understood that a person's states of mind flow continuously like a stream. Through this stream of mental activity, she works to differentiate herself from the external world. The stream is totally personal and individually accessible, constantly changing and quite selective, but at the same time connective to others.

Meares (2016) recognises the origins of this stream for an infant in the mother's face and voice. As she cares for her newborn, the mother sets up a playful game as if she is having a conversation (the proto-conversation) and in a short time the baby begins to join in. Meares suggests that "The emergence of self and symbol occur in childhood and early generative patterns of relating are carried into adult life" (p. 1).

Narrative capacity

Early trauma can interfere with a person's narrative capacity, or, in other words, her capacity to create a narrative that is cohesive or authentically pieced together. Van der Kolk (1998, 2002) came to this conclusion as a result of both his neuroimaging research and his direct therapeutic investigation with cohorts of adult subjects. The traumatised groups he studied initially seemed to remember a traumatic event in sensory fragments or somato-sensory flashbacks. They found it hard to put these memories into a sequenced, narrative form. It appeared to him that their trauma had been stored without linguistic components.

We are all probably familiar with the experience of finding words hard to come by when we are swamped with intense emotion. Not only may it be hard for a child to find her voice when traumatised, but as an adult she may have exactly this same experience if memory of the early trauma is triggered. Broca's area, which is the part of the brain most centrally involved in transforming subjective experience into speech, has been shown in neuroimaging studies to decrease its activation during trauma (Bowers & Sivers, 1998). Structurally, it lies close to the hippocampus in the central nervous system.

Whether or not traumatic memory is the same as or different than other emotional memory processes, neuroscientists and experienced psychotherapists agree that the body must be included if a person is struggling with the aftermath of trauma and its impacts on her memory.

Dealing with internal residues of the past

Van der Kolk (2006) says:

> A consensus is emerging that in order to keep old trauma from intruding into current experience, [a person] needs to deal with the internal residues of the past ... by learning to tolerate orienting and focusing [her] attention on [her] internal experience while interweaving and conjoining cognitive, emotional and sensorimotor elements of [her] traumatised experience (p. 11).

Both body and mind are needed for healing and resolution. Siegel's training is in paediatrics and child, adolescent and adult psychiatry. He describes the need to help a trauma survivor lower the somatic arousal she experiences when memories of trauma are uncomfortably cued or triggered. If the body is given due attention and the sensory arousal is moderated using a variety of body strategies, then the sense-making capacity of the hippocampal system can become fully functional (Siegel, 2010). In other words, the strength of somatic amygdala-activated memory can be moderated, and the person can begin to make use of the neural connections to her upper brain, seeking understanding and enabling meaning to be made of the experiences that have long been hidden behind uncomfortable and out of control somatic symptoms.

Van der Kolk (2017) says that trauma is about a whole organism being frightened. Mindfulness is needed so that attention can be focused. Emotions can be better regulated in a safe environment as a person is helped to move out of a stuck or frozen state. New ways of relating can be internalised when the person is no longer positioned defensively or aggressively.

Rothschild (2000) demonstrates multiple ways in which autonomic nervous system arousal can be modulated by the body and its resources and strategies. Perry (1997), Rothschild (2000) and van der Kolk (2006) all note the need for the therapist to encourage a survivor to look inward in order to become more familiar with and less afraid of the sensations and runaway emotions that have been overwhelming her.

Perry (1997) clarifies that the squelching of arousal (self-calming), once experienced, needs to be practised repeatedly if the brain is to learn new ways to perceive reality and to build new neural pathways. A person can become adept at accepting her body's over-reactivity and learn to be swift in immediately turning her attention in calming directions (Doidge, 2015; Siegel, 2010).

Trauma therapy requires embodied relational processes

Findings from research about interpersonal communication suggest that collegiality and mutuality and the underlying empathy and conditions in which the survivor can pick up resonance rely heavily on the language of the body and its implicit messages (Schore 2003). The interpersonal resonance of ideas can be said to rest on the ability of one person to tune in with the body of the other (biological attunement). Ford (1975) described beautifully the way the physical body, functioning in implicit ways, continually underlies and influences the mind:

> We first respond to verbal communication by an immediate change in our body. Our body then continuously changes in synchrony with the speaker's words. When it is our turn to speak, our voice similarly entrains the listener (p. 48).

A person makes use of body language and prosody, including tone, facial expression, emphasis and pitch, which is thought to be mediated in the right brain, as well as the explicit language of words, which is understood to be mediated by the hippocampus in the left brain (Mason, 2014).

The body language and the prosody of the therapist's words and even her gestures carry healing potential. Schore (2003) describes how important the behaviour of the body, including eye contact, is for communication. The tone and volume of the voice conveys so much and helps to determine the quality of a therapeutic interaction.

When body language as well as the language of words are experienced congruently within a physically close and collegial relationship, a once-traumatised person is able to begin to make use of the healing context. The safety developing relationally makes it possible for her to begin to make use of her own social engagement biology and to benefit from its intrinsic calming function. Her higher brain functions can then begin to do their clarifying work. The polyvagal theory emphasises this. A relational approach to therapy is necessary if a person is to move into a greater acquaintance with the vitalising and calming physiological capacity of her own social engagement system (Porges, 2011). Regulation develops at both physiological and psychosocial levels.

For an adult who experienced trauma early in life, the therapy relationship can be likened to the healthily regulating attachment relationship at the start of life, consisting as many researchers speculate, of implicit right brain to right brain connectivity (Schore, 2003). Some practitioners conceptualise the effective therapist as taking up a role as an auxiliary cortex (or a bridge) that enables a survivor of early trauma to gradually take steps away from her more primitive trauma biology and into the flexible use of her own social engagement system and its nuanced self-soothing means of connecting her in turn to her sense-making neocortex (Ogden & Minton, 2000).

Mirror neurons are described as the neurons that enable a child (or a person at any stage) to be able to learn almost by osmosis from those who relate closely to her. Siegel (2000) describes mirror-neuron research by Amanti and Gallese (2014) which he believes provides evidence that the body and the process of body-based attunement between one person and another creates what he calls 'social cognition' at both pre-verbal and post-verbal stages. This can also be described as 'human inter-corporeality', carrying the sense that for humans our bodies and our biology are at the heart of all our interactions and relationships. Siegel (2000) talks about the way a trauma survivor can gradually sense that she is 'in the mind' of another person. She is engaging face to face with a different, regulating and healing relational model. When she can feel in her own body the deep sense of being respected, the inequality, confusion and fear of past trauma or the disempowerment of a perpetrator-victim relationship is in the process of being 'out-faced'.

An interdisciplinary study of intersubjectivity by Beebe, Knoblauch, Rustin and Sorter (2005) arrived at the conclusion that, for resolution of early trauma when it is still affecting an adult, both the verbal narrative, which is explicit, and the implicit action dialogue, which operates largely outside of awareness, are needed. By providing a safe intersubjective space between herself and the person seeking therapy, a therapist can ensure that the co-construction of a narrative in both dimensions is made possible.

Both body and mind are affected by trauma, and therefore both aspects need to be addressed (Levine, 1992). If the predominant focus of a therapy approach is verbal, it is likely to miss crucial opportunities for healing.

Conclusion

A major aim of this chapter has been to explain some contemporary improved understandings of the impacts of early trauma. This cross-fertilisation of neuroscientific research and the observations of experienced trauma therapists has clarified that the impacts of early trauma are extensive, shaping both brain and body and impacting a person's sense of self and ways of relating.

Early trauma tends to repeat itself in a person's adult life because the brain makes associations with the past. Interpretations and expectations may be distorted by what has gone before. Sometimes trauma stimuli produce hormonal responses that suppress the parts of the brain that could be of help in sense-making: the signals are not able to get through to the upper brain where sense can be made of them. For both the pre-verbal child and the older child, teen or even adult, memories of trauma may be stored in a somatic sensory form only.

A child, and the adult she becomes, can become subjugated by trauma states similar to the original ones. Memories return without volition. Brain responses have an automaticity to them that contributes to behavioural and relational reactivity. High levels of nervous system arousal and/or dissociation influence the person's sense of self, her personality, her behaviour, her action patterns and all her relationships. Autobiographical memory is easily distorted, and a person's stream of consciousness is likely to be influenced by her implicit and unconscious somatic autonomic memory systems (Scaer, 2014). All these restraints can cause a pattern of internalising self-blame and the development of a dominant narrative that is negative, and which continues to subjugate. Fear and faulty neuroception (Porges, 2011) can cramp a person's life because she learns to retreat from experience in the attempt to stay safe.

In this chapter, I described how these understandings provide hope for the trauma survivor. In particular, Porges (2011), who linked new understandings about the social engagement aspect of the human nervous system to behaviour, demonstrated that it is never too late for a person to regain this more evolved capacity for self-soothing that gets lost in the trauma experience. He proposes that there is a thrust towards personal and interpersonal health once a person is helped to move herself forward to again make use of her social engagement biology.

Drawing on many disciplines, I have described how both biological attunement and the resonance of ideas are necessary for a healing therapy relationship. The creation of a collegial intersubjectivity with its implicit and explicit dimensions encapsulates this relational approach.

In the next chapter, I synthesise the theoretical underpinnings, research findings and practitioner experience of the approaches I have introduced, namely, narrative, contemporary somatic therapy and trauma therapy, into a new body-based narrative approach to working with people who have experienced trauma.

Chapter 4
The Magic Loom

A Monet picture is symbolic of a certain calm kind of feeling ... both a pond and a state of mind. Daniel Siegel

This chapter provides a pivot between the three strands of theory in Part One and the lived experience of those in the know in Part Two, where the body-based narrative approach is demonstrated. I expand on how my own experiential learning about trauma and the body evolved, and I open up the multi-dimensional metaphor of weaving from which the title of the book, *The Magic Loom*, is derived. The therapy conversations in this model are scaffolded by a weaving together of narrative language and strategies relating to the body. There is also a weaving together of therapeutic curiosity, attentiveness and resonant response with the responses and initiatives of the conversational participant. A guiding map for therapists makes further use of the metaphor.

The body as the first responder to trauma

The emotionally intense sensations with which we respond to alarming experiences can be described as the body's natural responses to danger. Trauma and its harms are never welcomed. A person's body is reactive from the beginning.

> *From his childish and personally unique perspective, frightening stimuli made Tim feel precarious. The death of the frog was anathema to him and his body reacted to it with emotionally intense sensations. His body raised the alarm. It sent out signals like a red flag waving madly, seeking helpful supportive attention. But no help came. Tim, who was now in his forties, told me I was the first person to whom he had divulged what had happened that fateful day.*

Without the relational support an infant or small child needs when she is alarmed, it's as if her body takes on a veil of fearful negativity that is symbolic of the traumatic experience. The memory of what took place becomes inscribed in her body and brain (Levine, 1992). The red flag of bodily panic coalesces with the traumatising stimuli of her experience. It's as if she continues to walk through a minefield or that she has a bomb strapped to her body that might explode at any moment.

Each person's body has its unique way of expressing impacts of past trauma. The lived experience differs according to the individual and to the traumatising contexts of her early life. The body-focused narrative therapist is not in the know. The generalised truth may be that trauma from the past disrupts an individual's relationship with her body, but the way this happens is idiosyncratic to each person, to her own personality and values, to the nature of the alarming experiences and contexts she has encountered and to her developmental stage at the time of the trauma.

When a person becomes more closely acquainted with her body, and more accepting of it rather than shunning it, she discovers that her body was never the problem. It was her reliable 'first responder' that had signalled 'danger'.

Privileging the voice of the body

In narrative terms, whenever I invite a person to notice her sensations, I am setting out to privilege the voice of her body. This occurs through what is often a playful kind of conversation. The sensation only needs to be noticed and allowed to be. I regularly observe a shift in the loading of stress and fear as a person begins to experience her body differently. She is more objective. As she feels more at home in her body, I observe that she often moves away from self-blame and shame. The problem of trauma begins to be experienced so differently that she can let go of the feeling that its effects are a part of her identity. She becomes receptive to something new. Ever-present fear diminishes. Attentiveness to somatic sensory impacts in the present helps turn the survivor of early trauma away from the past toward an entirely new story.

I began my progression into a new way of working by asking Tim to notice his body, to take a moment to give it his attention. I came to realise that what I was calling for was the application of body-focused mindfulness. I now regard this as a key protocol that makes it possible for the person to take the journey away from fear of her own body as the problem, into a new respect for it. Arguably, mindfulness makes space for incremental progress. However, such body-based awareness can also be immediately transformative. When the red flag of bodily sensation is experienced as a potent and useful signal instead of as a taunting time bomb, it becomes the pivotal turning point towards a re-authored story. As happened for Tim, the intense, panicky or uncomfortable sensations could be noticed, more readily tolerated and finally accepted. They began to make sense.

Agency and the process of re-authoring

White (2006) says that:

> *The restoration and/or development of this sense of personal agency provides an antidote to the sort of highly disabling conclusions about one's identity that feature perceptions that one is a passive recipient of life's forces (p. 151).*

White continues by discussing the immobilising phenomena of vulnerability and fragility, and negatively influential identity conclusions that include labels such as 'damaged' or 'messed up'.

For re-authoring to take place, he asserts that (2007):

> *Therapy conversations must recruit the person's lived experience, help her to stretch her mind, enable her to exercise her imagination and employ her meaning-making resources (pp. 61–62).*

In a body-mind sequence, the hardly conscious narrative of ever-present danger can gradually and effectively be made explicit by adding a focus on the body. Then, in a further step-by-step process, the dominant narrative, recognised now as being constituted by unmitigated trauma, can be named and explored so that its meanings are found, and contexts examined. It can then be gradually re-authored.

My understanding about collegiality became clearer. If a person's earliest traumas were interpersonal in nature, then the body-focused narrative therapist's respectful and collegial way of working can help the trauma survivor begin to internalise a new and transformative sense of safety and connectedness if she can feel that sense of connection (both implicitly and explicitly) as she explores. Throughout the process of negotiating unexplored present-day territory, she is being accompanied. She senses authentic fellow-feeling.

The narrative therapist thinks carefully about how she uses her influence when she sets out to help a client to re-author narratives that have been dominant and subjugating in her life. White (2007) describes the therapist's role as "de-centered, but influential" (p. 39).

Gene and Combs (2002) record their agreement with the term 'a co-research project' that originated with David Epston as a way of describing a narrative conversation. The therapist uses her skills of scaffolding by means of curious and investigative questions to ensure that the conversation remains collegial. It is the client who, in the case of developmental trauma, has experienced the original trauma and its repeated triggering. It is she who takes up the search for meaning and considers her own specific responses.

The therapist helps her to reflect and explore, and to develop and thicken her narratives. She helps her to think about the history and context of events, as well as the effects of what happened. There may be stands that would move her further into the present and away from the past. While the therapist might draw attention to the possibility of stand-taking, the naming of the stands and the making of choices belong to the person seeking therapy.

In Chapter 1, I drew attention to the influence of Russian educationalist Vygotsky on the way narrative practitioners scaffold therapy conversations into small and meaningful steps. In White's words (2004), the person learns "to incrementally and progressively distance [herself] from the known and familiar and move toward what it might be possible for [her] to know and to do" (p. 263).

Therapeutic scaffolding

The narrative therapist scaffolds the therapy conversation using specificity and yet employing a tentative approach to language by using with words such as 'perhaps' or 'might'. She orients her questions to the realm of ideas, beliefs, thoughts, values and dreams. She wants to keep the conversation moving towards increasing complexity and greater abstraction, so that throughout the exploration the person develops greater depths of understanding and can tease out the meanings she is taking from events. In short, the therapist aims to keep the client at the centre, while helping her to move forward, step-by-step, in the direction of new and preferred possibilities.

When she adds a body focus to her approaches, she can continue to use her words to communicate the spirit of investigation. However, now the therapist's curiosity is directed in such a way that the person is able to turn her attention to her body as distinct from her mind. The context remains that the expertise of the person consulting the therapist is what matters. She is the only one familiar with her bodily sensations, the one who can describe the over-reactivity that distresses her, and the one who is able to turn her attention towards those sensations. She is the one who can later begin to make use of her body's calming potentialities.

A three-phased body scaffold approach

I have arrived at a three-phased pattern of scaffolding that I call the 'body scaffold'. The three phases allow the therapist to engage a person in an incremental or step-by-step body-focused enquiry that again moves from the familiar to the transformative.

1.   Raising awareness of body sensations

It is through the process of careful listening to body language as well as to words, that the co-researching therapist is alerted, as I was with Tim. The sense that intense ongoing impacts of trauma are being described and experienced moves the therapist to engage with the signalling of the client's body and the wisdom inherent in that.

The therapy questions are oriented to help the person explore, in particular, what her body is saying. The mind of the trauma survivor is concurrently engaged through the process of mindfulness. She is learning to pay attention to her body, while also using her mind to provide the space needed for reflection.

The therapist hands over to the other person the task of listening to what her body's messages are telling her. The collegiality of the conversation is being maintained while the body scaffolding takes its progressive steps.

CHAPTER 4 THE MAGIC LOOM

Rick's sensations like Tim's had important and quite unique information to disclose. He told about moving through a range of intense emotional responses to some stresses which had arisen in his work during the preceding week. At one point, he was swamped with an irrational sort of anger. Then he felt sad. Finally, he fell into what he described as a kind of emotional frenzy.

I asked him if he knew which parts of his body were caught up in the frenzy of feelings he was describing, and he immediately said:

> *My neck's tight; my tongue is rigid and my breathing's shallow. There's pressure at the back of my head. It's as if there's someone behind me with a whip. I have to fix things or else!*

I wondered aloud whether, as he sat and kept his mind on those exact sensations, he could remember ever experiencing something similar in his body. A story arrived.

> *I was in grade four, about nine years old. I have no idea what I'd done wrong. But it made my teacher explode. He grabbed me by the back of the neck and shook me! It came totally out of the blue. It was so unexpected, it threw me into shock. I couldn't speak. I felt demolished. I was so confused that I thought there must be something wrong with me. But I was angry too. I felt what had happened was completely unjust. The thing was, I really liked that teacher. He was always very interesting and clever, and he really got us engaged. I felt so full of shame that I couldn't tell a soul.*

Rick was amazed at the way his body had remembered the sensations and the power dynamics of the event that had occurred that day at school. He said:

> *My well-loved teacher couldn't be to blame. Therefore, it must have been me who'd done something wrong. Now I can see. It's no wonder I blamed myself, no wonder I was confused – I was in shock. Nothing made sense. Part of me was outraged and I felt unjustly done by, but how could I blame my teacher? Actually, I can see that I felt powerless!*

The arrival of a unique body story or memory always provides the therapist with the opportunity to scaffold the conversation with further appropriate and curious questions.

2.   Exploring body strategies

As I saw Rick opening up his heart to his young self, I introduced the second phase of the body scaffolding process. I suggested he have a go at addressing his body with kindness. I asked Rick if he could remember his recent emotional frenzy and revisit the bodily sensations he had felt. Could he bring kindness into his responses to those sensations, just as he had opened his heart to his younger self? Rick engaged.

> *He commented on the intense pressure of the sensations he could again feel in his neck. He told his wife Linda and me that as he focused on the remembered tight sensations with sympathy, the sense of pressure and overall body-tightness diminished in moments. He felt excited and*

69

capable. He also shared a fresh realisation. He was beginning to understand what he had had to grapple with. The rigidity of his neck and his tongue said so much. In the classroom he'd been struck dumb! Now he had remembered the story, simply telling it to someone and finding his voice in this way, was helping him make sense of it.

We discussed this realisation back and forth for some time and then I asked Rick where his new discoveries might take him in the future. He said that:

It felt as if a mature part of him was able to offer to his younger self the human kindness he had been so in need of at the time the traumatic event took place.

Rick's difficulty with speaking fits with some neurological understandings about the impacts of trauma on the brain. This story also illustrates the lasting impacts that an authority figure can have on the young. Rick's experience may not have been physically life threatening, but it deeply affected how he viewed himself. The far-reaching alarm reaction in his brain and nervous system was still returning years later.

I asked Rick whether, since he was now making better sense of the past, he could speculate about the effect this event that took place in the far different past had been having on his working life.

No wonder stress at work can get compounded if it is triggering old traumas and I am unconsciously re-experiencing those, as well what is happening in the present. Now I understand why small stresses can accumulate and suddenly sort of go over the top. I can be instantly full of impotent rage and this sort of frenzy. Being able to consciously understand the dynamics, I can be kind to myself instead of coming down on myself the way my teacher did. And I can talk to someone else about my feelings!

Very often a person's experience of somatic sensory overload is the reason she has come to consult the therapist. It may be that she is focused on her disappointment with her over- reactivity to people or situations and concern that her out of control behaviour is at odds with her values. She may not have a clue that early trauma is being triggered.

When the therapist makes the person's concrete sensations the focal point of the enquiry, her body becomes her reference point. Asking her to name the part of her body to which the intense sensation most draws her attention, seems to make sense to her, although occasionally some time is needed. As she picks up the attitude of curiosity from the therapist, the participant herself becomes the investigator, directing her attention to her body and seeking to discover precisely what it has to say. She moves incrementally from fear of the intensity to curiosity, and eventually to an ability to tolerate and finally to accept what was quite recently found intolerable. Even this early on in the process, the person seems calmer and is more grounded. It's as if in becoming aware of her body, she is more able to inhabit it.

CHAPTER 4 THE MAGIC LOOM

A little further down the track, the body sensations may be helpfully re-framed as 'signals', and the world of metaphor and abstraction entered. During a gentle body-focused process, it's as if the fear, which has been expressed unconsciously in the body since the trauma occurred, is being diminished so that the mind is set free to take up its reflective and resolving work. I'm always surprised at the speed of the cognitive gallop that takes place once the body is perceived differently.

When attention to the signals of the body provides some relevant recall, the progression is immediately apparent. A small memory cued by the body in the context of over-reactivity connects to early traumas suffered. This led me to recognise that the body narrative provides an important opening. I have observed that when a person's body cues a memory via its sensations, the memory arrives in a form that is digestible. This is an important consideration in trauma work in terms of strategies that avoid overwhelming a person leading to them using defences such as dissociation. The therapist exchanges the 'body scaffold' for the 'language scaffold' and the person can start to make sense of the memory that was previously hidden to her. Facts, contexts and history can be pieced together. The therapist maintains the de-centred nature of the exploration.

Body-retrieved memory then seems to safely provide a window on the past, without every aspect of trauma and prolonged stress having to be obsessively or artificially reconstructed. It's as if resolving what the body has cued on just one occasion provides a template for future resolution and meaning making. Whenever triggering is recognised, the person has an immediate way forward. She can explore her own most effective body-related ways to consciously and routinely establish calm in place of the uncomfortable arousal she now recognises as a signal.

For Rick, looking inward with kindness was a body strategy he found immediately calming. The second phase of the body scaffold is all about the practice of self-soothing. The person is invited to mindfully explore ways of "putting the brakes on" the intensity or the pressure she is and has been experiencing (Rothschild, 2000, p. 115). She is in charge of every experiment she makes. Self-calming experiences multiply as she experiments with the wide array of resources or strategies that arise from her body.

The narrative therapist may begin an exploration of self-soothing body strategies already familiar to the person. This may be the first time these resources have been brought to mind, or made conscious. Old or new body resources begin to fill the resourcing gap.

Using body strategies to calm arousal

When full of steam, a pressure cooker has been known to explode. The pressure must be released one small 'pht, pht' at a time (Rothschild, 2000). A pressure cooker that is full of steam is an apt metaphor for the dilemma for trauma therapy. Explosive internal or outward reactivity is commonplace in the trauma survivor's life. By prioritising body strategies the person is able to immediately experiment and to calm the arousal one small step at a time.

A different body-related strategy emerged in conversation with Kerry. I asked her whether her senses had ever been of use to her when she felt the extremes of emotional reactivity. She shared this account:

> She loved gardening. One day she had been on her knees in the garden and she had had a vision. She felt as if she was "in the presence of God". It gave her a "totally connected" feeling. From that day the garden became a place of deep spiritual belonging. Being immersed in her garden always had a calming effect. Taking herself there when she felt overwhelmed had become a very tangible form of self-care. Whenever she made it into the garden she was conscious of it "doing me good". She loved every opportunity that came her way to be at one with nature. Kerry said that she had become aware that her children always benefited if she got to do some gardening or got out into nature. It replenished her spirit and her joy overflowed onto them.

Gardening or being in nature was not a therapy-suggested strategy, but because knowledge of this safe space arose from within herself, this noticing and naming helped to raise her awareness of her inner wisdom. She had a body-based resource on which she could rely and of which she could consciously make intentional use.

Rothschild (2000) suggests that when trauma is endemic in a person's childhood, it is important to find ways of building calm into her lifestyle. For such a person, life can feel desolate and desert-like. Rothschild recommends that the trauma survivor make calming use of what she calls 'oasis activities' in her everyday life. These are any activities that engage complete concentration. In real life or within a therapy conversation, Rothschild encourages the person to draw on her memory and imagination, thinking of safe people, places, pets, activities such as gardening or even focus on a beloved object like a tree or a beach. She calls these 'anchors'. By using all her senses, the person can enhance her memory of these anchors and make full use of their calming potential to 'put on the brakes' when unpleasant arousal is triggered.

Tanya spoke of a history of family violence, alcoholism and sexual assault. Until a year before, she had held her emotions at bay by using alcohol and drugs. However, she reported that she always had "a knowing" that life could be better. After many false starts she had been able to take a stand and she had succeeded in getting herself clean of ice (methamphetamine), heroin and alcohol. She had come to therapy to increase her confidence and to free herself of the emotional roller coaster that continued to dog her life. Hearing this context it was clear to me that the priority for Tanya's therapy was to have her focus on her sensations in order to help her to consistently lower the arousal they signalled and the sense of panic that was very familiar. She was not in a position where it would be wise to cue more trauma narratives than those she readily chose to talk about. When she did do that, helping her address the sensations they aroused with mindful kindness and strategies of body re-structure and then meditation was what worked. Sensations in her chest and stomach became important signallers.

Tanya was eager to experiment with self-soothing practices. She used to run and swim. She could do so again. She enjoyed her beautiful crystals and she loved to draw. She was intrigued by the idea that her brain worked on automatic and this led to the panic, and she liked the idea of being kind to her sensations. She needed to write down a list and to start a regular ritual, so she could remember what to try. She began to practise meditation. Tanya's body and the personal values that were precious to her, which centred on "peace instead of drama", became the guiding stars for her recovery.

Another body strategy discussed by Rothschild is what she calls 'muscle toning' (2000, p.135). A trauma survivor can be beset with bodily weakness, and slow muscle-strengthening exercises can be of help. Rothschild describes the way a person, even while sitting in a chair, can press her feet into the floor so that she feels the muscles in her thigh contract. This can often be of more use than relaxation techniques for the trauma survivor because it provides her with a sense of containment and strength. This was of help to Tanya.

Whether or not self-soothing through an activity like gardening is a remembered resource as it was for Kerry, the therapy conversation can be scaffolded so that the person is able to experiment with at least one calming body strategy immediately. Offering his concrete sensations an attitude of kindness was the strategy that gave Rick immediate agency while as already mentioned body re-structure and mindful meditation (Siegel, 2010) were of great benefit to Tanya.

A person only needs to bring to mind the raw intensity or pressure she has recently experienced in her body, and a body strategy can be put to work in relation to it. When she applies a body strategy to the runaway sensations (even if only their remembered intensity), I have observed that the felt somatic intensity always lessens immediately. Often the person has experimented with the strategy for only a matter of moments before a sense of agency arrives. The experience is transformative. She is managing the arousal. The problem of trauma is being outfaced, or defeated, through awareness. This moment is likely to be expressed as a pivotal one. It's an important moment to celebrate.

The use of concrete body strategies reveals to the person the amazing calming potential of her body and imagination. Even, for example, placing one hand over one's heart and/or over one's stomach can be self-supportive and calming (Ogden, 2016). I remember one client whose best way of grounding herself in a particularly fraught unsupported time of over-reactivity was to lie on the ground and to dig her hands into the soil. Another person finds the help needed by (secretly) putting her hand into her pocket to play with some pebbles or a squeegee ball, while another bends down and takes her time to do up her shoelaces, noticing in detail the texture and temperature of her shoes.

Like the small boy in Chapter 3 who wanted to jump out of the window but who revived himself by hammering, an adult I talked with recently instinctively turned to creative work with wood. He had been experiencing a triggered state of flatness and unbelievable exhaustion. By engaging creatively with wood, he was able to gradually revive himself. There was something about putting his hands on the timber, designing and making something new, that calmed and transported him.

The Rothschild strategy of anchoring (2000) has some obvious links with the narrative practice of inviting witnesses into the therapy conversation. If the narrative therapist asks questions that require the person to use any of her senses in regard to a significant witness to her life, she is helping the person to remember the witness holistically. Recalling and talking about a calming friend in richly embodied ways brings her to life as a supportive and down-to-earth presence and can immediately lower autonomic nervous system arousal.

The narrative practice of providing a person with a live audience in the therapy room enables embodied resonance-filled interactions, which help to calm and transport the person, and help her to begin to change her narrative.

As a person experiments with a wide range of grounding body strategies, real hope is engendered as space widens in front of her. One body strategy can be explored at a time. The sense of agency that follows carries its own momentum. The person sorts through the strategies to find those that are most effective in calming herself. She is exerting her own agency and naming the results of her own investigations, and in doing so is building new neural pathways in her brain (Siegel, 2010)

3.   Weaving a partnership between the body and the mind

The third phase of the body scaffold introduces partnerships between the body and the mind in the form of a measuring tool, mantra, metaphor and meditation.

Measuring the intensity of sensations

Making use of a measuring tool in a narrative style exploration enables the person to use her mind as she reflects or takes detailed notice of the way a body strategy modulates (soothes) her arousal.

It was late in our first conversation that I asked Kerry to think back to the chaotic situation with her children that had brought her to therapy, and then to revisit her sensations in that situation. I asked her to rate the intensity of the pressure she had experienced on a scale of one to ten.

> *She concentrated on her throat and quickly gauged the pressure as a nine.*

I asked her to focus on the same sensations in her throat, but this time to notice them with kindness and understanding.

> *After very little time the pressure reduced. Both her throat and her chest to which she'd addressed her sympathetic attention felt better. The pressure had lessened to a score of five or six.*

We repeated the experiment.

> *Because she was still aware of some tightness in her chest, Kerry engaged in further noticing, keeping her mindful focus on that part of her anatomy. After a while she reported that the score was almost nothing. She felt calm.*

I asked Kerry what it was like to experience managing her sense of being overwhelmed by using her value of compassion and kindness in this way.

> *She said that it was totally new and foreign to her, but she conveyed excitement. She wanted to try the same experiment in her real life situations during the coming week. She said that she was usually very harsh towards herself and her body, so just being gentle with herself in her awareness of her body would be a change.*

Kerry was expressing her desire to embody a new narrative. The experimentation, which she would take up in her own environment, would set the direction of enquiry for the next therapy conversation.

When a person notices the intensity of the internal pressure of her sensations, and scores it somewhere on a scale, she is taking her cognitive noticing a step further. There is a dual awareness as she is measuring what she is noticing (Rothschild, 2010; Siegel, 2010). The higher regions of her brain are being called on to gauge the felt intensity of her somatic experience. In an open-ended experiment, she can immediately contain her experience and put limits on it. To that point, over-reactivity had been dominating Kerry's life. In narrative terms, her new body awareness provided agency and 'vital exceptions' (Morgan, 2000) to the experiences that had been repeatedly reinforcing her powerlessness.

It interests me that even when a measuring process of this kind is introduced, the enquiry still only ever requires a minute or two of mindful attention. When the person has been living with the constant recycling of traumatic arousal, I notice that, like Kerry and Tanya, she is particularly eager to practise her newly discovered power to put on the brakes. The person's solutions are coming from a position of increased sensory awareness. The question, "Can you notice where your body is drawing attention to itself?" invites respect for the body and it is effective; the somatic overload is likely to decrease.

The ability to put the brakes on arousal increases with each experiment the person makes, much as a snowball running downhill gathers size and momentum. The person is reinforcing an attractive new sense of freedom. With repetition, she may find that she can use her newly discovered body wisdom to gradually and completely extinguish the sensory-arousal pattern. Trauma is being actively sidelined.

The use of a mantra

This third phase of the body scaffolding approach also helps a person to better appreciate the flexible co-operation possible between her body and her mind (Siegel, 2010). The use of a mantra depends on both mind and body. A ritualised form of words conveys important meaning, nurturing the mind, and when repeated like a chant, its sensory and auditory qualities can help modulate the bodily arousal.

As she reflected on the phrase, "no wonder I feel like this", Kerry described its meaning as follows:

> *When something happens like the upset with my kids, it's as if I get whisked back to a terrible time. But now I know that those things happened a lifetime ago. I don't need to keep going back there. What I didn't know then was that I handled myself pretty well when I was in the middle of all that trauma. At that time, I only felt a sense of being overwhelmed. The problems kept on coming. They didn't ever seem to go away. But now I know it wasn't my fault. Those events are over. Now, in my life today I am finding strategies I can use so that what happened in my childhood doesn't keep on affecting me.*

Exploring metaphor

Metaphor is part of the rich resource of language regularly explored in narrative approaches to therapy. In some of the conversations recorded in the second part of this book, metaphor is used to relate to the body. I observe that when this is initiated by the person herself, or explored in the collegial conversation, it can elevate the importance of the body's calming wisdom.

I met up with Samantha a few months after her therapy conversations ended to talk about the documentation of our conversations for use in this book. The first thing she mentioned was the metaphor of the canary in the coal mine. It was the designation she had ascribed to the pain in her side, one of the factors that had first brought her to therapy.

She told me how useful she now found the pain in her side if and when it arrived. It could quickly wake her up to an episode of triggered arousal and give her a push towards the story she preferred and away from the default of a dominant story of emotionality and despair. She was overcoming an old pattern.

These days, over-emotionality was itself a body signal she used to launch into self-soothing responses. A flood of tears immediately alerted her that the 'dementors' were in the vicinity. She now knew that they didn't have to be obeyed.

The body-focused narrative therapist can intentionally help a person to explore this kind of metaphorical language. When it relates specifically to an aspect of the body, the exploration immediately expands the person's sense of agency and contributes to her incremental learning.

Meditative space

There is a lot of evidence that meditation lowers stress. Siegel (2010) practices meditation for his own well-being for a period of about twenty-five minutes each day. He makes use of a metaphorical wheel that includes a focus on the body. He provides a description of this useful meditation in *Mindsight*, (2010, pp. 90–92) and it is also available in a version that can be listened to at http://youtu.be/ODlFhOKahmk.

The Magic Loom[1]

The idea that the therapy conversation can be mapped on to the interface between ideas and practice (White, 2004) comes to life in this final section of this chapter. As a mapping device I have developed the metaphor of the Magic Loom. It is an imaginary mythical structure for the weaving work of body-focused narrative therapy. (A little poetic licence is requested of the reader). The metaphor is designed to increase understanding about how the two scaffolding processes already described, one engaging the body and one the mind, work alongside each other. At the same time, it is intended to convey the interweaving nature of the collegial therapy conversation that could be said to add an almost invisible layer to the fabric construction. The image of an ancient Egyptian loom included at the start of Chapter 4 obviously pictures an ancient weaving process which relies on two people.

The survivor of developmental trauma is 'The Weaver'. Her narratives are always personal. She is the one who grapples with the questions being asked. New possibilities arise sometimes from her body and sometimes from the reflections of her mind. She is the only one who knows which storyline threads to pick up. She holds the shuttle. The Therapist is 'The Co-weaver'. She is the one who opens the space for the Weaver. She continuously orients herself to her conversational partner with her curious questions and also her responses in order to generate newness and provide the opportunity for resonance and safety. In her engagement with the Weaver she aims to ensure that new possibilities can be woven into a fresh, vibrant and unique fabric (a co-authored narrative which is in the process of becoming). Co-weaver and Weaver work together in concert.

The bi-fold magic loom relies on the fact that the two different ways of scaffolding the therapy conversation (body and mind) are always complementary. Two openings (sheds) separate the threads of the weft variously and the Co-weaver is the opener of the sheds. She interchanges the sheds by asking pertinent questions. When curiosity is applied to the expressions of a person's body rather than to the expressions of her mind, what the Weaver learns or takes from her body's expressivity, is, in turn, returned to her mind for reflection and exploration. The Co-weaver stays alert, alternately opening the appropriate shed at each stage of the conversation. New strands are constantly picked up by the Weaver. The body scaffold is always dependent on the language-based one, but the corollary is also true. Without the body scaffold, specific information and certain threads of possibility would not be made available for the weaving. The interweaving image is multidimensional, interpersonal and holistic.

---

1   Definitions: A loom is an apparatus for making fabric by weaving yarn or thread in two directions. The warp is the set of vertical yarns that are held in tension on the loom. The weft is the horizontal yarn that is woven over and under the warped threads. The shed is the name of the space that is opened up usually with mechanical help which alternatively pulls apart one set of warp threads and later another so the weft threads can be woven through. The threads are fastened to the shuttle which the weaver passes through the alternating sheds. Sometimes the weaver uses a pick-up stick instead of the shuttle so she can knot the weft thread directly around some of the warp threads. The heddle bar is a tool which is notched to fit over the width of the loosely woven threads so they can be tightened into a fabric. As the metaphor calls on many new threads to be woven in rather than one continuous thread, one can imagine that each loose thread will later need to be sewn neatly into the finished fabric.

The Magic Loom at work

What follows is a mapping exercise describing a hypothetical body-focused narrative therapy conversation or a set of conversations.

Narrative-based approach: The Co-weaver first brings her curiosity to what is uppermost for the Weaver. Using investigative questions, she might guide the latter to reflect on experiences never noticed or explored before. Some brightness may immediately come into view as the Weaver begins interlacing the warp with the threads of possibility that will create the weft of the weaving.

A conversational exchange focusing on the externalising of a problem might see the Weaver pick up new threads. A co-authoring process gets underway as she weaves in sections that begin to clearly show that the problem is outside of her as a person. She can thicken many finely detailed threads together and tighten the loose weaving which is taking shape with the heddle bar of a stand she is taking.

She might be helped by the Co-weaver to explore and to deconstruct societal attitudes never understood before, and this might show up in the fabric, tangibly marking a newfound ability to distance herself from past negative assumptions.

In the conversational exchange, an influential caste of characters might be noticed for their significance (Morgan, 2000) and the person's self-construction might become visibly richer, with an array of colours and textures discernible.

Body-based approach: In time the person might introduce a problem of great intensity. Her explorative weavings might even become quite frantic (tangled). (Note: This kind of intensity is explored at the time it arrives, sometimes right at the beginning of the conversation).

As the Co-weaver senses the intensity of emotion behind the person's words, she quietly opens the first shed (space) so the Weaver can thread body wisdom with her shuttle and weave it in to the fabric. The Co-weaver's curious questions highlight the body, and the person immediately starts to notice its intense signals and to hear its messages. She centres her attention experientially on the sensations in particular locations in her body.

If some recall is awakened by the person's focus on her intense sensations, an image or a belief or a memory from the past may arrive. Such an occurrence might provoke a pivotal moment. When the Weaver's excitement is matched by that of the Co-weaver, she is likely to pick up a piece of gold thread and to deliberately insert this into the growing fabric, as a kind of marker. Resonance is being experienced (White, 2006) and positive affect savoured (Pat Ogden, 2016).

Narrative-based approach: The Co-weaver now opens the alternate space so that the Weaver can thread the shuttle now in response to her mind's reflection about what is happening in her body. The Co-weaver might ask about the history and context of the body story. She is likely to help the person explore and understand the effects of the trauma that her body has revealed. Personal and societal influences may be explored. The Weaver may be weaving together dual awareness as she observes and gains new understanding of herself as a child. The shuttle may begin to move with more confidence as clear meanings about the past are deduced and agency arrives. Different thicknesses of yarn may be added to the weft and fresh design features appear.

In response to the arrival of a body-cued memory or story, the second story of trauma might also be explored. Discovering responses made at the time of early trauma or stress (White, 2006) is likely to bring new vigour into the weaving. The responses might be found in the body narrative itself or implied by the person's enduring life values, which might also demonstrate a consistency over time. All this might be woven into the fabric as a thread of glittering sequins.

Body-based approach: For a trauma survivor plagued with somatic sensory overload (Perry, 1997; van der Kolk, 2006), the Co-weaver will direct her investigatory questions so that the person begins to experiment with calming and modulating body strategies. The body-scaffolding space is opened up for the shuttle to pass through. Each strategy shows up in the different threads chosen by the Weaver. It may take time for the Weaver to gauge the effectiveness of the different body strategies she explores. Tags may be used as reminders to herself as further experimentation takes place.

If the Weaver experiences a despairing flatness (signs of dissociation), she might be helped to explore enlivening body strategies. It is likely to take some time for the Weaver to evaluate which of the strategies she is finding most agentive. She alone can make the choices and decide on her own unique ways of threading the shuttle.

Narrative and body-based approaches: The Co-weaver might open one space and the other in quick succession, so the person can use her mind to give consideration to the body-based soothing strategies or resources of which she has made intuitive and perhaps regular historic use. When she recognises her own body wisdom, an 'aha' moment might see her choosing a particular texture in the thread she picks up.

And so the weaving proceeds. At every point, the Weaver is growing in her sense of agency and confidence as she understands her body's messages, and modulates her nervous system's automatic intensity. Attitudes of kindness outbid judgmentalism. A new sense of freedom and of the felt sense of grounded-ness may show up in the growing fabric. Sometimes of course there may be miscommunication, failures of recognition and when the weaver is intensely triggered in particular, a loss of awareness of the body as friend. Parts of the fabric may end up recording the old and very familiar dominant narrative. Becoming visible within the conversation makes it very useful for further reflective exploration.

Narrative-based approach: A measuring tool may be called on to direct the mind when the Weaver needs to test the usefulness of the body-related grounding practices. Threads may be cut and layered together thickly so that another tangible marker shows up in the design. The exploration of a reinforcing mantra, of metaphorical language or of calming meditation might have the Co-weaver needing to open the two different spaces in rapid succession.

The narrative approaches when applied to the stories cued by the person's body can be described as helping the trauma-survivor to translate her intense sensations and emotions into what van der Kolk (2006) calls "communicable language, understandable to [herself] most of all" (p. 12).

Body-based approach: Excitement builds whenever a body strategy reveals its calming or its awakening capacity. As the weaving proceeds, the Weaver is finding that she is less at the mercy of her primitive brain reactivity (Perry, 1997). The measuring tool has reinforced her new attentiveness towards her body and her effective self-soothing practices. At each step, the objectivity that arrives as her upper brain is exercised is able to further advance the weaving process (Siegel, 2010). Terrorising or freezing sensations are losing their potency. The person weaves in her sense of agency as she takes up self-soothing body resources with useful rapidity. The agency experienced is more and more home grown.

A uniquely woven fabric has emerged: When the weaver chooses to cut the fabric free from the loom, she does so at a time when she feels that her weaving is finished. With the Co-weaver working right along with her, her mind and her body have expressed their wisdom in differentiated ways and their wisdom has coalesced. The richly configured textures have been woven between the two sheds of the warp and the fabric is ready. Freshly woven understandings and textured pivotal moments are all evident in the weaving and in its changed patterns. The quest to leave trauma behind has been rewarded and a dominant narrative has been re-authored. There are likely to be quite a few loose threads to tidy up but the fabric created collegially is the Weaver's own, to take away with her and to further manufacture as she has need.

PART TWO
The Practice

Chapter 5
Hannah's Experiential Journey

The bottom line is that clients need to be helped to think and to feel concurrently.
Babette Rothschild

This chapter describes the body-based narrative approach that I took in conversations with Hannah that led to her experiential journey from the effects of her early trauma experience to a new way of seeing and being herself. My thanks go to Hannah, who is our guide as she shares her up-close and personal experience of the legacies of developmental trauma and her quest to put them behind her.

What immediately caught my attention during our first conversation was that Hannah's body language and tone of voice were conveying the intensity of the distress she was describing in words as "a state of utter turmoil".

She told me how emotional overload had been interfering with her ability to function over the past several weeks. She could pinpoint the moment exactly it had started – when she was told about an error she had made that had complex taxation implications.

I invited Hannah to join in an investigation of what her body was saying. I hoped she might be willing to explore her body's sensations instead of immediately engaging with her thoughts. I asked her to try to re-visit the moment the recent intense anxiety had arrived and to consider her body sensations at that time.

It only took a moment for Hannah to describe the "punch in the guts", which had seemed to hit her with force right at the moment the taxation mistake that she had made at work was pointed out.

THE MAGIC LOOM PART TWO - THE PRACTICE

I asked her to simply sit with that punch in the guts sensation for a moment. In seconds, Hannah was struck with what she described as "a life belief":

"I'm not good enough!" She started describing an image of herself at a very young age. She could see herself in her mind's eye. Though only tiny, she was berating herself and hitting herself over and over. Her remembered words were, "Naughty Nannie, naughty Nannie!"

Because the narrative approach sees the other person, not the therapist, as the expert on her life, I asked Hannah how it made her feel that the pointing out of a mistake to her as an adult had taken her back to some of her earliest words and actions.

Hannah responded by first speaking about what she had recalled.

She was appalled that as such a tiny child, this was her reality. It was not the first time this image had come to mind. On an earlier occasion, alarmed by such memories, she had checked them out with her mother, who had confirmed that Hannah had taken to hitting and berating herself when she was around eighteen months old. Hannah mentioned how important it was for her to be sure she hadn't concocted the idea that her childhood had been riddled with trauma. She expressed her amazement that her body had corroborated this early life experience.

'Pivotal moments' are important in narrative thought. Duval and Béres (2011) describe them as pivotal because they provide a range of new possibilities, enabling the person to undergo a shift in meaning when they occur. If such moments go unnoticed, or remain unacknowledged, there is a risk that they will quickly disappear.

Narrative therapists do their best to avoid generalisations. Instead, they move the conversation forward by taking notice of unique and particular details. They seek to do this "tentatively and respectfully in a spirit of discovering meanings together rather than imposing an understanding or interpretation" (Duval & Béres, 2011, p. 93).

A responsible narrative therapist can use the body-awareness-raising conversational scaffold with similar tentativeness and for the same generative purpose. It is the person herself who, by attending to her body's intense reactivity, is able to make links with her early trauma narratives.

When I heard Hannah talk about feeling appalled, I was hearing her open her heart to the child she once was. Right now, she felt overwhelmed. More details emerged as, in line with narrative practice, I began to ask Hannah further questions about her history.

From infancy and throughout her childhood, there had been constant punishment. Hannah's mother had once explained to her the strict guidelines her father had imposed for her earliest training. Whenever baby Hannah cried after being put down at night, neither parent was to respond. If, after a period of prolonged crying, she ceased crying, her father would pick her up for a moment supposedly to affirm her decision to stop. But if she started crying again after he had returned her to

84

CHAPTER 5 HANNAH'S EXPERIENTIAL JOURNEY

the cot, both parents withheld any response. This pattern was often repeated many times before baby Hannah would finally give up and fall asleep.

I asked Hannah what she thought about her unwillingness to surrender, even as a tiny infant.

> *She liked that glimpse of her strong will. But at the same time, it felt confusing for her because she was often punished for it. Her strong will or personality became a label held against her.*

These dynamics were confusing for her. Therapeutically, however, I considered it was important to notice and name the strong will she had glimpsed. This aspect of herself would continue to emerge and it was a quality she came to respect.

I selected another narrative approach by asking Hannah about the parenting practices that might have informed her parents. I wanted to help her consider a little of the social context of what had happened to her. Deconstructing or exploring normative social practices in this way aims to help the person understand the impacts of wider influences, so she can move further away from a familiar practice of allotting blame to herself for what occurred.

Hannah explained that the context of her parents' own childhoods would have contributed to the way she had been treated. There was a patriarchal entitlement underlying her father's use of power in the family and in her mother's compliance. She could see that her mother's helplessness contributed to her own subjugation. Her father's misogyny and patriarchal power seemed to be matched by her mother's inability to put the needs of her vulnerable infant first.

I noticed as this discussion continued back and forth over some minutes that Hannah's previous distress seemed soothed. There was evidence in her body language that she was feeling energised by the process of the enquiry. With a sense of calm resolution, she took up my lead and expanded her historic storytelling. She now drew on her explicit autobiographical memory.

> *She recalled being punished by being put into rooms in the dark and being regularly hit by both her parents. She described what she called "hot smacks" and the welts and bruises that often covered her body. She called to mind a snapshot of herself taken at about six years of age. It revealed a state of neglect. Her dress was filthy and her hair a mess. She had a clear image of herself walking to school one day when she was in kindergarten. She was wearing shoes with holes in their soles. Cereal packet inserts had been wedged inside.*

From thinking about her infancy and early childhood, and in response to questions about the effects of these early events on her, Hannah said that throughout her adolescence and into adulthood her self-talk had been unrelenting:

> *You're dirty! You're unacceptable! You're not wanted! You're overweight, unattractive, unimportant. There's no place for you. You are not good enough!*

THE MAGIC LOOM PART TWO - THE PRACTICE

The self-punishing stance revealed in Hannah's image of herself as a toddler had turned into a patterned and habitually negative internalisation.

I was curious to again clarify how the conversation was going for Hannah.

> *She said she was excited about being able to put some of the pieces together. She was understanding why such an early belief and her later self-talk had become entrenched. She could intellectually understand that she wasn't to blame. However, try as she might, she couldn't do anything to change how she felt about herself.*

Van der Kolk (2002) provides the reason for Hannah's predicament when he explains that triggering directly impacts a person's rational capacity. Any triggering event automatically re-agitates a great cascade of neural activity, stealing a person's cognitive objectivity.

In the triggering circumstances of the accounting error, Hannah was emotionally overwhelmed and unable to think straight. Now she was articulating her perceived inability to change. Hearing this sense of helplessness, I was curious about what Hannah saw as her usual response to such triggering episodes.

> *Hannah described her impatience and anger at herself whenever she became emotionally aroused as she had been recently. She felt enraged by her helplessness and confusion.*

I suggested a rather quirky, but hopefully intriguing, experiment. I named the punch in the guts sensation Hannah had identified. I asked her to take a moment to reconstitute it in her body. Then I suggested she do her best to address it with kindness and compassion instead of with the negatively self-whipping attitude she had just described.

For about a minute, Hannah did exactly this, making a conscious effort to bring tenderness and empathy into her awareness of her gut's sensory reactivity. The calming effect was almost instantly apparent. Hannah articulated that she was now feeling much more settled.

This was the second phase of the body scaffolding. The first session with Hannah was coming to an end and I was keen to hear what she would take away from the conversation. Among other things Hannah expressed her desire to continue practising kindness towards any intense body sensations that might arise during the coming week.

Later I was to ask myself if the emotional intensity of a person's self-disgust contributes even further to the autonomic nervous system arousal. I wondered whether Hannah's change of attitude towards her body in the present was a factor that could energise a more calming pathway (Porges, 2011).

It was interesting therefore for me to read Siegel's (2010) general confirmation of the modulating strategy of kindness towards an intense sensation, when he said that "a non-judgmental, non-reactive and kind stance is what allows a person to tune in to herself and this is the foundation she needs, to build resilience and flexibility (p. 86)".

As Siegel (2010) points out, Hannah's focusing of her attention in therapeutic ways enabled her to strategically and voluntarily begin to change the neuronal firing patterns associated with terror, which had originally been laid down in a totally involuntary way.

Even while Hannah's dominant story was being thickened for understanding, and before a new one could be strongly articulated, the process didn't appear to be a re-traumatising one. Memories that her body had brought to light, and which her mother had corroborated, were fitting together alongside others that were more explicit. The process was increasing her understanding. The nature of the enquiry seemed to be having a calming and an energising effect.

There was again evidence to me of the accuracy of White's (2006) idea that helping a person string events together and to discover a sense of consistency over time can lead to internal reverberations that are themselves enlivening.

I could see that Hannah was already thinking differently. There was evidence in her body language and in her words that some hope had arrived and that she now felt she had the power to make a difference to her outcomes. When and if triggering occurred again, she could work with her intense sensations, rather than setting herself against them. I discerned that the body-mind processes were already having a re-authoring impact.

Just before our conversation ended, Hannah began to talk again about the matter of the tax error. She had come to a realisation while we were talking. Part of her reactivity had had to do with the intimidation she felt whenever she was around her accountant. Hannah was naming the complex relational aspect of her triggered trauma. I flagged this for exploration in our next conversation.

> *However, Hannah began again to describe the uncontrollable "stress" feelings that had been haunting her during the past month. She mentioned more specifics: neck and head pain, the way she seemed to hover outside herself, the experience she had of her skin prickling and her hair feeling as if it would fall out. She was feeling pain right at the roots of her hair, the follicles.*

The bodily symptoms Hannah was describing were indicators of severe hyperarousal and even dissociation. Unfortunately, time had run out. There were obligations that meant she needed to leave. There was little I could do but mention my availability if she needed support before the next session.

Complex developmental trauma and trust

Most developmental trauma is first experienced in the context of hostile early relational dynamics. Obviously, Hannah's brain associated something about the accountant with what had occurred in the past (probably with her father). Her brain automatically perceived threat and triggered autonomic nervous system arousal.

I was relieved that when flashbacks (signalling dissociative impacts) and other intense sensations began to overwhelm Hannah that evening, she had enough sense of trust in the therapy process and our relationship to ask her husband to ring for support.

I began the telephone conversation aware that it was important for Hannah to experience (implicitly) a sense of calm coming down the line. This was confirmed by my later research about the importance of the voice, its pitch and intonations, or what neuroscientists call 'voice prosody' (Meares, 2016; Porges, 2011). The voice is vital both during the attachment dance and within the therapeutic relationship because it can promote soothing and a sense of safety.

I quickly made use of the second part of the body scaffold by introducing a physical grounding strategy, which I hoped would help Hannah to engage the resources of both her body and her mind to quickly decrease the high level of arousal she was experiencing. She had only that day had her first introduction to the idea that she could do this. Now, in her very acute distress, she didn't need any advice, but more evidence both that she was accurately heard and cared for, and, importantly, that her own body held some answers.

Hannah told me later how helpful she found it was to notice her body's slump and to re-structure it. Step by step, she took action first to plant her feet strongly on the floor, to straighten her spine, to lift her chin and to slow her breathing. Her feelings of panic immediately began to recede.

When she felt a little calmer, she could then make use of her senses, which seemed to calm her even further. She kept her mind attentively on her feet, keeping them strongly planted on the ground and then she used her attention again as she ran her hands through the fabric of her scarf and, noticing its texture, she described its softness and delicacy and its visual details to me.

In neuroscientific terms, I was helping Hannah focus on exteroceptive information (coming from the outside) instead of only on the interoceptive information arising from her internal somatic memory. It was her internal memory that had been continuing to automatically trigger the reactivity in her autonomic nervous system (Rothschild, 2000). The focus on her tangible senses helped to bring her nervous system back into balance. Hannah was again deriving the sense that she herself could modulate the tyranny of her non-conscious somatic memory. As she mastered the reactivity, she was actively robbing the past of its power over her (Rothschild, 2010). By the time the phone call was over, Hannah felt reassured that she could maintain her calm.

At the start of our next conversation, I expressed my apologies to Hannah that she had experienced such re-traumatisation after our first conversation. Hannah surprised me, however, by making it clear that, despite the flashbacks and some hours of distress, she was already discovering a new and preferred story. She told me how pivotal it had been to get in touch with her body. She said that moving away from a total reliance on the intellect was a massive shift for her.

She assigned the decompensation that had caused her to telephone for support, as of little importance when compared to the new way she was learning to be kind to her vulnerable, younger self. Kindness towards herself was everything! In response to curiosity I had expressed in the first conversation about how she might extend her kindness to the child she had once been, she told me that she had put a picture of herself onto her phone and was gazing long and hard at the image of her child-self. There was a new empathy for 'the child within'. Looking into her young eyes was something she considered vital. She said:

I find I can offer her the kind of love I have for my daughter. There's a sense of deep compassion and joy bubbling up. I'm feeling different, all the way down deep, like I can feel it in my cells. The grounding strategies are also bringing a huge change. I'm feeling that I belong here. I have something to contribute.

I was learning a great deal from Hannah. As my co-theorist she was teaching me more about dual awareness (for example, when 'the adult' considers another part, in this case, 'the child') and about the vexed subject of re-traumatisation. She was knowledgeable and eager to move forward.

In our first conversation, I had only been able to introduce Hannah to the one body strategy of offering kindness to her sensations. This strategy had not been embedded enough in her consciousness, or perhaps was not tangible enough, to help her put the brakes on the hyper-arousing flashbacks she encountered later that evening (Rothschild, 2000). Despite this, it took me by surprise to hear that the kindness strategy had had the immediate secondary benefit Hannah was spelling out.

As we talked about her "sense of newness", Hannah described a vision she had had while meditating during the week.

It was as if I was wearing a heavy cloak of shame; shame for being alive, shame for just being me. The cloak was scratchy, and it was made of thick black wool. I took it off and gave it to both my parents. I made Mum hold it.

Next, I saw I had a scold's bridle on my head – that's an implement of medieval torture. It's made of metal and it has a bit like you put between a horse's teeth. I was tortured out of having any wants of my own or of articulating them. I've been dominated by everyone else's feelings and have always felt over-responsible for others. Now I was able to hand the scold's bridle back. It was a tangible action. It made me feel great!

I looked down at my body and noticed that there was something transparent, a bit like cling film, which was wound round and round my body. I was constricted like a mummy. Insecurity may be invisible, but it makes life impossible. It clings and constricts and imprisons. I was somehow carefully unwrapped, and I gladly stepped out free.

I looked down at my feet. I was wearing an old drunk's shoes without any soles. These "shoes of neglect" were replaced with well-made attractive ones. Then I saw that I'd been expected to wear another woman's dirty used G-string. I threw it away, realising it had never been mine. My fingernails, which grew like ugly talons for scratching and clawing my competitors, transformed into well-manicured hands that were the picture of health.

One by one, I took everything old and ugly and hateful, and handed it all back to my parents. It belonged to them. They had given me this costume and I didn't want it any more. The necklaces of candy, symbolising the junk food diet bequeathed on me, especially by my father, was torn off. Everything was replaced. It felt like God held out to me new clothes that were fresh and beautiful, healthy and clean. I had a feeling of complete renewal!

In narrative terms, Hannah had taken a stand. I was struck by the fact that she had done so on her own initiative and after a re-traumatising episode. Her vision demonstrated that some deeply implicit and unconscious change was taking place.

Hannah began routinely sharing situations of triggering, and, following my investigatory prompts, regularly described how she was modulating her sensations. Narrative explorations led to greater understanding of the past. Several conversations later, she described feeling inferior to a friend and how she had again noticed uncomfortably reactive sensations in her solar plexus. She responded to these as signals and I listened to the body story that was cued. Hannah made several discoveries within moments: she had been set up by her father to be in competition with her mother. An image flew into her mind.

> *It was evening. She was watching her mother get ready for her father's return from work. Her mother made herself beautiful. She watched her open her bottles and put on perfume. When her father walked in the door however, he ignored his wife and made a beeline for his little daughter. She was hugged and kissed and made much of.*

I was hearing Hannah responding to her own curiosity as she listened to a narrative cued by her body's sensations. The intensity of emotion when she'd been with her friend had made no sense to her but then it had become accessible because of her raised body awareness. She was immediately able to focus her left brain (using mindfulness) and to reflect on the meanings behind events that had become explicit in moments.

> *Hannah had come to dread her father's homecomings. She recalled an occasion when she caught a look, which she interpreted as one of sheer hatred, as it passed over her mother's face, as she was being hugged by her father. She had "a knowing" that she would be punished by her mother the next day because of her father's attentions. She lived in fear and helplessness because of this. But there was also a growing sense of rage within her.*

Therapeutically, my task was to continue to orient myself towards Hannah as she took brave steps away from a deeply negative dominant story and into a remarkable alternative one. It was important that I listen carefully and that my body language demonstrated my full attention. I was a supportive presence responding, often without words, to the sense she was making and gradually forming into a more life-affirming narrative.

As our conversation continued, Hannah enlarged on her hatred of her father's promiscuity. This awakened a memory of him molesting her when she was thirteen. He was drunk when he came downstairs to where she was sleeping. She woke up to find him lying on top of her, pressing down and touching her with his hands. In her rage, she pummelled at him and succeeded in pushing him off her. I asked Hannah what she could see of herself in this response.

She described herself as a fighter. She could think of other circumstances when the odds were against her, and yet she persisted and fought with everything that was in her.

This linked to her determination as an infant and it provided an opportunity to talk with her about the values she lives by.

From an early age, Hannah had vowed to herself that her children would not suffer the way she had. She talked about her first-born and her determination that she would never leave him to cry himself to sleep. This resulted in some periods of extreme anxiety, but she was intent on bringing him up to experience her love.

She further detailed her relationship with each of her children and more of the promises she had made to herself. Meanwhile, I was seeking to stay with Hannah moment by moment as the conversation continued and to listen with empathy. I remained in a position of not knowing. I was alongside her, putting my trust in her somatic processing. Hannah was her own expert; my role was to continue to help her to enlarge the territory she could explore by staying with the holistic investigation.

At the end of this session I again asked Hannah what she had found useful in the day's conversation (Morgan, 2000).

She described her happiness that she hadn't over-reacted to her friend out of the instant flare up of jealous feelings she had experienced. The reaction in her body had had nothing to do with the friend at all. It was a signal about much earlier pervasive and confusing stresses. She felt excited that she was learning to deal with triggers. She felt as if her childhood traumas were losing their grip. When triggers arrived, they didn't have the same power they had had in the past. As she noticed her body and calmed it, she knew how to reflect on the stories it brought her and on any other memories that came up. She felt that she was being freed of the past.

At the start of the next session there was a surprise. Hannah told me she had been mistaken about how she had responded to her father's molestation. She said:

I didn't pummel him, or push him off me, but that's exactly what happened in a dream I had some years ago. I got mixed up between my dream and what actually happened. I guess that response was what I wish had happened. I remember now what really happened. I just lay there. I was paralysed with fear and horror. Straight after the incident, I told my mother and she did nothing. I was alone.

Together we reflected about the meanings of both her remembered and her dreamed responses. What had not been explicit was becoming clear. More of her own responses to trauma and more of her values could be examined in the ongoing narrative process. I asked her about the benefits of lying still. Hannah could see the wisdom in what might have seemed to be passivity.

In answer to my further, more probing, questions about how her father had used his power, she elaborated on more of the history of her father's physical and verbal abuse.

> *She saw that the pain and suffering caused by so much severe punishment made "just lying there" actually her only safe option. Her response at the time of the molestation had been a very smart one.*

I asked about her mother's response, and we speculated together that perhaps her mother did take her husband on in private because there was no repeat of the molesting, but for Hannah,

> *there had never been any sense of solidarity, protection or validation. Her mother had done nothing to openly stand by her. Such lack of support was familiar. It marked her childhood.*

I asked her if she could talk about the values that were implicit in the fact that she had told her mother.

> *Hannah had absolute clarity that her father's behaviour should not be tolerated. It was wrong and had to be stopped. She acted from a deep sense that she deserved protection and safety.*

What is implicit in a person's behaviour forms an important line of enquiry for the narrative therapist because it speaks to important values they have chosen as their own (White, 2006). Hannah's respect for herself was now acknowledged and could be validated.

I was curious now to thicken the narrative about how she had differentiated from her parents and come to treat her own children so differently from the way she had been treated.

> *Hannah was struck by the divergence. She particularly recognised that she always did her best to validate her children when they brought her their upsets. She had continuously made choices and taken stands.*

I was curious to learn even more about how Hannah had arrived at the values she had made her own.

> *During her primary school years, she set out to observe what she called "happy families". When she came upon them as a result of sleepovers at the homes of some of her classmates, she watched them carefully. In so doing, she was willing herself onto a different path to that of her parents.*

White (2006) speaks of choices like this in positive terms. He says that even when left with few options, a human being can always find ways to reduce the power of trauma to cripple her life. Hannah's was an example of a life-giving response to trauma (White, 2006). Early trauma leaves a young child with a disrupted sense of self. However, the response the child has to that trauma also shapes them. Hannah's intentional decision as a child to observe families she discerned to be healthy can be interpreted as her best way to make up for what was lacking. She made an agentive contribution to her own formation.

As I explored this response with Hannah, it became evident to her that from a young age, she differentiated herself from her parents and from the parenting practices that marked her upbringing. She had chosen self-respect and had instinctively built her sense of self according to the values she preferred. She had not only an intent but a determination to make them her own.

Schore (2003) suggests that a child who learned to dissociate when very young might attempt to build a fragile sense of self by linking herself to (mimicking) the strong sense of identity of someone she admires. He calls dissociation 'an evacuation of the self'. I remember recoiling when I read that description. I found that I could relate easily to Hannah's courageous efforts at mimicking others, but not to the concept of an evacuation of the self. Perhaps the truth lies part way between the intuitions of the therapist and the views of the scientist.

Therapeutic rocking

Some months later, I invited Hannah to participate in a somatic process called rocking (or swaying), which is a little further removed from narrative approaches to therapy than the body-strategies already explored. However, I conceptualised this movement-based intervention as another territory of the body that Hannah and I could explore together. I hoped it would provide her with another fruitful way of listening to her body and lead to deeper implicit healing.

Therapeutic rocking or swaying aims to make a regulating impact on the brainstem, bypassing cognition and reliance on the intellect (Frese, 2005). Occupational therapists Elaine Masarik-Williams, Teresa Polizzi and Sarah Punshon (2016) convey the understanding that the internal sensations awakened by rocking can address the underlying physiological effects of trauma, bringing calm and emotional organisation while at the same time improving all levels of cognitive functioning. Proprioception is the unconscious perception of movement and spatial orientation arising from stimuli detected by nerves within the body itself and the semicircular canals of the inner ear. The body's vestibular system is a collection of structures in the inner ear that provide a sense of balance and an awareness of spatial orientation, that is, whether you are right side up or not. Such views seem to line up with Porges' research (2004, 2011), which describes the nerves of the face, beginning with the ear, as of vital importance for the activation of the nuanced calming of the social engagement system.

Since involvement in any intervention such as rocking has the potential to make a traumatised client feel vulnerable, I made sure that Hannah understood enough about it to feel safe to engage with it. It needed to take place within a reliably safe therapeutic relationship.

Once she confirmed her desire to proceed, I invited Hannah to take off her shoes and to lie down on a single futon on top of a king-sized sheet. Pillows were placed under her head and her knees. The sheet was folded over her and the ends from feet to shoulders tucked in firmly around her.

Once this was completed, I sat on a chair near her head and took up the ends of sheeting, which emerged from beneath and above her on the side where I was sitting. I asked Hannah if she could let the ground hold her. A state of bodily immobility would allow her to experience the rocking as it impacted all her senses, both internal and external. From the beginning and at intervals throughout the process, I verbally reinforced my presence.

Is that too tight? Is it okay for you, being here with me in this way? Does that feel comfortable? How is it going for you? Let me know if you want to stop.

Hannah was aware that I was with her, my gaze and my voice helped to keep me present to her. I began to pull the bunched sheet back and forth in a regular rocking motion similar in timing to the way a mother rocks her infant. Hannah's body slowly tilted, supported as it was by the sheet from above her neck and shoulders down to her feet. The regulating rocking rhythm proceeded for five minutes or so on each side.

Because this process provides an experience of repetitive movement, it can take on the form of a ritual. It takes place, according to the recipient's preference, within a co-experienced meditative silence or as part of the ongoing therapy conversation. Hannah chose to stay meditatively silent.

Changing to the other side of the mattress midway through the process involved me moving around Hannah, talking with her and again adjusting the sheets so that they were appropriately tucked in and could again be pulled rhythmically back and forth. I seated myself near her head but on the other side. When the rocking stopped, at my encouragement, Hannah took her time to sit up and to drink some water.

Then she reported that the process had been a spiritual one for her. She related that when she was rocked from the right side, she felt as if she was being rocked into God's chest. She said she was recalling a song about finding refuge. And then she added:

> It felt like "the Hannah essence" was being held physically. There was a full body sense of being safe.

When the rocking came from her left-hand side, Hannah reported a slightly different experience. Now she felt as if she was being rejoiced over with singing. She heard the words:

> I'm so glad you're in the world. Your Hannah-ness is there forever. You are my delight!

I was interested that Hannah's spiritual beliefs were central to how she interpreted her sensations during this body movement. There was a bigger story on which she could rely. I noticed that her immediate responses related both to her sense of self and to her sense of connection. They were linked to safety, identity and relationship.

A week later Hannah was reporting other more diverse responses. She talked about discovering the joy of her own physicality.

> She was finding a kind of euphoria in running. After being cut off from this part of herself for her whole life, now she described how she had begun to run early in the morning and that she had done it several times in the week. She said that as she ran, the experience of the rocking seemed to return. She described an internal change that had been brought about by the rocking and she conveyed a sense that it was bringing change into every other area of her life.

CHAPTER 5 HANNAH'S EXPERIENTIAL JOURNEY

A deeply entrenched eating compulsion seemed to be losing its power. Hannah was enjoying fresh food for the first time instead of the over-processed sweet stuff she had always found addictive.

The invigoration of the movement pattern of running, from which Hannah had been previously cut off (dissociated), was particularly striking. Fragmented or split-off dissociated parts of herself, in this case her physicality and the action system of running, were being reconnected. Hannah not only became explicitly conscious of this reconnection, but she was immediately engaged in integrating it intentionally.

She described behavioural change that didn't require an intense effort of the will, but which felt natural (organic). Hannah reported, for example, on some changes in her relationships:

> I have a different view of my partner. I'm letting him work on his own complicated stuff. I don't have to fear his disapproval. I have more compassion and gentleness towards him. I am not his rescuer. Even if he is emotionally reactive I can let him be.

She was sifting through her friendship groups. She could distance herself from people who were unhelpful or out of line with her values. She no longer had to feel responsible for their situations or feel guilty about not seeing them. At the same time, she was choosing to spend more time with the friends who treated her as an equal and helped her to grow and flourish.

She reported that what she had been attempting to do as a parent from an intellectual conviction, and with a level of emotional desperation, was now feeling as natural as breathing. I was particularly alerted when I heard about this development with regard to her parenting. Hannah was no longer putting pressure on herself in any artificial way. Her parenting felt more natural and authentic. My observation was that she was feeling better regulated and integrated.

As I thought more about what Hannah was articulating, it made sense to me that some of the outcomes and the integrative thrust she was describing, might have arisen from the cumulative processes of body and mind in which we had been engaged together over the preceding weeks. However, the rocking ritual was, in Hannah's view, pivotal. Porges (2004) theorises that once the cortical regulation of the brainstem structures that are involved in social engagement are activated, social behaviour and communication occur spontaneously. He calls the spontaneous outcomes 'natural emergent properties' of the biological social engagement system. The integrative thrust Hannah was conveying was startling. I wondered if including the wisdom of her body while operating within a collegial and intersubjective therapy relationship had taken her in the direction of her social engagement biology as well as in other healing directions.

Hannah has the last word

Several months after our first series of therapy conversations, I asked Hannah to reflect on the changes she had noticed in her life. She wrote the following:

One traumatic event triggered a chain of memories and responses in me that finally led to the big kahuna: the very real – but, oh, so buried – abusive childhood, complete with the dominant, manipulative, violent father and the passive, competitive, neglectful mother. Ah-ha! I thought, the magic key! It explained so very much about why I struggled the way I did. Transformation and healing were surely cresting just behind the door.

I dove into the deep with my therapist. The work we did, particularly the grounding strategies and learning how to be compassionate and gentle with my own terrified 'little girl', were invaluable. For the first time in my whole life, I was able to say – and truly believe with my whole being – that I am loveable and valuable. In my first session, I couldn't even mumble the affirmation, "I belong here". I sobbed and choked and simply could not get the words out. I didn't believe them for a second.

By the end of some months of therapy, I stood on the beach and shouted those words across the wide ocean, in gratitude, joy and full belief. The gift of self-esteem – where before there was only shame, self-loathing and fear – is nothing short of a miracle. I'm healed and healing; free and getting free-er, strong and getting stronger, chosen and choosing. It's an evolving, ongoing journey. And I'm so glad to be on it.

Much to my disappointment, all my self-defeating behaviours didn't disappear overnight. It takes intentionality and time and diligence to recover from a lifetime of pain. As a result of the work I did with the stuff that had been previously behind the door, I have new pathways, both neural and physical, but I still need to choose to train my body and mind to walk along them, when they are so used to responding to triggers in other, self-limiting ways. I still fall into overwhelm and find myself wanting to escape, although a lot less often, and rarely anymore with the voice of self-hatred that used to go with it. This, in itself, is a vast improvement. I am able to see what's happening, and I am, mostly, compassionate and gentle with 'the little girl within' who is still learning that she's safe.

Alas, there's no magic key to transformation that does it all for you. With my precious newly discovered sense of agency, it is now up to me to make consistent choices in the right direction. Like any new skill, I am clumsy and inexpert. I forget, and I fall over. Learning to walk is a cyclical, funny, messy business, not a straight, easy, neatly contained two thousand-word story.

Postscript

After almost a year's travelling overseas with her family, Hannah returned prematurely because of worrying heart palpitations. She had not been able to keep up her running regime during these months. Moreover, she had found it hard to continue modulating her triggered arousal when she was stuck in an unsafe living situation, from which escape was not easy. The heart specialist she saw immediately on her return told Hannah that her heart muscle was weak, and that she needed to take up exercise and a healthier lifestyle.

Van der Kolk (2017) explains that heart rate variability is a common symptom for survivors of complex trauma. Rhythms of the breath become disconnected from that of the heartbeat. He recommends regular yoga, where an instructor's calming voice can help a person focus her breathing at the same time as she is structuring her body in different poses.

Hannah resumed the therapy conversations and she was again able to practise modulating her autonomic nervous system arousal in triggering contexts. Gradually she found that she could routinely modulate her sensory affect. She took up a disciplined exercise regime and came to particularly love running on the beach.

Chapter 6
Making Theoretical Meaning of Hannah's Experience

The primary therapeutic task is the reinvigoration and redevelopment of the memory system called the stream of consciousness ... [and] of a 'sense of myself'.
Michael White

A body-awareness-raising practice quite naturally leads to interweaving cognitive processes, which help a person to integrate the right hemispheric somatic brain memories with the meaning-making capacity of the hippocampus and the left brain (van der Kolk, 2006). When attention is focused mindfully, the hippocampus, described by Siegel (2010) as "a master puzzle piece assembler" (p. 148), begins the work of integrating what was implicit and inaccessible before. Neglectful and abusive relationships set up hard to read and confusing maps. Therapy for early trauma seeks to re-create healthy, straightforward ones (Schore, 2003; White, 2004).

Intense sensations and neural firing patterns

Siegel (2010) talks about the importance of working therapeutically with what he calls the 'neural firing patterns' that replicate the original trauma dynamics. By helping Hannah to focus on the intensity of her bodily sensations right at a triggering moment, it seemed feasible that I was providing her with the space in which the traumatic dynamics associated with those original neural firing patterns could be changed.

Some neuroscientists (Siegel, 2010; van der Kolk, 2006) suggest that a part of the struggle for an adult whose early traumas are invading and biasing the present seems to be the implicit (unconscious) human tendency to retreat from sensations and emotions of terror and shame. Van der Kolk (2006) talks about the primary therapeutic task of helping a traumatised client to learn to feel safer about her inner messages. I understand him to be saying that the person will interweave the cognitive with the emotional and sensorimotor elements of past trauma as she is helped to become more tolerant towards her body and its intensely emotional sensations and to focus on them with greater acceptance.

Asking Hannah to give attention to her sensations was not only putting her into the driving seat of her healing, but also prioritising her safety. Unattended, the sensations had been promoting fear on top of fear. Porges (2011) describes how this can lead to faulty neuroception, which itself goes on contributing to over-reactivity. When her sensations cued an accurate memory that could be explored narratively, those same sensations began to feel useful. I observed that Hannah's sense of agency grew. Her body was helping her mind. Her familiar self-denigration, fear and helplessness were being replaced by something new, rather than reinforcing her dominant story. In Siegel's words (2010), exploring her cued memories narratively enabled Hannah "to hold them in the front of her mind" (p. 206). An experience of integration was replacing feelings of inner division and turmoil.

Raising awareness of the body leads to cognitive change

Because of early trauma, some of Hannah's left brain 'narrator function' had been at the mercy of the implicit memory storage of the right hemisphere (Siegel, 2000, p. 73). Her intense sensory and emotional disturbance and lack of functionality was expressive of the arousing (hyper-arousing) impacts of the primitive fight, flight or freeze mechanisms of her brain (central nervous system) in concert with her autonomic nervous system. It was as if she was a prisoner of the past (Siegel, 2010). She was unaware of the cause of her struggles when she arrived for therapeutic help, except in a very general and limited sense.

Attachment and regulation

Hannah's body helped her trace traumatic experience in her childhood right back to her infancy. Her corroborated memories revealed that her earliest caretakers were insensitive and unresponsive. They could be characterised as neglectful, even abusive. Bowlby's (1988) attachment theory recognises that this kind of start in life leaves children vulnerable to further stresses. Sometimes, a sense of traumatisation occurs somatically because the child's early attachment to her primary caretakers was insecure from the beginning. It is in her pre-verbal days, even partly during the last trimester in utero, that the infant's nervous system begins to be regulated or dysregulated by its connection to the mother's nervous system. The regulating process continues according to the way her earliest caregivers respond to her needs – or fail to.

Every healthily attached child continues to need mediating support from an adult throughout her childhood whenever confronted by trauma or ongoing stress. If given such support, she becomes resilient. Her own ability to handle stress is positively internalised, becoming part of her internal implicit knowledge (Schore, 2003). Infants who have received kindness, and who therefore have become well-regulated internally, have straightforward maps of behaviour patterns, secure sequences and embedded intentions of kindness and care to expect and rely on. Their mirror neurons produce empathy (Siegel, 2010).

Schore formulated regulation theory (2003) along these lines, and one of the conclusions he arrived at was that in childhood "the essential experience of trauma [is] an unravelling of the relationship between self and nurturing other, the very fabric of psychic life" (p. 134).

Insecure attachment, which can be categorised as avoidant, ambivalent or disorganised, always leads to some measure of dysregulation in the nervous system. When trauma has impacted an infant from the start, and she continues to be unsupported throughout childhood, any further stress that comes along puts her at risk. For such a child, the world is not a safe place and events are likely to terrorise. Close relationships are hazardous: who can she trust? Her thinking processes and memory structures are not able to support her. She is vulnerable to illogical conclusions that can be hostile to the sense of self, which has been in the process of its formation from the beginning (Schore, 2003).

Prolonged stress and trauma on a continuum

Rothschild (2000) makes the point that prolonged stress in infancy and during a child's developmental years can have similar effects to life-threatening trauma. She notes that:

> chronic, prolonged stress during the developmental years (from neglect, chronic illness, a dysfunctional family system, etc) can take its toll on the autonomic nervous system (ANS), just short of pushing it to the point of fight, flight or freeze (p. 81).

Rothschild may be referring to the stress-response cycle described by LaCombe (2014). Early childhood stress, whether chronic or acute, can impact on the brain's alarm systems and can affect the body's immune system and organs such as the heart (Perry, 1997). Somatic memories return without higher brain connections being made and, when this is so, they are hard to come to terms with or to resolve using talking therapy alone.

The rocking experiment

The regulating aspect of the work with Hannah came into even greater focus for me when I read about the neurosequential model of therapeutics for children and young people. This model, studied longitudinally over ten years with evidence of effectiveness, was pioneered by Perry (2006). He contends that within "developmental and age-appropriate regimens" that are tailored to the individual, "it is always wisest to start with simple rhythmic and repetitive activities that help the brainstem system become well organised and regulated" (p. 45–50).

Regulating interventions include music, drumming, movement, dance, patterned massage and other similar repetitive and rhythmic activities. A huge emphasis is placed on repetition.

Awakening maternal templates to improve regulation

Perry (1997) suggests that movement rituals like rocking may awaken positive state memories of maternal templates. The idea arose as a result of research into the infant human's final trimester in utero. Perry (1997) describes the somato-sensory patterns that make up a maternal template for regulation. He says for instance that "the neuronal apparatus of the brainstem is undergoing crucial processes related to building the organisational capacity to regulate heart rate, blood pressure, body temperature and respiration before birth" and, at this time, the primary environmental sensation for the infant is "the repetitive, relentless and rhythmic sound and feel of mother's heart beating at eighty beats per minute" (p. 8).

He further discusses the importance of rocking in many cultural contexts.

> *Is it any surprise that cross-cultural studies demonstrate that mothers in all cultures, rock children with the same frequency (Hatfleld & Rapson, 1993). It is between 70–80 beats to the minute, the same as a resting mother's heartbeat (p. 8).*

He postulates that this frequency of soothing may be the reason that similar patterns of sound and movement are utilised in a host of healing or soothing grief rituals, practices observed through history and across cultures. He suggests that therapists can learn much from traditional cultures.

Powerful evidence comes from hundreds of separate cultures across thousands of generations, independently converging on rhythm, touch, storytelling and reconnection to community as the core ingredients to cope with trauma.

Rose (2005) enlarges this vein of thinking:

> *Examination of the known beliefs, rituals and healing practices that remain from aboriginal cultures reveal some remarkable principles [for recovery]. The core elements include: first, an overarching belief system – a rationale, a belief, a reason for the pain, injury, loss; second, a re-telling of or re-enactment of the trauma in words, dance or song; third, a set of somato-sensory experiences – touch, the patterned repetitive movements of dance and song; fourth, a context which is intensely relational, preferably with family and clan participating in the ritual.*

Neither somatic nor cognitive approaches to trauma are relied on in isolation. Both Perry and Rose refer to storytelling and the importance of community input, as well as of repetitive patterning. In other words, traditional cultures have always promoted holistic responses to trauma.

Early manifestations of shame and terror

Schore (2004) contextualises shame as a social emotion relating to incompetence and embarrassment. It has been shown to originate in an implicit way even during the pre-verbal stage of development. Schore (2004) quotes Tomkins (1963) who differentiated shame from emotions such as terror or anger, which are induced from the outside. He deduced that shame is an inner torment, a sickness that besieges the soul. Schore notes that, like pain, the emotion of shame can itself act as a trigger and lead to a somatic response.

Perhaps it was the sense of shame induced by a voice (that of the accountant) proclaiming 'failure' that triggered Hannah's memory of her earliest shame-filled experiences. Now, however, despite the re-traumatisation that followed our first conversation, and within an extremely brief timeframe, Hannah was demonstrating that she was finding she could overcome the toxicity of shame and better integrate the harms of the past. Because her body had brought the past to light, her urge to meditate provided her with an implicit experience, a vision that was spiritually meaningful and healing. As she described it to me, she made it explicit.

What she shared vividly illustrated Hannah's preference to live out of a new narrative, one which was totally alternative to the narrative that had been so dominant because of a childhood of trauma and prolonged stress. What she described was at odds with the subjugating and dysregulating impacts of trauma and its themes of isolation and learned self-blame. In *Mindsight*, Siegel (2010) emphasises the healing benefits of receptivity. It was not hard to see this characteristic in Hannah's responses.

Changing disturbed physical action patterns

Van der Kolk (2006) considers that a major task of trauma therapy is to help the survivor of early trauma with her disturbed physical action patterns. Rocking was of help to Hannah in this regard.

I heard an anecdote recently about the life-saving value of boxing for a person living with PTSD. By making exercise with a punching bag part of his regular practice, he was able to manage his arousal and better regulate himself. I personally find rhythmic sessions of deep water running in a heated swimming pool, with a knowledgeable trainer poolside, builds calm into my lifestyle in a deeply regulating way.

LeDoux and Gorman (2001) demonstrated how memories of fear arise in the mid-brain, particularly in the amygdala. In turn, this part of the central nervous system distributes its output to brainstem areas that control the activation of the autonomic nervous system. In their research, these practitioners discovered that helping a person take effective action is a way of re-routing conditioned fear responses, while at the same time helping to manage arousal in the autonomic nervous system. Improvisational theatre, self-defence training and physical action programmes are proving effective.

Optimising the therapy relationship

I described in Chapter 5 how the therapeutic bond was developed and maintained with Hannah. Safety is clearly a pre-requisite for all therapy, but this is particularly so for people with complex developmental trauma, where often toxic or ambiguous relating, as in Hannah's case, was at the heart of the early childhood experience. The polyvagal theory describes how, under these circumstances, at an implicit level the autonomic nervous system learns to perceive danger everywhere. That can make therapy for trauma difficult.

Schore (2003) suggests that the brainstem can only be quieted and increasingly regulated using the kind of strategies and pathways suggested in this book, if the relational environment for the survivor is safe and healthy. Perry (2006) also emphasises the importance of a healthy relational environment in his work with traumatised children. It is his view that their states of arousal cannot be modulated if the trauma survivor isn't provided a deep sense of safety. We are born to be interdependent. He confirms that the neurobiological connections between self and other are part of what it means to be human.

While narrative therapy aims to help a person move towards an alternative story, the building of trust is not articulated as a primary aim. My point of view is that trust is intrinsically encouraged by the narrative practitioner because the approach she takes is always a de-centred one. The therapist is always orienting herself towards the other. The client is at the centre, rather than the therapist or her expertise. Doing therapy in a way that centres on the client establishes a trust that continues to develop with every conversation.

When the narrative therapist adds a somatic focus and herself trusts the soma of the client, I believe that trust becomes even more strongly embedded. Self-trust grows. Learning that her body can be trusted, and then also being able to explore the responses she made to early trauma, means that the person's trust in herself develops internally, and this, in turn, forms the foundation for learning to better trust the other.

Scientist-practitioners such as Allan Schore recognise that factors of biological attunement, resonance and empathy create an intersubjective experience. Congruent body language may often carry a greater impact than all the words spoken.

The de-centred focus of both somatic and narrative therapies sets the terms of the interpersonal engagement in this therapy model. I see here clear links to what Schore (2003) is describing when he says:

> *The interpersonal engagement that occurs in psychotherapy represents a potential medium in which an individual self can subjectively experience the 'need to know' and 'the need to feel known' in a safe, emotionally responsive context (p. xvii).*

Words and metaphors can connect and provide an experience of resonance within the therapy relationship (White 2006, 2011). Schore (2003) describes how a resonating empathic kind of interpersonal interaction aids the expansion of a person's positive emotions. In his words,

> *the therapist's empathic ability to receive, resonate with and amplify the patients often 'shimmering' transient states of positive affect [is important]. This can facilitate the interactive generation of higher and more enduring levels of positively-valenced states than the patient can auto-generate (p. 79).*

I relate what he describes as positively valenced (weighted) states to the pivotal moments that narrative therapists recognise and enlarge. 'Aha' moments, to which Hannah responded, were moments of insight. They were shimmering: light shone in. An understanding changed in a moment. Adding weight to a person's experience, joining in with her own delight, for example, can obviously help a person like Hannah to intensify a new understanding so that it becomes more enduring. Delight is shared through facial expression and eye contact, as well as through gesture, voice quality and tone (Meares, 2016; Porges, 2011).

Interpersonal resonance is available through words and ideas, but underlying this is always body language and a deep bodily attunement. Schore (2003) considers that the vital feeling of safety for the client always depends on the experience of this psychobiological attunement. It creates the therapy bond, which he conceives as specifically linked to the capacity of the right brain. He states that the therapist's ability to tune in with the body language of the client may be of more importance than words, which may at times be misinterpreted.

The term 'psychobiological attunement' can be thought of as shorthand for a grouping of abilities such as intuition, the ability to read body language and the micro-expressions of face and gesture, including the prosody of the voice. These contrast to the reliance on more rational processes, which are traditionally associated with the left brain. Schore (2003) describes what researchers see when a mother and a baby are engaged in what has been referred to as the dance of attachment. He says that:

> *Much of the exchange of essential subjective information in human relations is non-verbal and includes dynamic changes in facial expression, prosodic tone of the voice, touch, gesture and bodily state. It is the right lateralized brain which has the affect-regulating function that is dominant for coping with stress and uncertainty (p. xv).*

The collegiality of the therapy conversation was moving Hannah in the direction of her innate social engagement biology (Porges, 2011). The combined body-mind conversational scaffolding and the use of judicious investigative questions was helping her to trust her own body and to make good use of her mind. She was holistically expanding her own abilities. She was the expert on what her body was telling her. As she made meaning and chose her preferences and values, she was constituting herself. Initiating and responding within a collegial therapy relationship was building a foundation for relational change.

Even while Hannah's dominant story was being thickened, and before a new one could be strongly articulated, the process, on the whole, didn't appear to be a re-traumatising one. Memories that her body had brought to light and which her mother had corroborated, were fitting together alongside others which were more explicit. The process was increasing her understanding. The nature of the enquiry seemed to be having a calming and an energising effect. There was evidence to me of the accuracy of White's (2006) idea that helping a person string events together and discover a sense of consistency over time can lead to internal reverberations that are themselves enlivening.

Conclusion

In these past two chapters, I have shown that triggering the traumatic past implicates a person's somatic markers and indicates that old alarm patterns are contaminating the present. Hannah showed us that when a person learns to direct her attention to her intense triggered sensations, which may connect to what Siegel (2010) calls the original neural firing patterns relating to trauma, the changes can be immediate and far-reaching. Whether the triggering has plunged a person into hyperarousal or into dissociation, the body-focused approach provides integrating momentum. As she made use of more internal resources and developed more effective interpersonal maps, it seemed possible that Hannah, as science would have it, was building new neural pathways. She had a sense of newness deep down in her body's cells.

The conversations were scaffolded by weaving together the body scaffold and the narrative use of questions to engage curiosity and investigation. Bodily impacts as well as ideas, attitudes, beliefs, sequences, history and contexts can be explored in this integrative model. Hannah was in narrative terms re-authoring her story.

The chapter threw light on aspects of Hannah's experience, including neurological understandings of triggering, attachment, regulation, shame, re-traumatisation and the development of trust. They acknowledged what the West can learn from ancient cultures, which have always provided the traumatised with a tangible sense of community, a focus on ceremony and rhythmic movement as well as on story-telling practices. A holistic approach makes sense.

In the remaining chapters, I will provide further evidence of the effectiveness of this approach in different clinical contexts.

Chapter 7
Body-focused Narrative Conversations Featuring Isolation

What a difference it can make to people to be joined by others in their struggle to address the problems of their lives. Alice Morgan

The isolation that is common to the childhood experience of trauma is highlighted in the therapy conversations with Mindy, Tim and Rick that follow.

Mindy attains her own resilience

Mindy reported that she had worked at resilience all her married life. She felt prompted now, by despair, to seek help but she was also determined to find the resilience she craved. I asked her for more details.

Mindy said that she often felt like "a prisoner of war". The emotional and verbal abuse never stopped. She described the many times she had tried to fight back. She never won. Often the exchanges were loud and aggressive.

As the conversation unfolded, it became clear that there were issues of safety for Mindy in her relationship with her partner. In a narrative style conversation, therefore, we began to explore together the meanings of family violence. We explored the dangers of taking on 'the powers' directly and ideas behind acts of resistance as a way of staying safe, while at the same time holding onto a sense of self. It was obvious that the therapy relationship needed to provide a safe holding space but that explicit safety plans might also need to be formulated.

THE MAGIC LOOM PART TWO - THE PRACTICE

After a couple of conversations, Mindy reached a turning point. This was hastened by an act of physical violence against her, violence that up to this point had been blamed on her or minimised in her own mind.

Her husband had called her an idiot as he hit her and shook her by the hair. His rage was about whether there were enough vegetables in the kitchen cupboard. Despite the physical violence, it was the emotional power her husband wielded over her that Mindy described as having the power to make her feel stuck and paralysed. It was less tangible than the physical abuse and harder to put into words.

Mindy talked about her confusion. She was repeatedly told that she was to blame, and her husband's words had a way of causing her to cower. I decided to scaffold the conversation so that Mindy could take notice of how her body had reacted during the incident she had described of physical and emotional violence.

> Mindy described how her mouth had gone dry, her heart rate had soared, and her limbs had stiffened. She said that she could hardly speak. It felt like she was "covered in shame".

I asked Mindy to hold onto her awareness of these sensations and to let them take her back in history. Had she ever felt these exact sensations before? The following small and totally unique childhood memory immediately emerged.

> Mindy was with her sister at the Dodgem cars. She was about seven years old and her little sister was screaming in terror as the car she was driving crashed into another one. The crash and the screaming were already hugely upsetting for sensitive Mindy, but, in the same instance, her father's loud, blaming voice crushed her. What she could remember above all else, was the deep sense of shame she was left with. She wasn't all right! There was something wrong with her.

I offered my empathy without a lot of words. Here were all the components of early complex trauma. Mindy had from early in her childhood experienced undeserved blame and had internalised it against herself. I was most interested to hear what Mindy was deducing as a result of this very brief body-focused process.

> For Mindy it was a revelation that her husband habitually reduced her to the similarly traumatised and shamed state she had experienced at only seven years of age.

Using the narrative scaffold of curious investigation, I asked Mindy to speak more about the meanings behind her body story, and then to reflect on where this new understanding might be taking her.

> Mindy said that as her body revealed these truths from the past, she was at the same moment thinking more clearly about what was happening in the present. Even though she could enjoy the strengths that were in her family and in her children, a new realisation was flooding in. Her 'job' in the family system involved holding up an illusion about family stability and

happiness. She no longer wanted to be part of doing that. It wasn't the truth. She said that for years she had tried to be hopeful and compromising so that the marital relationship could move forward. Now she could understand her own vulnerability, and see why her husband's incessant negative labelling of her every move affected her so deeply. She always came out of the encounters with him pronouncing inwardly that it was she who was at fault.

I shared with Mindy her sense of amazement at her body's wisdom. As she reflected on this, I asked her to talk about the effects of her husband's behaviours on their children.

Mindy talked at some length about the effect her husband's routine treatment of her had had over the years. Her children not only witnessed his aggression and his verbal and emotional abuse of her, but they were often the butt of it as well. It had probably had a lot of negative effects; sometimes it made them feel angry on her behalf but sometimes they were angry at her. It must have demeaned her in their eyes. She couldn't protect herself and she couldn't always protect them either.

I asked whether, as she considered the effects on herself and on her children, there was a safe stand she wanted to take.

Mindy said that she understood that her husband's behaviours arose out of his own insecurity and pain. But now she was ready to stop minimising and excusing the aggression. It was continuing to do a lot of harm. She needed to take action.

I stayed with Mindy, showing my understanding as she put into words the stand she wanted to take.

She decided to make a long-held dream come into existence. She would apply to do some university study. There were times in the past when her husband had suggested she do this, so he could hardly object now.

I joined her in the joy that became apparent as she decided on this course of action. My therapeutic job was to continue to provide a safely attuned conversational space for Mindy. I needed to go at her pace so that she could continue to discover what Ogden (2016) describes as her own body's integrative capacity.

In the to-and-fro of the ongoing therapy conversations, I introduced a range of body strategies to help Mindy modulate her familiar arousal states. Week by week Mindy used her determination to experiment and to work out which of these strategies was most useful to her when the fearful and shame-producing arousal struck. She became good at slowing her breathing and standing her ground quite physically in those moments.

I also put into effect the narrative concept of thickening the story by seeking nourishing details about Mindy's sense of identity.

Once she began to study Mindy was startled to discover a change in the way she began to view herself. She was not 'stupid'! She was not without ambition. She was more than merely setting out on a course at university. She had every intention of completing it. She had her determination. By making space in her life for her own hopes and dreams, she was carving out a place she had not been in before.

As we talked, she grew in her own awareness that she was creating narratives that were alternative to the ones that had been bringing the despair. In exploring some of the context of the despair, which still often arrived, I also directed my questions to the recent past and the terrible isolation Mindy had endured up till now.

She said it was the burden of shame she had felt because of her marriage circumstances that had kept her in that isolation. At university, in contrast, she was allowing herself to enjoy a lot of encouraging interactions. She was connecting with, and observing, a much greater range of people, some her own age and many who were younger.

Mindy was becoming socially engaged (Porges, 2011) and breaking away from shame. I was curious about the values that were guiding her along this alternative pathway.

Mindy said she was enjoying learning to think critically and she was discovering her own qualities of openness and non-judgmentalism. Her values were strong. She had a generous approach to others and she believed in equality. She had a longstanding preference to work towards harmony and peace in all her relationships. She reported that she was using her determination to even change her language. Often-used words could be stripped of their negative power. She was re-naming her fears and labelling them as opportunities. She was reframing 'devastating' as a description of what occurred to her and intentionally describing each set back as a 'challenge'.

My curiosity about Mindy's determination led me to ask for detail about how this worked out in practice.

She told how afraid she had been of stating her own opinions. On one occasion, her fear itself was turned into an opportunity for change. She had experienced an overwhelming (triggered) reaction after speaking up in a tutorial. During it, she had felt "suddenly exposed". There was pressure hammering on the right side of her head. She went all shaky.

In a different context to her marriage, her body was letting Mindy know that the trauma from the past had the power to invade the present and cause a state of re-traumatisation. It could threaten her newly found agency. She had been quick to become aware of her body. I asked her now what she did with the shakiness.

Mindy reported that as soon as she became aware of her body and its sensations, she got herself away and found a way to ground herself. On this occasion, she did it by writing down her thoughts. She fairly quickly got herself back into functionality and found she was able to return to her lecture. The new ability she was finding to modulate the arousal in her nervous system by being aware of her sensations was increasing her confidence.

After this she began to do well in the group work that her course required. Speaking up was no longer something she had to force. She was conscious that she had the resources within her to master the triggers that sometimes assailed her. She could take her place as a worthy equal.

Mindy surprised herself with her excellent marks and she began to validate her strengths. Creative writing was becoming a passion. Her gift for capturing the mood of a story and for using apt and unusual imagery caught her lecturer's attention.

Despite this progress outside the home, Mindy continued to encounter circumstances at home that disabled her. However, it wasn't always her husband's behaviour or words that did the damage. Her computer, for example, could trip her up and overpower her.

She described moments when huge feelings of frustration would sweep over her. She began to see a familiar pattern. Intense frustration would be followed by periods when she would whip herself emotionally.

Noticing her body sensations on these occasions took her back to adolescence.

She had endured an unhappy and isolating time in boarding school, and she described a kind of 'self-talk' she was now remembering. In those years, feelings of loneliness were uppermost. Internally she was in the habit of judging and labelling herself 'pathetic'.

I asked her to talk more about what the word conveyed.

Mindy described a series of images: "physically awkward, not good at sport, nerdy and ugly". All these descriptors still had currency within her.

I used narrative's bifurcating approach, asking her if there were times when this was not so.

It was as if a light switched on, as Mindy began to talk about the singing lessons she had recently taken up. It was dawning on her that the musical talent of her children was not predominantly an endowment from her larger-than-life husband. This was a belief he had promoted for years with his cruelly articulate and undermining taunts. Her singing lessons had begun as a way of being true to herself. She had always loved to sing and, due to her teacher's affirmations, she was becoming braver. Her sense of herself was moving in new and transforming directions.

Focusing on her breath, the importance of which she was experiencing in her singing lessons, was of particular help. It turned Mindy away from shame and she began to think of herself in more nourishing ways. We shared a lively discussion about the aptness of the metaphorical story where an ugly duckling in her case (self-perceived) turned into a beautiful swan.

THE MAGIC LOOM PART TWO - THE PRACTICE

When I read back over this account, I could see Mindy's progression. She could look inward at her sensory somatic reactions, then turn her mind in the direction of her breath, and finally focus on her values and the new ways in which she was handling the present, which were congruent with those values. The past was losing its power (Rothschild, 2010; Siegel, 2010). The more she was able to manage the triggers and to leave her helplessness behind, the more assertive she could be even with her husband.

I asked her during one conversation to describe how she was doing this.

> Mindy said that she was able to literally walk away from many of her husband's subjugating practices, grounding herself firmly with long slow breaths. At such times, in her mind she could allocate the choice of abusive ways firmly to him instead of believing that they said anything about her.

Mindy herself was consciously weaving together the resources of her mind and her body. However, there were still times when overwhelming emotions took over. It became her practice to listen to her body, and I would help her to do so within the therapy conversation.

After one hurtful encounter, Mindy became aware that her body was very painful on her left side. She felt as though her husband's words had the power to cut like a dagger in her heart.

I enquired about these dagger-like physical sensations. As she put her attention on her side and her heart, several images came into her mind:

> She saw her father running around the house, so he could give her a belting with his riding whip; (there were) terrifying memories of him in a rage and throwing tools at one of the horses. As far back as she could remember she had experienced extreme fearfulness and linked with her terror was always a deep sense of shame because she could never measure up to her father's expectations.

We kept investigating.

> Mindy said she had grown up with a love of the horses that were at the centre of the whole family's life. She loved the exhilaration of riding. But now she was remembering a couple of incidents, including a fall, which had contributed to her loss of confidence. She had felt a failure. She described a time at a horse-showing event. She hadn't been strong enough to hold onto the horse she was responsible for. Her father's anger came down on her and immediately she felt the excruciating and familiar sense of shame. She was a failure.

I encouraged Mindy to reflect from maturity on these memories and their impacts for her.

> Mindy reflected that her confidence and foundational sense of accomplishment, along with much of her liveliness, had been eroded very early. The past of her childhood had been full of prolonged stress.

This caused her to think about her parents' 'marriage system', which was the norm she had grown up with. I didn't have to formulate further questions.

> She began to explore what precisely her mother had modelled to her. The role of wife always involved putting "a good face" on things. As a woman her mother always had to do "the right thing". She had to be nice. Anger was never expressed. There was no room for yelling or screaming. Such emotion simply wasn't acceptable. In looking back, Mindy realised that she had learned to play a similar role to the one she had been playing with her husband. She had to protect both her parents emotionally. During her reflections, she decided that she didn't need to play such a role for anyone anymore. It was time to stop protecting her husband from himself.

I was curious to hear Mindy describe how she might carry out this new determination.

> Mindy communicated that she had already been giving herself permission to express some of her rightful anger. Sharing more with friends and family was a constructive use of anger, and she realised that the choice to divorce her husband was also a righteously angry resolution to an impossible situation. She had already begun to distance herself from him emotionally, and now she began to make plans to distance herself geographically as well.

I asked Mindy about the place of her values in her decision making.

> Mindy expressed her strong desire that the separation between herself and her husband be a peaceable one. She was valuing herself as a communicator, and, as a result of this, she decided to use letters as a means of relaying a vision of the future, first to her husband and then to the family as a whole. In order to be able to be safe but also to stick up for her own values, Mindy said she had decided that she would move right away from the family property where her husband could continue to live. Her hope was that there could be family holidays there in the future.

I was interested in how she managed her husband's response to these initiatives.

> She told how, to her surprise, he responded positively, backing her up about this course of action. This was momentous. In coming to such a decision and taking the communication of it assertively into her own hands, Mindy was consciously working in her own best interest and in the best interests of her family. When she took up her own equal power, she found she was being respected for it. She had taken the lead on something fraught with difficulties, in a way that completely lined up with her own respectful values. She was keeping open options of good times for the family, while decisively removing herself and the younger family members from an unsafe and often harmful environment.

THE MAGIC LOOM PART TWO - THE PRACTICE

I saw that Mindy was experiencing an internal unity rather than feeling exhausted as a result of internal, as well as external, conflict. As I reflected on my conversations with her, it became clear that the body-focused enquiry had provided her with a deeper understanding of the similarly gendered power dynamics of her childhood. The two had become conflated in her brain and her earliest traumas had continued to have re-traumatising power throughout the many years of her marriage. I recognised that the narrative focus on her values had been crucial. The small acts of resistance explored became the stands she took that helped her to be safe and to build new confidence. Gradually, traumatising memories of failure were replaced with assertive initiative taking and transformative decision making. Mindy was leaving confusion and disempowerment behind, and her storylines demonstrated how she was embodying a preferred life narrative that was no longer thwarted by her early years of trauma.

Later feedback

Quite some time after Mindy moved away from her marriage, I was able to catch up with her in her new environment. She worked with me to make this account as authentic as possible.

> She explained that it was confronting as well as encouraging to revisit the therapy journey in its documented form. She wanted others to know that the journey to a new story can be bumpy when trauma has been part and parcel of how old dominant beliefs and emotions rule your life. These have the power to return sometimes out of the blue with what seems like even greater devastation. However, she said it was good to have the documented reminder. She could look back on how much territory she'd covered, and see the obstacles she had overcome, and how she had accomplished that.

After each therapy conversation therapists are invited to reflect further with the aid of the Magic Loom. It conceptualises the person consulting the therapist as the Weaver and the therapist as the Co-weaver. The task of the latter is to open up important space through which the Weaver threads her shuttle. In technical weaving terminology she alternately opens one of the two sheds in the weft so that the Weaver can weave new threads of possibility turning them into a woven fabric. In the metaphor narrative approaches are woven through one space and awareness of the body through the other.

The Magic Loom at work with Mindy

In the conversation with Mindy a context of family violence alerted the Co-weaver to issues of safety. She therefore made space in the conversation so that Mindy could weave narratively while exploring the nature of family violence. Introducing the metaphor of small acts of resistance gave Mindy the space she needed to begin to explore a safe path forward.

Mindy's despair and confusion in the face of physical, verbal and emotional abuse then prompted the Co-weaver to open space so she could focus on her body. Weaving began in earnest. Mindy gave attention to her intense sensations and the first small story highlighting the dynamics of her early trauma helped her find new threads with which to weave. The Co-weaver used investigative questions to give Mindy space to use her mind and make meaning of the body narrative. She fastened in a marker as it were, by taking a stand about a role she has decided to dispense with and yet another to demonstrate her chosen small act of resistance.

Opening more space for body-awareness as the conversation proceeded meant that Mindy was able to repeatedly weave her body resources into a calming narrative. Helping Mindy explore her values through the narrative space catalysed change perhaps showing up in a series of shiny threads. Mindy concurrently wove into the fabric her bright new awareness that her body's messages could be experienced as signals to which she could readily respond.

Throughout the conversation the Co-weaver maintained enquiry into the narratives of the body as well as those of the mind. She kept her own curiosity alive about the signals Mindy's body was providing. The story demonstrated that even nourishing contexts can trigger reactivity. Helping Mindy weave, using spaces for body awareness and for the reflections of the mind in quick succession, allowed important meaning to be woven into the new fabric. When Mindy cut her newly woven fabric free of the loom, there was evidence that she was embodying the narrative of resilience she had always hoped for.

Tim discovers a new way of relating

It was important that my enquiry focus on Tim's history and the wider context of the story he had remembered which was described in the Introduction and Ch.4. When he said that he had told no one about the incident with the frog, I expressed my curiosity about this isolation and Tim began to reflect.

It's come home to me that my parents were not truly there for me because both of them were working a lot. But actually, when I think about it, I couldn't have told mum any of my emotional fears or upsets anyway. She wasn't that kind of mum. In Papua New Guinea, where we lived at the time of the frog incident, we had a house girl, actually a kind of nanny, who worked in the house and looked after us before and after school. Although I remember her as quite affectionate, there was a cultural divide, which meant I obviously didn't reveal to her any of my deep thoughts or fears. As a child I didn't get on very well with my brother either. I spent a lot of time by myself.

THE MAGIC LOOM PART TWO - THE PRACTICE

At this stage, I wanted Tim to feel the resonance of my emotional support but also to gain a sense that his body could continue to help him. I asked him to talk a little more about what it had been like to lose his beloved pet.

He had felt abandoned. How could he go on?

The dynamic of isolation and lack of support was part of what had been triggered by his bodily sensations. By this time in the conversation, I had become aware of Tim's imaginative strengths. I asked him if he could stand up and imagine himself as a well-rooted tree.

He did this, strengthening his leg and thigh muscles and concentrating on how his feet attached him to the ground. He saw himself as a tree with roots spreading wide and deep into the earth, almost as far as the canopy stretched out overhead.

I asked him how he thought the tree fared when it was stormy.

He described the roots holding it firm. The flexibility of the tree trunk and branches allowed it to move with the wind, so it wasn't destroyed.

I asked him how the tree got what it needed.

He visualised the tree roots sucking up all the moisture and nutrients it needed from the earth. Attached to the strong trunk, the tree's branches were fed so that the leaves were fresh and green, and the flowers and fruit developed naturally.

As a nature lover, the tree metaphor appealed to Tim.

He began picturing the many ways the branches and the canopy provided a home to birds, animals and insects. Even humans, as well as larger animals, could benefit from the tree's shade or lean against its trunk for support. It had a purpose that went beyond itself.

I asked him how this metaphor could be of use to him.

He could imagine himself remembering the physical sensations of having roots that reached deep into the earth. He thought that summoning up the image could be of help if he remembered it at times of stress or loss or acute agitation in the future.

A week after our first conversation, Tim told me that he had forgiven his little boy self. I asked him what it was like to withdraw the earlier sense of self-blame?

He was finding a new pride in himself. He could see that he had responded as a child from what he now thought of as his true nature. The image of that little frog with its feet splayed was still very vivid for him. He understood that he was quite sensitive. But he expressed that he was feeling more 'okay'.

He described some changes that had resulted.

CHAPTER 7 BODY-FOCUSED NARRATIVE CONVERSATIONS FEATURING ISOLATION

During the preceding week, instead of making a regular visit to a relative of his out of duty and obligation, he had stayed at home. He was happy about the strength of this decision and he was feeling a new sense of independence and capacity to outface unnecessary guilt. Now I realise I can give myself some slack. A lot of the time I'm very hard on myself. If I take a snapshot, I'm mad at myself for not waiting a moment till the light gets that bit better! I'm always working. I'm too serious and I've allowed myself to be dragged down the wrong path for too long.

I had a sense that Tim was quickly moving into a new relationship with himself. As well as caring for and understanding the compassionate child he once was, he was questioning some of his identity conclusions. A re-authoring process was taking place (Morgan, 2000; White, 2004). He was exploring how he could embody a new and alternative story to the one that had long held him hostage. His body had helped him make useful moves. He was being transported. He was taking a stand.

Using the narrative approach, which seeks nourishing narratives within a person's own experience, I asked Tim if he had made any stands like this before.

He told me about his decision to move away from his parent's location and therefore also away from their expectations and control. He'd been seeking his independence for some time.

Tim wanted to talk more about the influence of each parent and my role as a narrative practitioner was to remain oriented to him.

When I was young, my dad was just unapproachable. I remember him working long hours. When he came home, he was always an authoritarian figure. Sometimes he had an explosive temper. My brother and I got the brunt of his anger a lot.

I prompted Tim to stay in touch with the sensations and the emotions that were aroused as he thought about his childhood fear of his father and quite quickly another story emerged.

I hated playing cricket with my brother. He was a lot older than me, and from when I was four or five years old we played with the kids next door. They were really good at the game. Every single time we played, my brother seemed to end up on the losing side. Then he would fly into a massive rage and throw the bat around in a way that terrified me! So, you can imagine my feelings when one Christmas my father made me a full cricket set.

Tim was holding his head and I enquired what his gesture signified. He was feeling despair; his head was heavy and there was that earlier tightness in his chest.

It wasn't the kind of present I wanted, but I could never have said so to my father. I finally told my mum that evening, and she yelled at me and called me an ungrateful brat! I remember running into my bedroom screaming my head off. I was probably six or seven years old.

This led Tim to reflect on what he described as a more complex relationship with his mother. She always tried to live out of his achievements. It was very confusing for him. He was his mother's golden child, but it wasn't a happy fit.

> *She saw me as talented and special. When I would plan to go bushwalking with friends, Mum would spoil my enthusiasm. I needed her to back me up. But she would come with us and take everything over. When she supported me like that I always also felt as if there was a price to pay afterwards – I owed her. I had to support her projects and do whatever she needed me to do with her.*

This dynamic continued through adolescence and into adulthood.

> *It was mum who pushed me into the sciences when I was much more drawn to the arts. I was good academically, but I ended up feeling manipulated into a career that didn't suit me. I'm learning now to withstand the guilt when mum pressures me for involvement in her next project.*

I asked Tim if he could go back and tell me a little more about the history of his stand for independence.

> *He expressed surprise as he recognised the reality that he had made several stands before coming for therapy. On one occasion, he had taken himself on a long trip to have time for reflection. He explained how he had been able to face up to some of his intense emotions of grief and anger while on that trip. He felt he had had some success in understanding and coming to terms with his emotions.*

I asked him what it was like to recognise that he had had the ability and the inner wisdom to take such strong stands in line with his own preferences and needs.

> *Tim expressed his pleasure in this achievement. He talked about the changes he had begun to make in his life in more detail and expressed his pleasure at his hopeful new journey. Recently he had begun to put down his roots in a locality of his own choosing.*

I introduced a second metaphor into the conversation. We talked back and forth about the way skiers crouch close to the ground as they swerve round dangerous bends. In a session not long after this, Tim described changing his responses during one of what he called "regular guilt-producing telephone conversations" with his mother.

> *He had discovered that physically adjusting the way he was standing, tightening his thigh muscles and lowering himself closer to the ground, helped him to change his emotions and his sense of himself. As he thought of himself as a large well-rooted tree, it was as if his roots went down and he felt stronger and more impervious to the barrage of words. He heard himself speaking more confidently. Instead of being manipulated he was assertive.*

Active muscle toning (Rothschild, 2000) was the practice Tim was making use of in conjunction with his reflection on these two visual metaphors. He was learning to feel safe and solid by using metaphor, mindfulness and a body strategy together. Narrative emphasis on language and then the body resource of re-structuring his body were working together to help Tim mindfully support the vulnerable child he had once been.

Rothschild (2000) describes how traumatised individuals tend to pay more attention to internal stimuli associated with traumatic memories whenever these are triggered, and that they give less attention to other balancing information which can be drawn from outside the body. Now Tim was getting more balance. He was thickening his new story of independence as he re-negotiated his family relationships. He was using the strengths of his body and of his mind and practising embodying a preferred and alternative narrative for his life.

Later feedback

Tim discussed this account with me some time later.

> He alluded to the sense of shame and inadequacy that had had such a powerful influence on his life. The overwrought state that had been triggered repeatedly, and which had cost him his first career, had continually increased his sense of shame. As an adult and as a scientist, he had always had the belief that he should have been able to manage life rationally, but he never could.
>
> Now he had become proficient at picking up his body signals, and he could recognise the familiar overwrought state before it took over. He reported that his new body awareness helped him calm himself quickly. By using body-restructuring strategies, he was growing in confidence. He mentioned how the tree and the ski metaphors continued to be of help as he cemented his new patterns and stories. He reported that the speed with which he could now catch and moderate the overwrought state was importantly helping him to wipe out his old sense of shame and inadequacy. His independence as a person was growing and he was finding healthy ways to build his own life and friendship circle.
>
> The explorations into his childhood context had also freed Tim in another unexpected way. He was finding himself altering the stories he habitually told himself about his parents, his father, in particular. He was taking the initiative to build a freer and truly adult relationship with him and enjoying the many aspects of life they had in common.

This reminded me of the narrative 'team of life' metaphor described by Denborough (2007). A person can sift through her relationships and begin to make revisions about the influence she wants to allow significant people. I'm intrigued that after several body-focused narrative conversations, Tim spontaneously set out to revise his conclusions about the place of his father in his life. No further therapy was needed. Tim had developed an inner certainty about how to improve his relational life.

THE MAGIC LOOM PART TWO - THE PRACTICE

I was seeing the way that organically sound brain processes are set in train once a holistic enquiry allows the body to have its say alongside the mind within a collegial therapy conversation (Porges, 2011).

The Magic Loom at work with Tim

Tim, whose negative view of himself had been fed by his panicky response to catching a frog on his fishing line, suffered traumatic impacts in part because he had no one with whom he could share what had happened on that day. He couldn't resolve or makes sense of his own actions.

Opening space for him to gain awareness of his body was what made it possible for Tim to weave a somatic memory into the therapy conversation. Then the Co-weaver could open narrative space for further investigation, particularly helping him research the context which had left him without the support he needed. Tim began to weave colours of understanding into his fabric. Recognising Tim's imaginative skills, the Co-weaver rapidly flicked between the body and mind spaces so that Tim could weave metaphor and bodily wisdom together. This helped him to calm his autonomic nervous system arousal and develop a somatic awareness of grounded confidence, which showed up in uniquely woven features. The Co-weaver sometimes opened space for the body almost incidentally as she noticed and named what Tim's body demonstrated (body language) in the midst of his storytelling. She used her therapeutic curiosity to throw light on transforming moves that Tim has made before engaging in the therapy conversations. He was able to put tags on the new idea of his own expertise as he wove through the mind-focused narrative space. Gradually by weaving through both spaces, one after another, he was re-authoring a story which was very different to the old one of shame and isolation. He began more confidently to choose and weave together threads which would shape his fabric entirely differently.

Rick increases his emotional cohesion

In Chapter 4, I described how Rick's sensations of frenzy in his work environment cued the specific body narrative. A teacher whom he had previously found very engaging had grabbed him by the back of the neck leaving him so shocked that a primitive part of his brain was activated.

Rick hadn't felt he could talk to anyone about the incident with his school teacher. I asked him to explore why he thought this was so.

> I didn't tell anyone. The culture of my family is that you can't not know. You can't ask for help. Uncertainty is a sign of weakness, so you have to camouflage it. Often for me there's been this huge fear and terror and a sense of impending doom. There was a lot of disharmony between

> *my parents, but they both held their anger in and then got busy doing something else. There wasn't a lot of affection shown, and my dad, in particular, punished us kids by withdrawing affection. He would ridicule you. I remember a sensation of shrinking.*

Hearing Rick name this new sensation, I asked him to focus on the 'shrinking feeling' for a moment. As Rick centred his mind on the sensation that accompanied the experience of being brushed aside by his father, it cued another memory for him.

> *I was still at primary school. I usually did well at school. One afternoon I got my report card. It was a good one. I remember being so excited on the way home. I was so looking forward to showing it to my parents. When I arrived I gave it straight to my dad. I think the main hurt I felt was that he didn't respond as well as I had hoped. It seemed as if he was somehow disappointed or that I should have done even better.*

Rick described how inconsolable he had felt in that moment. His hope and excitement had been shattered. Rick had come for therapy because he had again experienced a deeply agonising experience in his professional life, which his brain associated with his early upsets in a particular context. It routinely left him full of shame and with a deep narrative of humiliation. I asked him what sense he was now making of this personal history.

> *In his estimation, his family's patterns and the parenting practices followed had left him devoid of skills. He hadn't been equipped with the knowledge of how to handle or express anger safely. He didn't know how to assert himself nor did he feel validated as a person. All he knew was a negative pattern. He knew how to ignore himself and, like his parents, how to bottle everything up. It had never been articulated or demonstrated to him in childhood that mistakes are acceptable, and that they are part of being human. He talked of the resulting perfectionism he often fell back on. He could see that, like his old teacher's outbursts, this perfectionistic mindset seemed to be able to strike from underground at any moment, even if he hadn't done anything to deserve its whipping.*

The one-off incident with a teacher had remained unresolved partly because he had no one he could readily turn to for help. Once we had explored the childhood context a bit more I asked Rick what he was making of his body's capacity.

> *Experiencing the way his body sent him empowering messages made him realise that he mattered. Injustice was never okay. He was allowed to be angry. He could speak up about unfairness and he could make sure he got the support he needed.*

I was interested that experiencing his body's wisdom was providing Rick with an impetus to change. I was curious about his sense of identity, and so I asked him to describe a little more about how he was now looking at himself.

He could better appreciate his vulnerable self. He said that he wanted to learn how to encourage that more needy part and to know that when he felt anxious he could get on his own side and stand up for himself. At no time did he have to just accept it when others brushed him aside or treated him badly.

I saw that Rick was not only more aware of his body, but that he was also developing a healing dual awareness (Rothschild, 2000; Siegel, 2010). This gave me an opportunity to thicken the new story of internal emotional cohesion I was witnessing.

Rick had mentioned setting a goal to get on his own side whenever anxiety or intense emotions reduced him to a state of frenzy in the future. He wanted to resolve the stresses unresolved in childhood. I asked him if he could think of a mantra that he could call on to help him at those times.

Rick couldn't come up with a mantra immediately but the next time we met, he shared that he was making use of the self-validating phrase, "I am Rick and I'm okay".

He had found a simple and straightforward way to reinforce the practice of offering kindness to his embodied self, which was the first body strategy with which he had experimented. A mantra is both a cognitive and a bodily resource. By making use of the one he had coined, Rick was enjoying benefits that people from Tibetan and other ancient cultures have long enjoyed. Simple calming chants are embedded in their regular religious rituals (Perry, 2006). The use of this mantra was helping Rick embody and thicken an entirely new life story.

Later feedback

Some months later, when I asked Rick what had been of most help to him in his therapy process, he wrote the following:

What's been of huge benefit is acting on the principle of being kind to myself and of understanding that there are reasons for my 'not okay' behaviours. When I accept these things about myself with kindness (as I try to do with others around me as well), it takes away all of the self-doubt and negativity. Then I can get on with living and doing the best I can. Over time, this has meant that what I call my 'not okay' (frenzied) behaviours are a lot easier to pre-empt so that they don't escalate like they did previously. The process of identifying triggers and the associated body sensations has also been really helpful. It seems like I have a lot more awareness of my behaviours and actions, as well as strategies for dealing with difficult situations. Quite often, I have insights into previous times where I've behaved in a way that I didn't understand, and I can now see reasons for these behaviours, and I can process them with kindness towards myself, so that they don't become 'baggage' for me going forward.

The Magic Loom at work with Rick

Rick used the narrative space opened up with investigative questions, to begin to make sense of the story his body had remembered. He wove the context, history and effects of his family system into his understanding. The Co-weaver slipped space open for new body awareness so that mindful attention was given to a sensation which could further contribute to his sense-making. Rick then wove threads through the narrative shed and tagged his understanding of the automaticity of the triggering of a dominant narrative and the way it could interfere with his working life. Keeping the narrative space open meant that an 'experience of experience' question about his new body awareness led him to consider his identity construction. This in turn provided re-authoring impetus. The Co-weaver moved swiftly between the narrative and body-focused spaces, and Rick could take a stand thus tightening his weaving into a firm fabric. He described the benefits of experimenting with the regulating rhythms of a reinforcing mantra. He now had ways to calm himself whenever that was needed.

Chapter 8
Body-focused Narrative Approach to Transforming Emotions

The elusiveness of emotions and feelings is probably an indication of ... how much mental imagery masks the reality of the body. Antonio Damasio

One of the strengths of the body-focused narrative approach is its ability to deal with any experience a person brings to therapy. Everyone's body holds in it the experiences of their lives, and once accessed through listening to the body's cues, the narrative strategies provide scaffolding that enables the person to make meaning of those sensations, the memories they hold, and the way they have affected their sense of their identity.

Because body-based narrative therapy is an approach, rather than a rigid set of techniques, it can be applied with a flexibility that is responsive to the needs of the person who has sought therapy.

The three therapy conversations with individuals in this chapter emphasise how different each person's life and weaving process is. Kerry wanted to discuss the disempowerment she felt when she lost her voice when triggered by her children, Pearl was upset by her angry reactivity as a mother, while Gerry was having trouble with what he describes as his "irrational fears".

Kerry takes hesitant steps towards self-compassion

Kerry's reactivity to the incessant squabbling of her children was the factor that originally brought her into therapy. The week following our first conversation about this issue, she became aware of a body sensation that she hadn't previously noticed. When she had been in a highly aroused state with her children, she had been making every attempt to raise her voice as a way of trying to control their behaviour. Only a high-pitched squeaky ineffectual voice had emerged.

My voice was like an eight-year-old child's. That's how old I felt. No wonder I couldn't get them to take any notice!

I empathised with her sense of helplessness and with the meaning of powerlessness that the physical loss of her voice communicated. Together we discussed a little more about what neuroscientists describe as 'the automaticity' of the phenomenon of triggering. It is not something a person has control over. Old unresolved trauma can be triggered suddenly by a dynamic in a person's later life that has similarities with the early trauma circumstances (Damasio, 1994).

The Broca area of the brain, nicknamed the speech centre, often becomes suppressed, along with other significant parts of the brain, as a result of traumatic experience. Voice production is often weakened or even lost completely (Rothschild, 2000; van der Kolk, 2002). When the trauma is triggered, so too is the person's inability to speak. It all happens automatically.

It was hard for Kerry to fully comprehend that she was in no way to blame for her reactivity. As she had become more aware of her own body and its signals, however, I noticed that Kerry was becoming better able to make use of calming body strategies to manage the arousal in the future.

Later, she shared how her voice weakness or loss became a sensory signal that could alert her. Sometimes the stimuli of loud ongoing childish conflict would again automatically trigger her neural networks, causing somatic impacts that affected both her vocal and her other cognitive abilities. Now she was aware of it, she could respond to this signal.

Kerry was increasing in her self-understanding, but I noticed that she continued to be harsh in her self-assessment. I decided to weave a different narrative approach into the conversation. I asked Kerry if there had been a witness to her life whose contribution had always encouraged her.

She told me about Alison, who, straight after her mother had died in her early adolescence, had become a mother figure to her. Kerry talked of her warmth and affection.

I asked Kerry what it was like to use her senses as she thought of Alison.

Kerry found she could not only bring a picture of Alison to mind, but that it was as if she could immediately hear her voice and experience her gaze. She recalled the warm way Alison looked at her. She spoke of the numerous times she heard her encouraging words. Alison had always had a way of mentioning Kerry's strengths and her courage. One thing she often remarked on was the unusual empathy and the attribute of compassion that she saw as central qualities in Kerry's life from that early age. Alison became a constant encourager in her life and, right up to the present, she still visited and supported her. She reduced Kerry's stress and helped her in very practical ways such as taking over the care of the children, so Kerry could have some respite. She would tackle the clothes folding or take care of a pile of dishes.

CHAPTER 8 BODY-FOCUSED NARRATIVE APPROACH TO TRANSFORMING EMOTIONS

I asked how it made Kerry feel that this significant person in her life had noticed how precious being compassionate had been to her from a young age.

Kerry said that she felt a huge debt of gratitude. She appreciated how Alison's voice was supporting what she had discovered about herself as present even as early as eight years of age. However, she reiterated that along with the gratefulness she always felt that she was unworthy. It was a sense that constantly returned. She couldn't get away from it.

Raising Kerry's awareness of her responses to the triggered memory of her childhood had brought to light her amazing sense of compassion towards her mother when she was very young. Now I wanted Kerry to consider the scope of her compassion. Would this word describe her attitude to herself?

Kerry's answer was strong and immediate in its negativity. She had never liked herself. She had entirely uncomplimentary pictures of herself in her mind. She thought it would be very difficult for her to begin to think generously towards herself or to treat herself in the loving way she treated others. However, she did agree that she was definitely feeling more sympathetic towards her younger self, since her body had shown her how she had responded to support her injured mother in the midst of being traumatised herself by her parents' violence and the blood.

Here was news of an exception to the constant negativity of the dominant story. The exception was founded on dual awareness. We talked about Kerry's own children and she thought about offering her younger self the sort of compassion she was good at showing them.

I used the rest of the session to take Kerry back to what her body had been showing her. I wanted her to have a chance to come to evaluate its wisdom. I asked her to think back to the chaotic situation with her children which she had described in our first therapy conversation and to revisit it.

As described in Chapter 4, addressing her bodily sensations and their intensity on a scale from zero to ten was impactful for Kerry. She found she could reduce the internal pressure. She then explained what it meant to her that she could contain her own emotional arousal.

It was totally new and foreign to her to notice her body with kindness, and she conveyed her sense of excitement. She wanted to try this in her 'real life' situations during the coming week. She repeated that her usual attitude towards herself in general, and her body in particular, was very harsh so just being gentle with herself as she noticed pressure in her body, would be a change.

Here was the second exception. As well as having compassion for the child she had once been, she was finding that she could offer kindness to her body and all its uncomfortable sensations. She had some evidence now that this new self-acceptance was effective and the body resources of mindfully noticing and assessing her sensations and their intensity could lead to modulation. Perhaps this exception would widen in the direction of a new attitude of compassion towards herself as a whole, and evolve into the formation of a new life narrative.

THE MAGIC LOOM PART TWO - THE PRACTICE

The Magic Loom at work with Kerry

Kerry arrived and through the body space, she immediately initiated the process of weaving a new awareness of her body, in particular in relation to what she had realised about the impact of stress on her physical voice and the accompanying sense of shame. The Co-weaver responded by opening the narrative space so that Kerry could develop new understandings that showed up in the fabric she was weaving. Narrative space allowed for research into related brain processes and more discoveries were woven in.

Noting the hold that negative self-assessment had on Kerry, her weaving companion helped her weave back and forth through both spaces. More colourful threads were chosen as Kerry explored the influence of a significant witness and wove her sensory experience of her through the body space. She also drew on her cognitive autobiographical memory when mind-related space was made available.

As Kerry expressed some compassion towards her child self, an exception to what has seemed an intransigent self-denigration emerged, and she briefly wove with a particularly shiny thread. The Co-weaver helped her work further with some of the patterns woven earlier. She then helped her to measure the difference she could make whenever she picked up a new thread of kindness and wove it through the space of greater body awareness. Kerry found another exception and as a result added a vibrantly different thread to her fabric.

Pearl moves into a new relationship with her anger

At the start of the conversation, Pearl said that it felt as if being a mother was testing all her capacities. Her behaviour as a mum often failed to line up with her values. She described the intensity of the rage she often felt unable to master. It seemed to be repeatedly triggered by day-to-day conflicts with her children. She said that she would find herself escalating into hysterical outbursts.

Pearl was articulating that her present resources were not enough to help her. When I re-introduced the body scaffold, Pearl was able to readily search out the sensations that had arisen that week in the vanguard of her over-reactive rage.

> Pearl was aware, as she had been before, of a strong irritability in her gut. However, this time as she kept her awareness on the sensation, an image of herself in her teen years came to mind, rather than one of herself at the age of four that was described in Chapter 2. This time her body sensations cued memory of the exact moment she discovered that her parents were separating. There was an intense sense of betrayal and she confided that any hint in the present that she is being betrayed in any way still has the capacity to undo her.

I asked her about the context of her parents' break-up.

Pearl recalled that she had had a haunting fear throughout her whole childhood that this would happen. However, she had never imagined that it might come about as it did. It was a secret affair on her mother's part that was the catalyst. Her mother went off with her new man and Pearl was left to pick up the pieces with her devastated father. She wasn't at all comfortable with being left with the stressful role as a pseudo-parent to her father. It was towards her mother that her most intense adolescent anger was directed.

I wondered how thinking about this was making Pearl feel now, towards her adolescent self?

It was helping her understand herself a lot better. She could appreciate how the separation of her parents had added to her insecurity and to her sense of powerlessness. In addition, it was a surprise to clarify that it was the seemingly more stable parent whose desertion so distressed her.

I asked where this new understanding might take her?

Very quickly, Pearl began to describe inner change. She now knew what her anger meant. She understood the layers of helplessness she had felt and why her emotions had been so intense.

As I stayed attuned to her, I asked her about what was coming out of her new understandings.

She was taken by surprise that as a result of this new understanding she could see her mother with different eyes. Comprehending more about where her own rage had originated seemed to be enough to begin "to clear the anger out of the way". She was no longer blocked. She could see back beyond that adolescent emotion. It was as if she got her mother back!

I was curious about what this meant.

She began to talk about some of the ways her mother had cared for her as a child. Though she rarely offered her praise or verbal encouragement, she consistently made beautiful costumes for her to dance in. Pearl found herself being able to more fully appreciate her mother's quieter character and to remember how much her mother could be relied on, year in and year out. She had always been affectionate and had quietly provided constancy. This was obviously why 'the betrayal' had felt so devastating.

I wondered if she could describe more about how her perspective was changing.

She said that it was as if she could now as an adult attempt to walk in her mother's shoes. She felt free to do this in a way she hadn't before. From an adult and a very human perspective, she could now see her mother's hidden affair as part of a lifelong pattern. Her mom had never been able to talk things through. Secrecy ruled and everything bad was regularly pushed under the carpet. As Pearl contemplated her mother's life as a whole, it was with new compassion. Sadly, she recognised that her mum had gone from her bad marriage with Pearl's father into another equally unsatisfying partnership.

I recognised the generational transmission of trauma in this story: Pearl's mother had had demons of her own with which to contend.

As a result of reconnecting with her mother in this body-focused narrative exchange, Pearl went on to retrieve an important memory. She remembered an incredibly honest conversation she had once had with her mother, about circumstances which probably had a lot to do with her struggles.

> Her mum had told her that around the time of Pearl's birth, she had, in her own words, "behaved like a witch". She said she had subjected baby Pearl to a regime of controlled crying and had many times abandoned her to cry in her baby basket. Her mother apologised. She communicated how much she hated the way she had behaved. Pearl wondered whether her mother had been suffering from post-natal depression, although this hadn't been mentioned and the diagnosis may never have been made. Her mother had described her remorse at the way she had been influenced by parenting practices of the time which she now looked back on with horror.

How may early trauma influences and an unresolved past have affected Pearl's mother? How much did these hidden influences underlie her post-partum depression and the way she parented Pearl as a tiny baby? Could such legacies have affected the architecture of Pearl's own developing brain?

Schore's (2003) discussion about the way an infant's distress is a "plea for regulation" (p. 62) seems to apply. He clarifies the way that, even for a tiny infant, anger works as a protective mechanism. In baby Pearl's case, no one was listening or taking action with regard to her pre-verbal distress. She was left to cry.

> Pearl said she was better comprehending how deep her own fear and rage went and, therefore, how easily these emotions could be triggered when she felt opposed or neglected.

Perry (1999) explains how years after the original fear or alarm was experienced by an infant, the brain still acts in response to a false signal. Earlier, it developed a pattern of neuronal activation associated with fear, and its response now is disconnected from the upper brain's ability to make sense of things.

> "It's no wonder I feel like this" became meaningful to Pearl, and use of this mantra seemed to play its part in helping her to get to the point of self-calming and of making meaning of the triggering episodes she regularly experienced. It began to help her to moderate her reactivity.

Pearl's own body had succeeded in bringing her into a dialogue with her rage. As a result of discovering what her body remembered, together with reflecting on her history, Pearl was finally able to become adept at calling a halt to a lifetime of self-blame and shame. She understood that the legacies of trauma in her own mother's past had caused her the kind of harm that kept on unpacking itself.

Before the therapy journey, Pearl had no idea what was behind her reactive rage or how it could be resolved. Now she was feeling hope. Generations of children can go on being impacted if complex developmental trauma remains unresolved. Pearl was eager to interrupt the automatic triggering both for herself and to prevent it similarly harming her own children.

For her there was another journey. It arose out of her bifurcated response to the kind of isolation that had been the result of her mother's inability to speak up for herself or to deal with conflict. Pearl had become part of a support group where she was learning to take her turn in telling her stories. She was taking a stand and moving herself out of isolation.

In one of our conversations I asked Pearl how she had calmed herself during the week.

> She told me about having the courage to pick up the phone. It made such a difference to have someone to talk to immediately when she was feeling overwhelmed.

In response to my curiosity, she described more of the benefits of her support group.

> It gave her space to test her own wisdom and later to take a share of leadership. She became more and more ready to celebrate the way belonging to a mutually respectful community was helping her.

This brought to my mind what scientists now claim about the wisdom of traditional cultures and their communal responses to trauma. Protocols for emergency mental first aid after traumatic events (Kelly, 2010) involve the practice of providing support for people in an embodied and tangible way. Perhaps this also helps to explain why twelve-step programmes are so empowering for people who, like Pearl, carry a legacy of isolation and a learned fear of connecting with others.

The Magic Loom at work with Pearl

The body-focused space was opened and Pearl recalled her body's sensations in the midst of recent angry reactivity at home. Focusing on her sensations cued a narrative of her parents' marriage break-up. The Co-weaver opened the narrative space so that Pearl could weave in meaning; the threads she chose helping her make new sense of her anger. When her collaborator made an opening so she could reflect on what she had just experienced, she wove in brightly the benefits of her new body awareness. She took up another thick strand as she re-instated memories of her mother and added a shiny thread of empathy. The narrative space exploration even enabled Pearl to weave into the developing fabric a remembered conversation with her mother. The angry reactivity she'd been struggling with was made even more understandable as contexts far back into infancy were woven in.

THE MAGIC LOOM PART TWO - THE PRACTICE

> Pearl was able to weave her threads between body-focused and narrative spaces, as a mantra helped her both understand her younger self and 'get herself back' from somatic triggering. Notice how the Co-weaver kept the reflective mind space open so the Weaver, Pearl could describe ways she was moving herself out of isolation. She was re-authoring her story. The new story was different from both her own negatively dominant narrative and that of her mother. Her new fabric recorded the way she was removing the power of traumatic legacies from another generation to affect her well-being and possibly that of the next generation as well.

Gerry finds new self-definition

In Chapter 1, an externalising process with the Captain allowed Gerry to work at changing his verbal aggression towards his wife. In later couple conversations, I observed that he was taking re-authoring steps. His life narrative was changing. On this occasion, Gerry came on his own, to talk about what he described as "irrational fears" that had a way of dominating his life.

> *Most recently cycling in his head was the fear that his wife might leave him. He knew it was irrational and his wife assured him it had no basis in reality. She loved him and was increasingly hopeful about their relationship.*

I recalled that Gerry had been in the grip of similar fears about losing his job just a month or two before. His work review had happened since I had seen him last. I asked about its outcome.

> *Gerry laughed as he reported that he had passed with flying colours. He had been assured that his employment had never been in any danger.*

We set out to explore what might be promoting the fears that he felt were irrational. The evidence from his workplace showed him that it was irrationality he was up against. Suspecting the impacts of trauma, I asked Gerry if he had noticed any sensations in his body that went with his fears.

> *He didn't find it difficult to remember his body on the occasion when he had so recently been plagued by fear about his wife. He identified that the sensations hit him right in his core. His chest felt weak. "It's a falling apart feeling I get. Now I think about it, that same sensation's been turning up for a long time."*

I suggested that Gerry stay with these sensations.

> *In moments, he was talking about a romantic relationship he had had as a schoolboy. When his girlfriend's mother left her father, she had become the victim of her father's physical and emotional abuse. Under the influence of alcohol and drugs, this man made sure that Gerry also bore some of the brunt of the abuse. There was venom in the father's voice when he*

132

made his verbal threats. Gerry found them terrifying. This was totally different to his personal experience of family. On the day Gerry helped his girlfriend get away from her father and move interstate to be with her mother, the father made repeated threats against Gerry's life. He detailed a timeframe within which he would come and kill Gerry.

As quickly as Gerry completed this story another traumatising event came into his mind. My curious questions again helped him fill out the details of this second set of influential circumstances.

It was the night of his 21st birthday. He had been driving a bunch of his mates from his home to another venue. They were cruising along happily but luckily not at a high speed. As the car crested a hill there was a body right in front of the car, lying on the road. Gerry wasn't able to stop in time to avoid a collision. The aftermath of this event was fearful and quite prolonged. There was the arrival of the police and the ambulance and eventually a court case. The drunk pedestrian (who recovered fully) was found to have caused the accident himself. Gerry was completely exonerated. However, he described both his overwhelming panic at the time of the accident and the length of time it took him to get over the shock and strain which followed.

As we talked about these events, Gerry recounted how any sense of threat, even if not directly addressed to him, could trigger these same fear-related sensations in his core. He gave an example from the near past.

His little family was living in a duplex, and every day the man on the other side of the wall was loud and aggressive towards his family. For Gerry it triggered repeatedly the same irrational and unrelenting falling apart fear. It produced such angst that eventually Gerry and his wife decided they would have to move house. It seemed the only way to escape what had become an emotional roller coaster.

As Gerry was thickening the dominant narrative, which was so related to trauma, he emphasised his eagerness to find ways to manage this fear. I noticed that already he was changing his narrative away from self-denigration.

I introduced him to some body-based strategies, and over the following weeks he practised moderating the intensity of "the falling apart feeling" whenever it arrived. In particular, Gerry articulated the benefit to him of restructuring his body by slowing his breathing, straightening his spine and flexing his thigh muscles. It always provided speedy relief. Gradually, he accumulated evidence that he could rapidly settle his fears.

He said that he was already practising mindfulness and so noticing his body sensations in a mindful way made sense to him.

In our following therapy conversations, his embodiment of a re-authored narrative was taking place. There was a new optimism and agency. Although Gerry's body hadn't taken him back into childhood, the experiences from early in his adolescence and young adulthood had had impacts so

THE MAGIC LOOM PART TWO - THE PRACTICE

terrifying for him that they split him away from being able to make sense of their meanings. They had been strongly remembered in his body in only emotional and sensory somatic ways.

I had already explored Gerry's family context with him. There had been many stories of parental support. I knew that Gerry lived with a diagnosed bipolar mental illness and that he routinely took low range antipsychotic medication. This exploration of what he called his irrational fears was quite pivotal for him. He speculated that the extremely traumatic events remembered and held in his body may have triggered his illness, which was first diagnosed soon after his 21st birthday.

As Gerry mastered his irrational fears using his own body and its wisdom, I was in the vanguard of a new self-narrative that celebrated, among other things, how much more Gerry was than a diagnosis.

The Magic Loom at work with Gerry

In this conversation, the Co-weaver opened space for mind-related reflection so that Gerry could explore the nature of his irrational fears. Exploration of a different territory added threads of understanding about this dominant narrative. When she opened space so body-awareness could grow Gerry wove it in via his sensations and two cued trauma narratives from adolescence were also woven into the fabric and better understood. The Co-weaver used narrative curiosity to open up for Gerry an investigation of his history. The body-focused space was again opened and Gerry wove, perhaps in dark threads, the impacts of a repetitive trigger that had been showing up and adding its dominance. This alerted the Co-weaver to open space for body awareness again so that Gerry could weave in calming body strategies of a lighter colour and begin to thicken an alternative story. Narrative curiosity was transferred from the Co-weaver to the Weaver and Gerry made weaving experiments inside and outside the therapy room, which no doubt showed up as bright embellishments in his fabric.

Chapter 9
Weaving Body-based Issues into Narrative Conversations

> *In response to the investigative questions ... the people in therapy also assume an investigative-reporter-like position ... building an exposé of the character of the problem. Michael White*

This chapter provides further examples of how the body-focused narrative approach has a flexibility that enables a responsiveness to the needs of the person seeking therapy, whether, as in these examples, it involves transforming apathy, developing agency or overcoming procrastination.

Anton reconnects to his roots

Anton came for counselling to talk about "a frustrated and apathetic feeling" that affected him regularly. He often found himself going on the dole because this feeling interfered with his ability to work. At around forty he wanted to get his life more on track.

As this pattern, probably partly a dissociative one, obviously had a long history, I was immediately interested in raising Anton's awareness of how the emotions he was feeling linked to his sensations. I asked him whether he had ever noticed how the frustration and apathy impacted his body.

After some hesitation Anton began to speak of a tightness in his chest, throat and face. When I asked him to focus on these sensations for a little more time, an image of his baby son at about one year of age came into his mind. Anton was emotional as he told the story that was linked to this image.

> *Pending fatherhood had brought him nothing but conflict. The birth had been the upshot of an extremely short relationship that began almost accidentally. Because of the aggression he faced, Anton had broken away very rapidly. He recounted how he had needed to keep his distance from the mother of his child. However, after his boy was born he found that he wanted to visit and to get to know his small son. He visited him regularly and quickly began to bond with the baby. It was going quite well. Then at around his baby's first birthday, without any warning, the mother moved her family (including his child) out of the area. They completely disappeared. He wasn't given a forwarding address or any hope of staying in touch. Anton said that he had been left with a mix of confusion and guilt. He felt helpless and full of grief.*

I asked him what had kept him going throughout this time and he described how when he couldn't track them down, he fell into a practice of storytelling. He told himself:

> *"My little boy's life will be okay without me." Over and over he repeated to himself. "He has a life and he has an older brother. He'll be okay." And now he said it all a couple of more times. "That's what I have to believe."*

Anton had found a way to ground himself by repeating this story (mantra) and giving himself some hope for his child's life in a situation where he experienced himself as completely without power. Later, we were to return to consider his complicated grief and to hear more about his feelings of loss. But at this stage, we simply sat quietly together. No body strategies were offered.

Instead, after a few moments I sought out the narrative pathway and began exploring with Anton what meaning fatherhood had for him. He talked a little more about the happiness he had felt at emotionally bonding with his baby. Then he moved the conversation to memories of his own childhood and his own father. He said that when he was six or seven, he remembered feeling that he was a burden.

> *It never felt as if Dad was on my side. He was an authoritarian and life was complicated because he was my teacher as well as my father. I'd get the cane at school and the belt at home. I remember thinking that my parents didn't love me. My mother was different from my dad. She was sort of intense and smothering, occasionally pulling me in and making much of me. On the other hand, I often felt neglected. Sometimes she would write big embarrassing letters, over-praising people or trying to help people out. She turned to religion and, when I look back, she seemed pretty detached from reality. I know she suffered from depression. Her own mother had bipolar and committed suicide and, at one stage, I heard that my mother's first boyfriend also committed suicide. When I was born, it was after she'd had several miscarriages. Probably there were lots of things that affected her. My memory of life at home was that it was very monotonous, and I didn't like school much either. I got into quite a bit of trouble in my teens.*

As Anton reflected on his aloneness, he began to talk about a workshop he had once attended and the metaphor of 'rootedness' it had him exploring.

> *We had to draw a tree, and at the end of the time the facilitator commented that my tree didn't seem to have any roots. She wondered if my life was like that, without roots. That question and that image seemed valid to me. As I consider my life now, that's what it's like: it's a life without roots.*

Narrative practice relies on the idea that a person's identity is socially constructed. Exploring a person's relational history and mutual influences often leads to an expansion of her sense of identity. Similarly, Rothschild (2000) takes the position that simply raising a person's awareness of significant people in her life can somatically calm and anchor her.

Together, Anton and I began to explore the image of rootedness he had introduced. I asked him if he had had any people who had been important to him when he was younger. He immediately seemed enlivened and he discovered that he had quite a lot to explore.

He described a loving relationship with his two older sisters. Though they were quite a few years older than him, they continued to be significant in his life. They always had been. Talking about them reminded him of his older sister's boyfriend who also had a big influence on him as an adolescent.

> *What he did was to take me away from the monotony of my home life. He rode a motorbike and seemed to be interested in everything in life! He got me into all sorts of things: surfing, shooting, photography. I had found someone I had a lot I common with. Yes, he was very significant. He encouraged me to begin to think for myself. His friendship was important. He felt like a big brother.*

> *There was a place, a bit later in my teen years, where I got a job. It was on a farm. The husband and the wife there became almost like a second set of parents. I had a lot of meals at their place. The guy was a bush craftsman but a bit of an intellectual as well. He talked about all sorts of things. He showed me how to weld, how to build, how to do hefty sorts of work and at the same time he told interesting stories.*

Rothschild (2000) notes that "Concrete and observable resources such as pets, places and people, even objects like a tree or a place like a beach, can provide people with relief and well-being both physically and emotionally" (p. 93).

As I stayed engaged with Anton, he began to weave the present into the past. He began to reminisce about a recent job.

> *He had been dragging logs about with an excavator. While doing the job, he had had moments when he felt real achievement and a sense of happiness.*

I asked him to focus for a moment on these sensations of achievement and happiness he was describing, and this immediately took him back to his experience on the farm as an adolescent. Later, I noted that narrative approaches had enabled Anton to focus on a somatic experience, which, by being made explicit, moved him away from a dissociating or fragmenting way of thinking.

He talked of skills learnt and values cemented on that farm. He had developed a love of craftsmanship. Right now, he described being engaged on commission to make several wooden tables out of recycled timbers. It was so satisfying. He compared how he valued craftsmanship over mass production. It felt excellent to be refining his techniques and to be able to feel pride in the results. He described his love for the timber and what it meant to him to be able to recycle old fence posts and other timbers. He talked of the pleasure he felt in building strong joints. He had found the perfect work space and he enjoyed the job's complexity. Underlying it all was his love of environmental simplicity and sustainability.

The somatic experiencing (Damasio, 1994) that Anton was responding to was linking something positive in the present back to old and positive somatic memories of adolescent experience on the farm. Rothschild (2000) describes this kind of positive somatic memory as empowering to the person because it is "able to help to offset and divert memories of prolonged stress and trauma" (p. 92).

Anton continued.

Perfectionism can stop me. But it's been good having a work order and using my accumulated skills to meet a deadline. I really like the sense of accomplishment that comes. And the process has its own intellectual challenge to it. I have to do the research. I like utilising my own ideas. I like gaining new knowledge, the creativity. People tell me they like what I make. It's good to have the feedback. But I've got to be happy with it. Yes, I think it's the self-validation that really matters to me.

As I drew attention to the many values Anton had been describing, I named that final value because it stood out to me, namely the importance he was placing on having a sense of integrity within himself.

Anton expressed "the newness" of being able to see the way he lived out values that he had taken as his own along the way. He was recognising who had influenced him. But he was able to own the evidence he had of the attributes and values that he had taken into himself. He had put down some deep roots after all.

My reflection later related to the importance for me of staying oriented to a person's narratives and of noticing and naming the values being discovered. At the next session, I reminded Anthony of the roots we had explored and of his sense of integrity. This led to further, more mixed, memories, a thickening of the story, but also to the articulation of another value.

Anton began to describe some attributes of the farmer he had talked about that had not been so positive. There was some deviousness in him. He described him as "tricky" and he enlarged on some of his manipulative ways. He also said that there was "a manic quality" to the way this man often went about things. "You always had to be careful of the highs and the lows in his moods. I really don't like that. I prefer straightforwardness."

CHAPTER 9 WEAVING BODY-BASED ISSUES INTO NARRATIVE CONVERSATIONS

Anton jumped from this realisation of a preference to a judgment about his own adolescent years.

> There were times when I seemed to behave in quite a manic way myself. I did some silly things and made some really bad decisions. I did things that weren't right. I think they still make me ashamed of myself and solidify this sense of shame I carry around. Sometimes I feel a deep despair and at other times there's just this emptiness, a sense that there's nothing in my life, only worthlessness; it's a feeling that can just hit me. It can come along out of the blue.

I was curious about whether his sense of shame was ever lightened.

> Looking back on that time, I remember how I made a good decision about what I was doing. I decided to walk away from "the manic". I desired stability. I wanted my life to be calm.

I was reminded as I reflected on this later that the narrative philosophy includes the belief that our stories don't just reflect life but shape it. Telling his stories was shaping Anton's sense of himself. It was in the subtext of his relational story with this influencer that he named "manic and manipulative ways", in response to which he had chosen "straightforwardness" as his preferred way to conduct relationships. While there was much about the farmer that had influenced him positively, there were other aspects from which he had differentiated himself and moved himself forward on a completely different trajectory. Evidence of his own intentional moves was coming to the surface as he talked.

Anton's working life became an ongoing source of alternative discoveries.

> He described another line of work presently open to him. He was setting up BMX racing circuits for kids in local council areas. He articulated his desire to develop his "professionality" as he went about this work.

My enquiry about the meaning of this term took Anton into immediate memories of his father.

> Professionality was part and parcel of who his father was. He was reliable.

Articulating this, Anton began to change some of his earlier statements about him. In effect, he began to re-instate his father into the list of positive influencers (White, 2007). He had had a definite emotional connection with him.

> Now I think about it, BMX racing was a sport that Dad really encouraged me in. He took me to the track every single week for a long time up to the age of sixteen. He was always very steady. He really got involved and he supported me with that training. I remember what a great sense of adventure there was in it.

Again, I couldn't help noticing that Anton's relational and connecting memory of his father had come to mind as he was reflecting on his engagement in the kind of work or activity his dad had once helped him to love. As he reflected, this somatic experiencing seemed to put him back in touch with a stability that was perhaps a more deeply established part of himself than he had appreciated. One of his earliest caretakers, his father, was being restored to him. This was important because "the emptiness" he had mentioned might suggest difficulties with attachment at the start of his life.

139

Now Anton's body was resourcing him with memories that he could take hold of quite consciously and intentionally. The beneficial choices that Anton had been making about his occupations were arising out of an alternative story of rootedness, which contrasted with his earlier more dominant one with its implicit belief that roots were lacking.

I thought it might be helpful to invite a witness from Anton's present life into a one of our conversations. Anton chose his partner. I asked him to tell me what he thought she might have to say if we asked her to give him a reference. He found he could do this without real difficulty.

> *Well, she would probably say that I'm a kind person. She would describe me as a bit different, an idealist, that I'm excited by ideas. I'm a stable role model for her young son, I can be playful, I have an empathy for how it feels to be a kid. I'm good at the argy-bargy of father and son sort of mateship. She would say that I'm even-tempered; that I make her talk about feelings; that I stimulate emotional connectivity; that I'm persistent and aware of good timing, that I'm genuine.*

I asked him how it made him feel to consider her views.

> *Anton said that he would need to take time to draw some satisfaction from it. He would have to be really conscious in thinking about it.*

But having said that, he began to speak about seeing that "the two of us" have a real "teamwork situation". Earlier in the conversation, he had been describing himself negatively in comparison to her. Now he was seeing an actual and beneficial complementarity.

At this point, Anton wanted to re-describe his times of emotionality. He talked about how his life tended to repeat itself. He often seemed to be dogged by a deep sense of self-doubt and anxiety. He referred to the following sensations without prompting.

> *There's a tension in the throat and stomach and it can move about a bit. In the emotions there's negativity and that sense of blankness I've talked about before. It's like there's just emptiness and undirected bumming around, like I'm in limbo and just caught wallowing. It's like the shock absorbers on a car. I just don't seem to have any! The suspension system needs repairing. When life's like that "the pity party" is always very seductive.*

Anton was again using a metaphor to convey the intensity of somatic arousal. I noticed that now he was using his language to describe the dominant story he had come to better understand. He had become more aware of his sensations. He could identify his emotions and to be aware of his instantaneous tendencies to plummet emotionally. His mind-based metaphor had physical dimensions. He better understood how an automatic kind of dysregulation had the power to keep stealing his freedom.

Just articulating his descent into the negative seemed to empower Anton to take a move away from it. Something more positive (a bifurcating of direction) came to the surface. Anton recalled a time

CHAPTER 9 WEAVING BODY-BASED ISSUES INTO NARRATIVE CONVERSATIONS

when, in the middle of "the negative", he had taken a stand. What he said next sounded like a sort of announcement.

> *When I stopped smoking pot a while ago, it really helped my life. What I came to know at that time is that I am capable of consciousness!*

I perceived that Anton had himself arrived at the narrative idea of taking a stand without any therapeutic help. His reflections resonated with what Siegel (2010) calls:

> *a simultaneity of conscious attention in which you are focused both on the past and on your present-day self re-experiencing that past. [This] is an active engaged process that initiates hippocampal assembly of those strewn puzzle pieces of implicit-only material (p. 164).*

Therapeutically, I was able to point out to Anton that he seemed to be providing himself with evidence that the expertise to "repair the car's shock absorbers" was within him. His imagery was a true fit for his experience. When his therapy came to its conclusion, it was with a clear articulation of his strong sense of agency. How he managed "the downers in his life" was up to him. He knew how to act consciously.

I asked him to detail some of the things he was taking away with him from the therapy conversations as he moved forward.

> *He felt he could notice his body more, and that he had evidence from his own life that he did know how to take a stand whenever emotions pulled him down. He had made beneficial choices before and now he was clearer about his values. He could see how he had chosen them from among others, during interactions with people who had influenced his life. What was of most importance to him was that he owed it to himself to be true to who he was.*

My time with Anton taught me more of the impact of positive somatic experiencing. The nature of a person's own body wisdom can become available when the nature and effects of anchoring relationships or the influence of significant witnesses is explored in therapy conversations. Somatic and narrative approaches work together in a complementary and effective way.

The choice of scaffolds always depends on what the individual shares and the way the therapist orients herself in the other person's direction. Anton's body spoke, but he often also used the powerfully explicating language of metaphor.

The Magic Loom at work with Anton

The Co-weaver opened body enquiry immediately in response to Anton's dark-threaded news of flat affect and frequent loss of functionality. A piece of Anton's history was cued by his body and an opening made so he could weave narratively. The Co-weaver then helped Anton move past his first story to explore some of the meanings of parenthood and his family history. The metaphor of "a lack of roots", which the Weaver introduced into the fabric, led the Co-weaver to provide space for mind-based reflection and an extended weaving in of witnesses and anchoring relationships in Anton's life. The body space was briefly opened when Anton described some positive somatic experiencing. Weaving through the narrative shed allowed him to focus on his own values, and he added a shining thread as a re-authoring process began. The Co-weaver helped Anton to recognise stands he had taken by himself and to weave earlier choice-making into his identity fabric. With narrative space open, exploration of the word 'professional' saw him weave his father back into his narrative as a positive influencer. His partner's witness to his character helped him further thicken the sense of identity he was choosing to consciously construct. Anton initiated a dark-threaded weaving, back through the body space as he re-described his familiar somatic dilemma and then opened his mind by making use of a potent metaphor. Narrative curiosity helped him recognise the truths that go with the word 'consciousness' that he had threaded into the weaving. When he took his quite complex fabric from the Magic Loom, he articulated the sense of agency that had been evidenced in the stands he had taken and his recognition that he could continue to take such stands intentionally in the future. Loose ends would need his attention.

Kerry finds a new sense of agency

In response to my enquiry, Kerry described feeling caught by a set of contradictory impulses during the preceding week.

> On the one hand I'm off the hook. My upbringing doesn't define me. But then on the other hand, if I'm off the hook, well, it's open slather. I can eat what I like: a whole container of ice-cream in the dead of night, do what I like! Housework can go out the window! It's almost like "the worst version of me" is free to come out! And when this happens, it's totally out of step with my values and in no way living in the nourishing way I want. I'm flung back into depression and disappointment and the cycle of anger within me starts all over again. Sometimes I don't know who I want to be.

Hearing Kerry's litany on this day warranted some quiet moments of reflection. She seemed on the brink of a new consciousness about the ambiguities of life, as she sought to make sense of the contradictory nature of some of the internal conflicts she was grappling with. On this occasion, she was expressing the full range of the conflicts she was facing with clarity and honesty. She was owning but struggling with her complicated confusion.

Van der Kolk (2006) observes that in the process of "negotiating somatic and behavioural residues from the past, traumatised individuals can experience emotions that appear out of place and actions which are bizarre" (p. 2), and further, that "confronted with chronically overwhelming emotions, they lose their capacity to use emotions as guides for effective action. They often do not recognise what they are feeling and fail to mount an appropriate response" (p. 2). Meares (2016) on the other hand explains what Kerry was struggling with as a universal human experience.

> *The co-existence of sameness and change in self and the world contains a ... paradox: that of unity and multiplicity. The state of existing is sensed as coherent, as a relative one-ness, yet it is made up of multiple states. Perhaps it might be said that paradox is a quintessential feature of what we mean by self (p. 20).*

As the intensity of the ambiguity and paradox Kerry was negotiating waned, I pursued a bifurcating direction. I asked if there had been any area in the past week where she had not been disappointed with herself. Out of the blue, a new tone of voice emerged and suddenly Kerry was launching into a very different and a very particular narrative.

> *There had been a night during the week when she got up to her young baby, Esther, who is a terrible sleeper, and on this occasion, there was no frustration.*

As I leaned forward and asked for details, I found myself matching Kerry's tone and body language. She was eager to explore with her mind what was for her a body-focused problem.

> *I found I could just pick her up and hold her and love her. Usually during the day, I do take great pleasure in her doings. She has such a unique personality and I have a lovely bond with her. But she's a terrible sleeper and I've been suffering from sleep deprivation for years. Over the past few months with her it's just felt like the final straw!*

I asked her to tell me more about the "sleep deprivation" factor.

> *All her children had been or are bad sleepers. Since her husband's work takes him away during the week, he is not available except at weekends to take a turn at getting up. It's been all up to her.*

In an externalising way, we began to explore some of the effects of the factor.

> *Kerry remembered journeying through a myriad of efforts to get rid of the problem, and how, instead of going away, the problem only seemed to get bigger. She had been to doctors and naturopaths and read every self-help parenting book imaginable. She had listened to all her friends and worked on diets and regimes for the children and for herself. She had raged at God, questioning His goodness and feeling like she was the butt of some cosmic joke. She had indulged in many a "pity party". She had wondered how she would ever get through and she had tried her very best just "to live for today". Often, she had found herself obsessing about her lack of sleep all through the day and then the next night her sleep would be interrupted again and again. Nothing ever improved.*

THE MAGIC LOOM PART TWO - THE PRACTICE

"So, what was different with you and Esther this week?" I asked.

> *Well, I just decided the problem wouldn't get to me any more. Sleep deprivation wouldn't have me – I wasn't going to be a victim!*

I heard a new assurance in her voice with this stand and she explained further.

> *I'm not being unfairly treated. I've stopped thinking about sleep deprivation's power. Any time it's come into my mind during the day this week, I've just refused it air space. I've made up my mind: it's too hard to find the cause of the problem; it just is what it is.*

Then I heard Kerry make some strong statements.

> *I don't have to worry about other people's expectations. I can turn away from advice-givers. I can reject the 'should'. Now I'm taking any situation when I'm deprived of sleep as an opportunity. Each time Esther wakes me, I take it as an opportunity to hold her peacefully and just love her. I know I can do it, so I'm just going to follow my heart and live by my own compassion.*

We reflected on this narrative and I asked Kerry to compare it with the other stories she had brought that day. She said that "remembering her values" was the key. As I asked the 'experience of experience' question about the source of the victory over sleep deprivation, I was curious to hear Kerry's own conclusions.

> *Hesitantly, Kerry acknowledged that the victory was all her own. She had found her own solution, and, contrary to the disappointments she had suffered and described during the week, here she was face to face with what she described as her own "best self". She was at one with herself and she had made her own success happen. This was the way she wanted to be.*

This narrative externalising conversation was a significant one for Kerry. She had created her own template, which could be applied to any future disappointment. Her inner wisdom and ability to take a stand was clear. She knew how to live by her own long-standing values. She was no longer subjugated by societal assumptions of superiority. Narratively, the alternative story that was now being embodied by Kerry was totally different to the first story she had brought to the session, which had been characterised perhaps by the uncertainty and inertia of somatic clouding or perhaps by a universal human experience of paradox. Neurobiologically, Kerry was demonstrating to herself that when she didn't internalise a body-related problem as if it defined her, she could move in a direction of 'straight thinking', using her own cognitive processes. Her own brain and thinking power could set her free from any disabling inner or outer sabotaging influences. She knew how to let go.

Therapeutically, offering my curiosity in a direction that led away from despair and disappointment was important. It allowed Kerry to tell her alternative narrative, moving her in the direction of hope and providing her with evidence of her own agency. The process of externalisation helped her to find a language that clearly separated her from the problem. I was interested in the way that the agency that had resulted from earlier body-focused narrative conversations had been embodied by Kerry within her lived experience. She was on her way to being her own embodied narrative therapist. In the face of an intransigent body-related problem (which may have been triggering old intense trauma repercussions of self-disappointment), she was moving away from the assumed superiority of the opinions of others and a tendency towards shame, towards a new sense of inner unity. She knew how to live according to her own agentive preferences.

The Magic Loom at work with Kerry

A set of contradictions was explored as curiosity opened space for reflection. Notice how the Co-weaver kept the narrative space open and used a bifurcating question to provide a new threaded direction away from disappointment. Kerry wove in a body-state problem named 'sleep deprivation' and the Co-weaver quickly opened the narrative space into which Kerry could weave the results of an externalising investigation. The Weaver described the history and effects of this problem, threading the shuttle through the alternate spaces herself, telling of a self-initiated personal stand, which included the deconstruction of certain social assumptions and unhelpful influences. This stand, which continued to be woven through the narrative space, revealed to Kerry some of her own values. She took up shining threads as these become pivotal in moving her towards an alternative narrative. When encouraged by the Co-weaver to do so, Kerry signified in her weaving a new way of constructing her identity recognising herself as a problem-solver. A stronger section of weaving came into view. Kerry had made an important move away from her earlier dark-threaded self-denigration.

Hannah chooses passion over procrastination

At the outset of the therapy conversation, I took up the problem of procrastination, which I knew was on Hannah's mind, asking her how long it had been in her life.

> I remember the pattern from the time I was fifteen years old and studying for my Year 10 certificate. There were too many things I needed to be brilliant at to be acceptable to myself and others. So, I just gave up. I was diagnosed with glandular fever. I slept all day, actually spending weeks in bed. Now I look back, I was escaping from overwhelm. This pattern in my life is associated with heavy shame. It doesn't yield to rationality. I remember falling into it once years later after I'd applied for a job that I was totally fitted for. I had all the qualifications, all the skills and I just didn't turn up for the final interview. Over and over again, I procrastinate. It's deliberate self-sabotage. All responsibility is blocked out.

Therapist: "It sounds as if procrastination has quite a few effects?"

Oh yes there are lots! Loss of opportunity, the end of achievement, good job opportunities sabotaged, degrees not completed, social adventures and fun nipped in the bud.

Therapist: "So, do you think its effects also include how you see yourself?"

Of course! I hear words in my head: "But you can! So, what the hell are you doing?" Then I hear the reply that I'm "just not up to it".

Therapist: "Sort of makes you doubt yourself, and your relationships as well?"

Yes exactly. There I am in my dressing gown, wearing a cloak of despair. My body is full of aches and pains. My partner's the one who has to carry the load of two people. He has to catch up on the housework, cook meals, care for the kids. When I "drop my bundle", to use his words, it sours the relationship. And yes, it has lots of effects on the kids as well. For them life is unpredictable. You can't trust mum's word. She's physically in the room but she's not connecting with you. This week I heard them wondering what might happen. We've been talking about having a great family adventure and doing some travelling and my kids are wondering what will happen if mum gets sick or tired when we're not at home and everything's foreign. It's burdening them isn't it? They're feeling anxious and having to sort of, be the parents looking after me instead of me looking after them. This procrastination thing has impacts on our wider group of friends as well. It means they really can't rely on our family. We're unpredictable. Something good is planned but we might let everyone down at the last minute.

Therapist: "Can you think about how this thing recruits you? I mean what are the tactics procrastination uses? How does it creep up on you?"

Oh yes, I see. Now I can see what it does! It always uses "tiredness". That's it! There's something significant in my family about tiredness. People in my family don't say, "How are you?" It's more, "You must be tired, you poor thing." I remember when I was studying for those Year 10 exams. I was really enjoying it. I got such a buzz out of being a hard worker. I wasn't tired. I was thriving on it! And there's my father coming up behind my chair, massaging my neck and saying, "Oh, princess, you mustn't get too tired. You mustn't let all this hard work get you exhausted." When I think about it, it seems as if tiredness has been a dominant power in my life. I've spent weeks in bed escaping from feeling overwhelmed. Of course, my mum went to bed for eight years with depression when I was a kid too, from about when I was seven years old till I turned fourteen or so.

Now I see it! It's a thief – "the procrastination thief!" It's doing to my kids what it did to me when I was young. It's been creeping up on me with tiredness, making me believe a lie. It's a spoiler, it's a major thief. It's talked me into believing my father and copying my mother! Now I remember its earlier history. When I was little, going to bed was always a major battle with my parents. It was terrifying … that's the link with that other story about getting punished every time I refused to fall asleep, being left and neglected and then punished. That's the overwhelm isn't it? That's the trauma! The procrastination thief has used my earliest terrors to keep on spoiling my life! But it's over – this is not me. It's not going to have me anymore!"

Helping Hannah externalise her body-focused problem gave her many memories to explore and meanings to discover. As she explored the phenomenon of physical tiredness, the historic review helped her to discover that this present intransigent somatic problem in her life originated right back in her early infancy. She had encountered complex trauma. It wasn't her fault.

A pattern of thinking in her family about tiredness had also influenced her. She could find connections between incidents and patterns over time. As a result, she was understanding herself better and experiencing inner resonance (White, 2011). As the holistic externalising exploration advanced, both the impacts of trauma and their links with repeated conditioning over time could be explored.

When her values, and particularly the wellbeing of her children were discussed, it was important that these were properly acknowledged and seen to have prompted Hannah to take certain stands. Understanding the history and exploring the effects of the 'procrastination thief' on her sense of herself and on others helped her not only develop insight but to find the alternative story of her energy and passion for the action and behaviour patterns she preferred.

I noticed the pivotal moment when Hannah got in touch with her own bodily excitement and her love of hard work and achievement. These are the opposite of tiredness. A fork in the road opened up in front of her and she could choose the way she wanted to go. Her own natural impulses to action and to responsible and empowered behaviour were more available to her. Hannah was finding answers within her own life experience and personality preferences.

I noticed that the despondency with which the conversation had begun had disappeared. Probably the most important turning point was when Hannah identified the procrastination thief's way of 'tricking' her. She discovered a counter-story within her own experience.

The narrative approach of externalising can be applied to every kind of problem, including those that relate to the body. Such exploration can help a person make sense of past trauma.

The Magic Loom at work with Hannah

In this conversation the Co-weaver used the narrative language of externalisation from the start. Hannah found the space to weave in the history and effects of procrastination. She explored with some sombre colours its effects on herself and on others, including her children. The question about how the problem had recruited her took her into a brighter-threaded understanding of history. Space for body-awareness was opened briefly, providing space for a thick-threaded identification of tiredness as a family-wide problem. Then again as reflective space was opened, Hannah wove understanding of more family history. Chronologically, she added glittering threaded experience with its news of an exception, into her story. She continued uninterrupted to trace the parental influences around the body factor of tiredness until she discovered original traumatic stimuli way back in her infancy. She marked this strongly as her mind did its weaving. She came up with a new name. The procrastination/tiredness factor was described as s a "thief". This was the pivotal moment and Hannah contributed a wide satiny strand into her weaving as she made her stand clear. The problem had now been woven over with new strongly chosen contrasting threads. Hannah had found a way of weaving a sparkling alternative story.

Chapter 10
Rocking as a Body-focused Narrative Therapy Strategy

> *We have no human voice without our body as a sounding box ... without a body we do not resonate with experience. Stanley Keleman*

Because body-focused narrative therapy is an inclusive approach to working with survivors of early developmental trauma, it can incorporate a range of techniques and methods that access body experience. The body intervention of rocking is one effective way of working with trauma that uses the body rather than the mind (Masarik-Williams, Polizzi, & Punshon, 2016). In this chapter, I describe this practice with two survivors of early developmental trauma.

Simeon acknowledges his own inner wisdom

Simeon took our collaboration to a different level. Taking the shared therapy notes home, he wove his voice in with that of the therapist. At times he shares his thoughts as well as his words.

> *I thought I'd be the last person to need therapy. I was raised in a home where my parents loved my three sisters, me and each other. My dad had always worked hard making a living and mum had given up her job and worked hard being a mum. I had done well at school, gone to uni, built a successful business and married a beautiful girl. Now I was raising a young family of my own. I felt I should be happy, satisfied, content. I wasn't. I didn't have a clear idea of what was missing or wrong or why, but I wanted my life to be more than simply trying: trying to be better, failing, feeling guilty, trying to make up for that, promising myself and others to do more, to become better, failing, and on and on.*

THE MAGIC LOOM PART TWO - THE PRACTICE

When Simeon, a professional man with a young family, first came to have a therapy conversation, he didn't tell me this context, but he seemed to have trouble focusing his thoughts. He would mutter my words over and over as if trying to pin them down, so he could find his answer. He said his memories were hazy and he had over-the-top anxious and agitating reactions to any sense of not being appreciated. He described himself as "a shopaholic, a person who spreads himself over twenty-seven different surfaces, someone always moving from one thing to another". He was particularly concerned about his parenting.

While the quality of Simeon's self-presentation was indicative of anxiety, I nonetheless felt that my first task was to bring my curiosity to the theme of parenthood, which Simeon was presenting as a major concern. I began to research some of the nourishing stories that might have been overlooked in his usual narrative-making about his life as a parent. I was curious to find out what he was pleased about in his relationship with his children. Here is some of what he said.

Firstly, I could only think of my failings and regrets – being too hard on them, my lack of patience, their lack of obedience, but slowly there were some good things. I love being outside with the kids. I have enjoyed some fishing trips with Aemon – we seldom fight, though I have to battle with the desire to take over when I feel he isn't "doing it right". I'm trying to learn to let him be and to simply be alongside him.

Letti and I can really work well together, and we share a similar sense of adventure and drama. Some of my happier memories are of spending time with her, the companionship when we look after her horse together. She likes adventure, even jumping into the water hole in winter or making a fire in the fireplace. She also loves bedtime conversations. Mind you, she's like me in that she also likes to argue on and on and her words can be cutting.

Seeking to weave his body and mind together into the conversation, I asked Simeon about his senses and what it was like for him to visualise himself nourishing the lives of his children and forging a way of parenting that seemed to be consistent with his values. He was surprised to be able to acknowledge his pleasure in this. I commented on how much more relaxed and articulate he seemed as we talked about the joy he felt in building strong emotional connections with his children. The outdoors had come up noticeably in the stories and in the back-and-forth exchange as we talked. I asked him whether there were other areas of his life where grounding himself using his senses in this way was beneficial.

I didn't really know much about grounding, but I knew I did find myself captivated at times by the beauty of nature. Arrested by a glimpse of cherry blossom, I would literally pull the car over and take photos to try and capture this, in order to share it with others. Actually, this was becoming a regular practice – clouds, sunsets, misty mornings, starry nights, a flower beginning to blossom. I always seemed to feel better and somehow more healthy when connecting like this. Now I was learning this was inner wisdom, an intuitive use of a body-focused grounding technique. For me you could call it a spiritual experience.

CHAPTER 10 ROCKING AS A BODY-FOCUSED NARRATIVE THERAPY STRATEGY

The body had been brought into the conversation through a typical narrative investigation. As I noted Simeon's lived experience of his body's resources, I continued with the language scaffolding to help him explore more of the context and meanings of parenting for him. I asked Simon to talk about some of his own experiences as a child.

> *It took some time to find memories. My parents were good people [who] loved each other and loved me. We had everything we needed, yet somehow my memories didn't add up. I didn't want to blame them – I just wanted to understand. My dad, he was (and still is) so affectionate, but for the most part of my early life I don't really remember him being around. When he was, we didn't seem to talk about important things in life, and I think mostly what was best for me was simply chosen by someone else, so I tried to like whatever would make the most people happy with me.*

> *I remember getting smacked at home and school – fundamentalist church culture: "Foolishness is bound up in the heart of a child, but the rod of correction will drive it far from him". There was the sense of it being a duty to God. I needed the punishment because I'd made a mistake. It would make me better. At home it was mostly Mum, because Dad wasn't there. As I got older, I think she and I just fought more. I can remember us both getting so angry; sometimes it was like she wasn't an adult, she could be resentful and tit for tat.*

I had heard Simeon share some of his own values when he described his way of relating with his children, and I noticed that he was differentiating himself from some of the practices mentioned in the narrative about his childhood. He was also alluding to bigger societal, in his case religious, influences. I asked him to talk about the values he and his wife were choosing to live by as parents.

> *Above everything else, we want our children to know that they are loved. We want to create a sense of openness so that our kids will always feel they can talk with us about anything.*

As we again talked back and forth, Simeon clarified and thickened his narrative about this differentiation. He was pleased about the stands he and his wife were taking. Several times, however, he mentioned a problem he had with "big over-reactive moments" with one of the children or with his wife. I thought it was time to take our enquiry in the direction of his body, as we explored what he was calling "over-reactivity".

I asked if Simeon could remember and attempt to re-configure his body into the same reactive sensations he had experienced in his household recently. He spent some time thinking about his body and then adjusting it in line with the intensity of tension and sensation he was remembering.

> *Suddenly I realised how tight my jaw was feeling. As I concentrated on that tightness I also noticed that my face felt flushed and that my insides were ready to explode. What's more I could feel my fists clenching and unclenching.*

I asked if he could recall his body responding in a similar way at any other time in his life.

151

THE MAGIC LOOM PART TWO - THE PRACTICE

When I put my attention on these reactions, I immediately got an image of myself lashing out at mum. It was the same memory I'd had earlier. Now I was seeing that my body had reacted recently just like it had in the past. It was when I came up against unfairness or disrespect or if I didn't feel appreciated.

Remembering what he had said earlier about being calmed by going for a walk or by getting involved in making music, I asked Simeon to imagine himself taking notice of his fists and his jaw and that explosive sensation, and making a move such as taking himself outside for a walk into nature or walking away into another room and picking up his guitar. I was seeking to engage his own curiosity and imagination as I asked him to speculate.

I have to admit it seemed strange to be focusing on my body, and yet the experience was so tangible I was drawn into it. I felt that if I could get outside, connect with what my senses were experiencing I would be calmed. Even sitting there, thinking about doing it was giving me some confidence. This was such a different idea to consider. Again, I was being told I already had the skills I needed, to calm my nervous system via my senses! And if I listened to my body – the tightness in my jaw or gut – these could be my reminders. I just needed to be aware in the moment of what my body was telling me and conscious of the resources within me.

When Simeon acknowledged his intuitive knowledge (which I had called inner wisdom) about how to calm the arousal in his nervous system by using his senses, this proved to be a starting point for experimentation for him.

From then on, he began to try to practice self-nurture at any moment he became upset. He was able to work on becoming more aware of his uncomfortable sensations. Over several weeks, he reported progress. He would describe his efforts at modulating any arousal when he was aware of it in his body. Simeon was recognising that there was a level of dysregulation in his life, which may have begun for him quite early in his life. While he had shared a sketchy narrative of childhood that suggested certain stressors, he was discovering that he did not now need to delve deeper into memory in order to be able to heal from the prolonged and stressful dynamics which had been influencing his self-narratives in a dominantly negative way and holding his life back.

The Magic Loom at work with Simeon

Look for the ways in this segment that the Co-weaver stayed present with the Weaver as he curiously searched out his own richly coloured and textured threads for weaving. When Simeon alluded to his somatic resources, the Co-weaver noticed and named this, and resonating with this he tagged a place in the weaving as a reminder. She kept narrative space open, researching history and context with him, and he wove in lighter threads of understanding. When Simeon mentioned the dark threads of over-reactivity with which he was unhappy and which also fitted in with his earlier body language, the Co-weaver re-opened space for curiosity about the body. Simeon's weaving demonstrated the two major phases of the body orientation, focusing first on sensations and then mindfully modulating them by making use of other body resources. As these were explored, Simeon picked up glittering threads to mark his excitement. Through the narrative space, Simeon took up threads of recognition while also using the wisdom of his body to take him colourfully forward to create his unique and well-woven fabric.

Simeon's experience of rocking

After several therapy conversations, Simeon was becoming more adept at using his body and its wisdom to better regulate his life. The therapy relationship had also developed in collegiality and trust. I decided to introduce him to the body strategy I call rocking, explaining the details before we started. He was intrigued and receptive to this body-focused process.

I couldn't see how this was going to work but I was willing to try it. As I lay down, my inner voice began: "Make sure you think of something to talk about. Try to get it right." But as the rocking began, I was able to concentrate on the motion and on my breathing, giving myself to the sensations and quieting my mind. I succeeded in letting myself be in the moment. It seemed as if I travelled through some of my life's stories that I never think about. Zooming in on particular moments and then pulling back out to see sweeping panoramic views. I remember Mum playing tennis, softball and squash – I would have to go with her because Dad was away. I saw myself playing sport too, though I don't have strong memories of my parents being there. Despite my high levels of enjoyment, my participation in sport stopped for me when I was only nine. It felt like what I liked to do, wasn't important enough.

Another memory was that my parents thought I was amazing (conforming to the school system, becoming an academic success and a leader of my peers), but this contrasted totally with my own feelings of inadequacy. I just wanted acceptance but instead the word for me over all these years – in caps lock – was AWKWARD. I didn't know why but I was repulsed by myself. I remember looking into a mirror, dressed for my formal at the end of high school, feeling utterly rejected, thinking, "How could anyone kiss you?"

Towards the end, the rocking experience became more meditative, almost like chanting. I began to let go of 'awkward' and 'self-repulsion' and thoughts of my parents. I just let myself be. Tension seemed to melt away, and it was like I was coming out from underneath a weight. Who is Simeon? He's okay. If 'awkward' had been the word dominating my story, I could sense it fading as 'acceptance' flooded in.

It was remarkable to hear this review of how the rocking affected Simeon and drew him into the meditative moments he described. In the weeks afterwards, he had more to report.

> *I'd be trying to get our baby off to sleep and I'd find myself immersed in the lullaby music. As I lay there listening, I would find myself getting calm. I could let everything go and I could just be, just as I had at the end of the rocking experience. Then I had another experience. One night I couldn't sleep because of anxiety and tension. Finally, I did fall asleep in the early hours of the morning and I had a very significant dream. In the dream I felt myself being kissed on the forehead. I felt such warmth and acceptance that every anxiety simply melted away. This dream encounter was so tangible and transforming that subsequently just bringing it to mind has gone on having the power to calm me.*

For Simeon, the experience of rocking seemed spiritual and connecting. Allowing his body to be rocked seemed to help him shift the old ingrained sense of unworthiness (shame) and disconnection (isolation) that had dogged his life. The dream experience, in particular, showed that a depth of internal change and transformative self-acceptance had occurred at a healing level beneath conscious awareness (implicitly) It was deeply relational and evocative of healthy social engagement biology (Porges, 2011).

The Magic Loom at work with Simeon

The focus was on the Weaver as he responded to this specialised somatic experience. The body weaving space was being held wide open by the Co-weaver, but narrative exploration was able to occur at any point. The surprising outcomes of the rocking that Simeon encountered in lullaby and dream enabled him to weave a new sense of self-worth into his fabric.

Samantha finds new confidence in re-authoring her narrative

Samantha first came for counselling because of what she described as "floods of emotionality". She had a tendency to break down in a storm of tears which she couldn't stop, no matter how hard she tried. She described a pain in her side that kept returning. She couldn't get rid of it, even though she had sought a variety of medical and homeopathic remedies.

I began some narrative investigation with Samantha, but I focused it on the first body phenomenon she had mentioned. I asked her what her tears would say if they could speak. She replied, "Let your passions loose!"

I was curious about when her passions had been heard.

> *As a child, they had "never been heard". Indeed, they had been "stomped on". She enlarged*

on her story of growing up with a single mum who always worked two jobs to try to make ends meet. She particularly recalled her fears when left alone in the house with her younger brother. She was speaking of her tears now as being related to an all-encompassing fear. Then she was remembering a range of expectations, such as being required to take on a lot of chores. It seemed to her that she was never able to do them well enough. She said now that she also had a lot of tears of "failure".

As I continued to show my interest, Samantha began to unpack more of her life history.

Her own father had left her fatherless when she was tiny and then her brother's father also abandoned her at the age of eleven. It had only been at this point that she had learned that the man she had been looking up to from two till eleven as her 'dad', had not actually been her birth father. She remembered it bursting in on her that she had never felt as if his love was really there for her. He had always offered her brother more attention, more time, more money. She had responded by becoming a tomboy. Now she reported that her tears were also expressive of her sense of "forsakenness, jealousy, grief and loss".

Recently, when I told Mum how I had felt back at the time of Dad's leaving, she could only focus on her own pain. There was no understanding or empathy there for me at all. With Mum I always felt I was somehow wrong and that's the feeling that takes over when I can't stop crying: "I'm wrong!"

I asked Samantha a question that might take her in the direction of an alternative story, within her own experience. Could she remember her emotionality being supported in any other contexts at all? Samantha paused and then she looked up, with a brightness in her eyes.

She was recalling a recent incident in her art class. During the class proceedings, she had become very emotional. However, she told me that, contrary to a lifetime of experience, this time her emotion was honoured. She was given time and her feelings were not disparaged or blocked in any way. Moreover, she was asked in a positive way to talk about what had touched her.

I noticed that in her narrative her sensitive point of view and her passionate engagement had been validated. As she told this narrative it was obvious that it thrilled her. There was a setting where her passion had been being seen and validated. Together we savoured this pivotal moment. I then asked a 'how' question. I was interested in exactly how she had found herself to be in such an environment.

It was because she had stepped out bravely. As an adolescent she had been pushed by her mother into the sciences. At university, she completed her training in the health sciences. She went on to find work in that area. But she was never happy. Only recently had she had the courage to launch out on a quest to study the art that was close to her heart.

I asked her what she saw in the self who was following her quest. Samantha could see "a determination to branch out". As a child, she felt she could never have what she wanted. Tears were brimming as she went on:

Mum's voice was so very loud! The direction I wanted I couldn't have.

I was curious about whether there had been any signs of this branching out of hers earlier in her life. This was a way to thicken her branching out narrative, so its significance was given greater weight in her mind.

Samantha responded eagerly, remembering that as a student she had branched out in the way she dressed. There had been a sense of defiance towards her mother's way. Though she was doing a science course, her clothing was always very arty. She emphasised: I wanted to be me. I wanted my individuality and I found it by being very quirky.

I named this determination to stand by her own passion and wondered if her branching out could be described as a kind of inner wisdom. As she shared her excitement at this idea, Samantha gave another example of branching out.

She had chosen to travel. Having toed the line in her job for several years, it felt like she had paid her dues. At work she often felt like a performing porpoise. Though leaving was difficult, she badly wanted freedom, and so she made a stand. She had long dreamed of learning a new language, thinking it would help her experience the newness she craved. She wanted to grow, and, in the end, she did it by removing herself completely from everything familiar. She said it was like going cold turkey and that then she had to "make life up as I went along".

I enquired what it was like for Sam to be remembering herself taking such a strong stand.

It was enlivening. It was so good to remember the fact that she had actually done it! Her list of achievements was admirable: I remember I was good at problem-solving. I was spontaneous, creative and resilient. I got an apartment. I learnt a new language. I learnt a new culture. I felt accepted. I widened my horizons and then I met my husband-to-be.

I asked her to describe further what it meant for her now, in the present, to be looking back on herself pursuing her quest to be herself by branching out in those earlier phases of her life. She said it gave her a greater sense of self-confidence.

I'm on a similar path now by doing my art course. Mum's tone of voice always reminds me of the role the Dementors play in Harry Potter. (I've been reading it to my kids). They suck the life out of you! It's so good for me to see that at other times in my life I have been able to turn against their loud criticising, dogmatic voices.

I was curious to hear more about whether there were different (alternative) voices she had been taking notice of recently.

She was learning to listen to her friends and to take notice of more nourishing voices in her life. Leaning into her individuality was not only allowable but it made her feel satisfied inside and more comfortable with herself.

As we neared the end of the session, I decided to address the second body concern Samantha had raised at the start of our conversation. I asked her what her usual attitude was towards the pain in her side? She said she was impatient and critical towards it.

As she ruminated on this impatience, I asked her what she thought would happen if, when she noticed the pain, she could refuse the Dementor's pathway of criticising it, and instead treat the pain in her side as a friend? What would happen if she could increase her awareness of it and offer it tenderness and understanding and sympathy? This was obviously a new idea but as she sat in the chair Sam responded to this line of enquiry which engaged her with her body. She began to experiment.

> She concentrated on remembering and re-embodying the tense pain that was quite familiar to her. She said she could reproduce the sensation of it easily. Then she practised noticing it in a kinder, more welcoming way. In a matter of minutes, she reported that its intensity was decreasing.

I asked her to think about the intensity of the pain in terms of a number on a scale from zero to ten. She said that the score she was allotting to the pain had diminished from about a seven to a three. She began to describe an image:

> Perhaps this pain in my side is like my canary in the mine.

We talked together about how the proverbial canary saved lives when gas seeped into the mines.

> She was saying that her pain might well turn out to be a life-saver for her, a kind of signal that, at a specific moment "the toxic old dementors were hovering", and that rather than reacting emotionally she could choose a path of kindness to herself. A new way of escape was open to her.

The metaphor she had chosen heralded a change in her thinking. All of Levine's (1992) aspects of experience, namely sensation, image, behaviour, affect and meaning, were being explored as a result of Samantha reflecting on her intense bodily sensations.

Rothschild (2010) suggests that a person's body can act like a sort of gauge for her. If, like Samantha, she can identify a sensation, or a mix of sensation and emotion, which accompanies her intense experiencing and link that with an image, this becomes a jumping off place for change and healing. The canary in the mine was a positive image which carried a potency that made it memorable.

Discovering her own wise pathways, which could be described narratively as small acts of resistance, was important as Samantha searched for emotional freedom from the past. As a narrative therapist, I noticed the healing power present when I did my best to add weight to the pivotal moments which arrived, helping Samantha to thicken her branching out narratives.

The Magic Loom at work with Samantha

Hearing Samantha, the Co-weaver was being made aware of an intensely emotional somatic issue.

She briefly opened space for the body each time 'the tears' entered the conversation but then swiftly opened mind-focused narrative space so the emotion could be thoroughly explored. Samantha was weaving in darker shades as she thickened the dominant narrative and made it visible in the weaving. However curiosity opened the way for a more nourishing narrative to be found. You may recognise that as stands earlier taken were examined, the Weaver began to weave into her fabric a bright and alternative performance of identity. Her Co-weaver maintained the opening of space using the narrative method of enquiry. Re-authoring was occurring narratively and showing up strongly in the fabric. However she didn't lose track of the body problem of dark-threaded pain that had been presented along with the description of intense emotionality at the start. She opened the body space so Samantha could weave in what arose as she raised her own awareness of her body. The Co-weaver then opened space so Samantha could mindfully apply bright new threads of kindness aimed directly towards her bodily sensations. Textures of confidence came into view as the Weaver herself began to use her body's resources to intentionally put the brakes on her autonomic nervous system arousal (pain). Notice that Samantha promptly signalled for narrative space to be again opened up, so she could weave in the meanings that she saw as a result of exploring a powerful metaphor using the spaces woven between mind and body. Her newly woven fabric began to present a strong contrast with the dark heavily textured dominant story that had been forged by over-emotionality and dissociated or psychosomatic physical pain.

Samantha's experience of rocking

It was some weeks later. After due preparatory explanation, the rocking began. Being tucked in in preparation for the rocking reminded Samantha of some of the good aspects of her childhood.

She immediately spoke about how much she loved being tucked in firmly as a child. She and her brother both loved it when mum tucked them up tight when she finally got home from work at night. It made them feel snug and safe. She had a feeling she was completely safe in the space with me. However, she was feeling some anxiety in her stomach about the idea of the rocking. Her body was letting her know about the anxiety that was accompanying the idea. She asked if it was all right for her to talk during the rocking process.

I reassured her that she was safe to be herself and to talk all she wanted. As the rocking continued

Samantha immediately started talking.

The image of Harry Potter is coming to mind. He's finding out he's a wizard and I'm finding out that I'm an artist.

For a few moments she was quiet. Then she mentioned that the pain in her side was drawing her attention. I asked her if she had some kindness to offer her side.

Samantha intentionally let kindness in and in a short space of time she was reporting that her tension had diminished. The pain wasn't worrying her any longer.

I observed her relax and she became more fully engaged conversationally as she began to be able to consciously take in the sense of being rocked. After we changed sides, Sam remarked on a different image. She was recalling her brother.

I can see him where he always sits on mum's balcony to have a smoke. [He had recently been unwell.] I can be less anxious about him, I can let him be.

She revisited the huge stress she had experienced at finding out that her brother's birth father was not her real father. There was an accompanying deep sense of rejection. Now she was realising that she had, for a long time, carried anxiety and fear that her brother would also reject her. Samantha closed her eyes and when she opened them she communicated that she was very sad that she had lived with this fear of rejection for so long.

It took time for her to move her inward eyes away from that dramatic internalising fear and grief. As the rocking proceeded, however, something more life affirming popped up.

Samantha began to describe a series of scenes in which she and her brother were enjoying light-hearted connection. She could visualise the two of them having fun at the beach, in the house and at the football.

I asked if these happy times at the beach had anything to say to her about her sadness.

Samantha began to bring playful images of herself and her brother into her grief. She described how the sense of rejection was being replaced by a deep sense of connection and togetherness.

An alternative story was appearing. After the rocking was over, Samantha drank a glass of water. She had more processing to do. I became aware that she was thickening the new narrative.

As the older sibling, she had always experienced herself in the role of caretaker to her brother. Now she was recognising some of his leadership capabilities. She was remembering that he had been the initiator when it came to risky behaviours like jumping off the shed roof and into the backyard swimming pool. Over the years he had taught her some of the skills you might associate with a father's role, helping her with her bike etc. As she thought about this, she named him as a "bridge person" who somehow ensured that she didn't grow up un-resourced by the gifts of maleness. Far from rejecting her, he gave her some of the sense of herself as important and as a relating and sharing person. Samantha talked of this as a real shift. She had a new sense of equality with her brother. She was no longer the caretaker and he was no longer dependent on her.

In her imaginative way Samantha then returned to her first image.

Harry Potter's self-talk revealed doubt in himself as a wizard. This is just like my own doubts about myself in every way and now as an artist. But by doing this art course, I'm finding out that I'm not alone. I'm not the only one who can tear themselves down.

I was curious about how the tearing down process manifested itself.

Samantha responded again using metaphor, this time the barbed wire fence of assumptions and perfectionism up against which she and others often got squashed and torn.

But, she went on, Hagrid opened a door for Harry to step through. I feel as if the door is open for me. I am walking through it. I am in transition to a new kind of self-acceptance – trust in my body and being aware of it seems to be increasing. It's okay to be myself.

The conversation was drawing to an end. Samantha raised some concerns she was having with both her children. But rather than talking further about these, she said:

Today in remembering the aliveness and excitement of my own childhood and how, despite its negatives, me and my brother grew and discovered so much together, I can see that I can trust my children to be children. They're going to be all right. It's true what I tell them, that I've never done this before, that is, parented children of ten and eight years. But it's reassuring that children of ten and eight years somehow have an inbuilt knowledge about how to be kids of the age they are!

For Samantha, there was a sense of transportation. In a conversation engendered by a rocking experience, she had moved into a new sense of agency which might not only influence her but also provide a legacy for the next generation.

Rothschild (2000) explains that emotional overload is one of the implicit residues of early trauma. During the earliest explorations with Samantha, I did my best to stay therapeutically attuned to her and to give due honour to the tears that welled up from time to time. As her sensory somatic experience of emotionality was explored narratively, the weaving together of the scaffolds produced explicit meanings: details of events, of history and of context. The past could more and more easily become differentiated from the moves forward that were being explicated and thickened.

Noting and naming the nourishment of near at hand adult witnesses to her life proved crucial for Samantha. She was able to begin replacing the dominant narratives of early subjugating stress in relationships, with stories of significant present witnesses to her life. The way they embodied nourishment and connection was vital as she made clear in her feedback months later.

Several themes to which White (2011) draws attention were apparent in Samantha's narratives. Her strong values and the insider knowledge long recognised by narrative practitioners which provided a fruitful orientation for my interest and my questions. Samantha didn't have to rely on knowledge from the outside. She had internal wisdom and was now experiencing what White (2011) called "aspects of her life being revalued through a range of resonant responses" (p. 125). "Reverberations through history" (p. 128) were concurrently providing her with inner resonances. Samantha's use of language, and particularly of metaphor, was often the vehicle that brought such reverberations to light. With every experience of resonance and reverberation, a dyadic engagement was creating a bond and underlying all the words.

White (2011) explicates the way that physical senses (the body) are always being woven into the processes of the mind when he says, "This process sponsors the development of an inner world that can be visualised and a sense of aliveness that displaces a sense of emptiness and deadness" (p. 128).

I was interested to see that one experience of the body strategy of rocking helped Samantha not only find an alternative image of her mother (the one who tucked her in snugly), but also enabled her to explore and to expand her view of her family eco-system (Bogdan, 1986). Addressing the pain in her side, which had been acting as a red flag in her life, was the body process which, when woven with the more narrative-based attitude of kindness, became pivotal.

Early pervasive stresses had kept on taking their toll on Samantha well into her adulthood, as the brain's primitive mechanisms and the arousing impact of autonomic nervous system activations through the amygdala often whisked her back into the past. Helping her to explore and to modulate her emotional states holistically meant that her hippocampus was being activated and was helping her to put the puzzle pieces together (Siegel, 2010) as routinely happens in a brain unencumbered by early trauma. All her mental resources could become more available to her.

Samantha's story also bears out Porges's (2004, 2011) assertion that connectedness is a biological imperative. She was demonstrating that the social engagement system aspect of the autonomic nervous system can be promoted with a focus on a person's everyday relationships. When a person feels witnessed or accompanied, the more primitive patterns of arousal and dissociation are overridden by the more nuanced calming capacity of the person's social engagement system. Noticing and naming a person's emotional connections can expand her range of exploration. A therapy that combines a co-regulating body focus with rich and similarly intersubjective narrative exploration can function to help a person learn to calm herself within her everyday contexts.

THE MAGIC LOOM PART TWO - THE PRACTICE

The Magic Loom at work with Samantha

As the Co-weaver makes the body shed available, watch for how she responds to the Weaver's conversational initiatives. She responds to the way Samantha's pain weaves dark threads of anxiety into her expectations. She calls on the second phase of body-scaffolding introducing body resources and strategies so that Samantha can modulate her bodily arousal and immediately brighten her weaving with threads of kindness. Her pain dissipates. The narrative shed is opened so that Samantha can weave in aspects of her history and her family dynamics and add bright and confident threads of self-understanding, particularly into her memories of her brother. The Co-weaver helps her to weave into her sadness positive textures from her own felt sense of pleasure. She maintains an attitude of open enquiry and flexibility in opening the narrative shed so that the Weaver has the space she needs to integrate her emotional and sensory expressions with her other more mindful processes. From the outset of the conversation, the Co-weaver is intrigued by Samantha's explorations of the metaphorical threads that she is drawing from the Harry Potter chronicles. These often bring both sheds together in ways that richly impact the co-created new fabric being woven.

Later feedback

Months later, I asked Samantha what she had taken from the therapy journey.

> She immediately mentioned the metaphor of the canary in the mine. She described how useful she found the pain in her side if it arrived. It could quickly wake her up to an episode of triggered arousal and give her a push towards the story she preferred and away from the default of a dominant story of emotionality and despair. She was overcoming the old pattern. Over-emotionality was itself a body signal she jumped off from these days. A flood of tears immediately alerted her that the Dementors were in the vicinity. She now knew that they didn't have to be obeyed.

> She described as well how much better she had become at absorbing or taking in the positive messages of nourishing friends. She gave an example, describing how a friend had recently observed that she was "in a bit of a slump" and had simply put a hand on her shoulder. She said how incredibly powerful it had been for her to be thus seen and grounded by her friend's touch. That very day she had been able to ground herself and to reinforce in her own self-talk. She said she had a sense of her own strength and validity.

As she explained this detail I noticed that Samantha had just straightened her spine and lifted her head: her body telling the same story as her words of moving out of a slump into a vital sense of her agency in taking care of herself.

Chapter 11
Body-focused Narrative Therapy with Couples

It turns out that the only part of your consciousness that can change [the] deeper structures [of the brain] is this self-reflective part. Dr David Van Nuys

Body-focused narrative therapy is effective when utilised in the context of relationship therapy. In this chapter, the interweaving of body and narrative approaches scaffold conversations with three couples.

Linda discovers an intergenerational understanding of her early trauma

In this couple session, Linda's therapy conversation and her narrative discoveries about intergenerational impacts of trauma are witnessed by Rick. Linda had been growing in her awareness of her body and its signals. She had already been experiencing new opportunities to leave behind her dominant story and to welcome alternative narratives. In an earlier session with Rick, he had talked about how Linda sometimes got 'a look' on her face that made him feel stupid. She was totally unaware of the look, and so we agreed together that we would explore this factor in the next session.

The idea that the look could be named and explored in such an externalising and less personal way enabled Linda to do away with shame and defensiveness. From the start she was ready to talk, and Rick was eager to witness the therapy conversation and to listen carefully.

Linda told us that as she had anticipated the session, she had begun to be aware of the sensations that made up the look when it arrived.

When someone like Rick says something I don't agree with, I can actually feel the look coming over my face.

Narrative therapists always look for specific and detailed reflection, so I asked her to describe exactly what her sensations had been.

I feel pressure, particularly here [she touched the area around the front of her neck]. I also feel very anxious.

I wondered tentatively about the sensation's history and I was surprised with Linda's quick reply. "I've got a theory." Her eyes filled with tears. She had trouble speaking, but when she was ready the following narrative emerged:

When I was seven and my sister was about eight years old, my sister peered out the lounge room window and saw the postie coming. Dad was with us in the room. My sister yelled something silly like, "We don't want any mail today". Inexplicably, Dad absolutely freaked out. He grabbed a tea towel that was on the back of a chair and he started to push it into my sister's mouth. He seemed to be shoving it right down her throat till suddenly he stopped and stormed out of the room. I was rooted to the spot with terror. My sister could hardly breathe. She was sitting still, with this ghastly thing hanging from her mouth and tears running down her cheeks. I had seen her eyes nearly popping out of her head. I can't remember anything else; how she recovered or who came to her aid or anything.

As we talked about the meanings in the story, Linda had a realisation.

Perhaps I am still reacting in some situations as if I have to protect myself from an onslaught like that.

We talked for a bit about what it was like for her when she was triggered into such self-protection. She described again the anxiety she felt and the emotional intensity of the sensations of pressure at the front of her neck. I was curious and asked Linda how she talked to herself about these sensations and her feelings of intense anxiety.

She said she always got mad with herself and felt frustrated and angry.

As I oriented myself towards Linda, hearing about her almost automatic negativity towards herself, I asked her about turning that attitude around. What might it be like to experiment with bringing kindness into her awareness of the sensations in her neck. Linda was keen to take up an experimental trial.

After she had concentrated mindfully for a few minutes on this task, she reported that she was already feeling much calmer.

We talked back and forth as she compared what occurred when she offered herself judgment and how different the outcome was when kindness was brought into the picture. Gentleness towards her

CHAPTER 11 BODY-FOCUSED NARRATIVE THERAPY WITH COUPLES

sensations, and thus towards herself, had a settling effect and even though practised for only a very short time.

Linda had the sense that it was lowering the tension and stress to which she had also been reacting. She expressed her amazement that she had managed to settle herself so quickly just by noticing her body in this more sympathetic way.

Taking up the narrative scaffolding I now asked Linda if she felt it would be useful to talk more about her father's history and the contexts of his childhood and hers. She was keen and soon enlarged on some of her father's history and his social context of extreme poverty.

> *I know that Dad came from an underprivileged background. What I've pieced together is that many times in his childhood, bailiffs would be seen approaching the house to repossess his mother's sewing machine or the television. I don't know how many times that happened. Anyway, when the bailiffs or whatever they were called arrived, Dad and his siblings would have to be quiet and to pretend they weren't there so the bailiffs would go away. Obviously "the enemy" still bulldozed their way in and got what they wanted. It must have been terrible!*

> *I think my sister must have triggered him on that day and instantly Dad was back in the middle of the trauma of those experiences. He was terrified that the postman had heard my sister's innocent remark and that there would be some dire consequences. His reaction was completely irrational, but it makes sense now that I'm understanding what triggering can do. And when I think about it, I can see that Dad often had the look on his face when I was growing up too. It made me afraid and affected my whole childhood.*

We continued to explore this legacy and how it played itself out for her. Linda talked about how, out of fear, she must have also developed a tendency to overreact when she met any kind of opposition. As she considered this, she came to the conclusion that her body had gone on holding within it her terror of her father's actions on that day. It was just one example. But she wondered if, in addition, she had also learnt the look from him, because he also dealt it out if he was ever opposed.

> *Living with my Dad was always scary. My mother had us all walking on eggshells around him. She would rush around getting tea ready and we would tidy up the house ready for his arrival, so he wouldn't get upset when he got home. He was always a fault finder. He would come home from his job, which I assume he hated but felt locked into because he had to provide for our large family, and he would yell and scream at us if we stepped out of line in any way. He portrayed himself as a bit of a victim without a lot of joy in his home life. I believe it was a chore for him to be at home and that what he really wanted to do was to go to the golf club as soon as possible. We [the seven kids] were considered a huge burden – a bit like the cross Jesus had to bear. I can see he had a huge effect on me, and now I can see that that influence is still affecting my adult life and how I react.*

165

THE MAGIC LOOM PART TWO - THE PRACTICE

This became an opportunity to follow the narrative approach of exploring and deconstructing some of the assumptions or taken for granted attitudes that often lead people to experience subjugation in their lives (Morgan, 2000).

It was Linda's view that the stigma around poverty, which her grandparents must have found terribly demeaning, would have been nothing short of traumatic for the children. She recognised that even these days there is a lot of stigma around poverty. She said that she was seeing how these social attitudes had then affected her generation. Her mother's life as well as her own and that of her siblings had all been impacted.

When Linda and Rick arrived the following week, Linda had another story to tell about the look.

> *Linda told how stressed she felt about getting the girls into the car and off to school in the mornings. On this occasion her older daughter, Casey, tried to tell her something on the way out of the driveway and Linda said that she snapped. At this her daughter burst into tears. Linda got a shock and she suddenly noticed pressure at the front of her neck. She pulled over and stopped the car. She asked Casey whether the way she had looked at her had been part of her upset. She said, "Yes, you made me feel stupid".*

> *Linda said that she was hearing the exact words her husband Rick often used. Along with the body sensation itself, the other thing she had also become aware of was the intensity in her voice as she had snapped at her daughter. It was an emotional intensity that was totally out of proportion to anything either child had done that morning. No horrible crime had been committed. Linda described her apology. She told both her children she never wanted to make them feel stupid. In fact, the very opposite was true. She wanted them to know she was interested in what they had to say. She loved them very much. She said that she would do her best not to use that kind of look and tone. "And if I do," she told them, "please tell me, so we can sort it all out together".*

Linda and Rick were excited to see the way another generation could begin to be set free of the long-term legacies of trauma. Linda was listening to her body and feeling a new sense of agency, which she could pass on to her children.

Some weeks later, Linda and Rick described a visit to the home of Linda's parents. They explained what a difference it had made that they could both see Linda's father's behaviour with more understanding eyes. They found that they could let him be and not take his behaviours as personally as they had done previously. As a result, the intergenerational atmosphere was much improved.

I asked what it meant to Rick to have been a witness to what Linda's body had revealed and to have watched how the exploration of its meanings unfolded.

> *Rick felt his increased understanding of Linda and of his father in-law was in turn helping him to see with new eyes. He could support Linda in a much more realistic way and not take the reactivity so personally.*

Working all this through in the presence of her partner, and having him join her in so much more understanding, was making Linda feel deeply supported. Rick was showing a willingness to tune in to the meanings that were behind her reactivity. This was providing an added resonance for Linda, in line with White's ideas (2011). Both her therapist's and her husband's orientation towards her and her stories allowed her to feel the sense of attunement and resonance she so needed.

Linda shows what it means to embody a new story. Not only do we see how her body had held onto an old story related to prolonged stress and trauma, we can also observe her not just choosing a preferred story but also finding ways to inhabit it. Beyond articulating a narrative or having an idea or even values in her mind, she has described herself embodying them. She has demonstrated ways in which she is living out her re-authored story. We see her determination to understand and leave behind a body-language behaviour that has taken her back to early trauma and proven harmful to her way of relating to others. Her willingness to leave the past behind by experimenting in her interactions with both her parents and her children is clear.

I found myself asking another question about what Linda had shown me about her values. What was absent but implicit in Linda's story was her desire to live in a loving way. What White (2006) would describe as her intentional-state notion of building loving relationships both within her partnership and across more than one generation, was very clear.

Later feedback

Months later, I asked Linda if I could use the above snippets from our conversations for this book and we modified some of what I had written to better fit the way she would express herself. I also asked her what in our conversations had had the most impact on her. Here is a part of her reply:

> *Before I started therapy, I would often have sharp jabbing pains up and down my neck if I was stressed; for example, if I was going to be late for an appointment or if I had to voice my thoughts or wants or desires. At such moments, my throat would close up, and while I could think of what I wanted to say, I couldn't make the words come out. So, when we discovered in therapy how my neck was responding to the arousal in my nervous system, being able to make this connection with my other experiences made a huge difference to my recovery.*

Reverberations through time

Linda had made many connections, from what was happening in her face to her history of childhood trauma and how that history had affected her view of herself, kept her fears alive and had had the power to affect another generation. It had cost her her voice at times in her workplace as well as within her home and in other relationships. Making all these connections proved pivotal.

In just such ways, "diverse experiences of life" are brought together "into a storyline that is unifying of these experiences" and that provides Linda with "a sense of personal continuity through the course of her history" (White, 2011, p. 124). White refers to the way this also creates "reverberations through time", which displace a linear world of "one damned thing after another" and introduces complexity into a person's sense of their life (p. 127).

Intergenerational trauma

Perry (1999) says that the memory of trauma is carried not only by individuals according to their neurobiology, but it is carried in the life of a family though family myths, child-rearing practices and belief systems, literature, laws and social structures.

When I discussed with another narrative practitioner the way the body's wisdom can help resolve generational legacies of trauma, he added several examples of the way that non-verbal behaviours can be the vehicles which carry the continuation of the impacts of trauma down the generations. He mentioned the collective responses of Jewish people to the holocaust as an example of an intensely traumatic culture-shaping set of events, which have had ongoing impacts on socio-political life, both good and bad for future generations. This, no doubt, also sheds light on the ongoing conflicts in the Middle East.

Similarly, he wondered whether guilt and shame among white Australians regarding the way we have treated Australia's original inhabitants might cause defensive reactivity in us. When defensiveness sits in the body, causing discomfort and often unrecognisable sensations, it is usually pushed away rather than being traced to its source or really understood.

It was beneficial for Rick to be present throughout Linda's conversation. It opened up room for him to consider his own defensive reactions to her look. This was something he was able to consider further in other conversations, and on several occasions Linda was able to take her turn to be a witness to his processes.

The Magic Loom at work with Linda and Rick

The conversation started with Linda ready to explore the look on her face that her husband Rick had found intimidating. The Co-weaver opened space so Linda could use her mind and weave in a responsive way to language which focused on externalising the problem body language. When Linda, pictured as Weaver shared her somatic awareness of unusual sensations that related to 'the look', her Co-weaver kept the body space open and a relevant story line was shared. Linda excitedly wove some glittering thread into her fabric. The Co-weaver only had to ask about history and Linda began to weave in more important meanings. She added strong markers as she moved the shuttle and made links between her behaviour in the present and what had occurred in the past. The Co-weaver encouraged Linda to weave swiftly between the body and the mind space as she experimented with a new attitude of kindness towards her sensations. In response to the curious explorative questions asked by the Co-weaver, Linda embroidered her weaving with new understandings about the social assumptions around poverty that had affected her father. Then she chose textures to draw attention to the sense she was making about generational legacies of trauma. This was so pivotal that Linda wove shiny sequins firmly into her fabric, telling stories the next week about embodying her re-authored story in her relationships with two generations, her children and her parents. Rick was so struck by what Linda was weaving that he wove a new fabric of his own as he set about embodying a new narrative in his relationship with her parents.

Clem weaves a path to liberation

Clem and his partner Angela's conversations began separately. They had agreed together to seek therapy but to come individually at first because of the escalating conflict between them.

As I enquired about the reason for his coming, Clem was quite clear about his motivation. He described feeling over-controlled by Angela. Conflict between them kept erupting, yet previously they had had a great relationship. They had had so many hopes and dreams.

I first scaffolded my enquiry in a way that meant he could explore in some detail the nature of these positive dreams. After this, I returned to his first words, and asked Clem to recall his most recent conflict with Angela, and to notice how his reaction to the sense of over-control affected his body.

He could feel a constriction in his chest.

I didn't have to probe much before I heard him describe an image that went with this sensation.

His hands were tied behind his back and he was being told to dance.

It was a powerful image and worth close enquiry.

The image took him straight back in time and place to his very early experiences of his parents bickering. After describing what this was like for him, he went on to describe the parental breakup, which occurred when he was about eight years old.

But the image then took Clem further.

He began to describe his empathy for his mother. He remembered the way he saw her "being controlled and degraded" by her own mother and by her male siblings. He remembered watching powerlessly again and again as his mother was "made into a laughing stock". He told the story of his helpless childhood fury when at a family party he watched his mother again being humiliated by one of her brothers.

As Clem told this narrative I stayed with him, noticing a change in his body language. I enquired about how his body was feeling.

> As he talked about his mother, the sensation in his chest had changed. Now it was feeling kind of hollow and empty. This new sensation led him to begin to talk about his mother's death, which took place not much later, when he was only nine. From that moment his life was never the same. He was sent to live with the family of one of his mother's siblings. It was the uncle who had most put her down.

Before hearing too much about this, I thought it was important to fill out a little more of what his relationship with his mother had meant to him.

> He shared some of the warm details of his mother, but quickly talked more about the loneliness her death brought into his life. His grief almost swallowed him up. All he could recall of that time was that he had to immediately make his way in a totally different world. The family he entered operated according to what he described as "a highly organised and controlling kind of regime". There was no softness or affection, and nobody ever attempted to help him grieve for his mother. Life for him consisted of toeing the line. He had to make sure he never made waves. He was under control.

When I asked about his father, Clem described an absence. He said that he saw very little of him and that he always had the feeling that his father viewed him as an inconvenience.

I suggested we explore more about the meanings of the image his body had brought to mind, but focus our enquiry on the present.

> Clem said it made total sense to him. He could see that any hint of over-control that he might receive from Angela could cause a big reaction in him. It was if he was instantly back under the power of the heartless regime he had described.

Clem's potent metaphor spoke of power misused towards him and earlier towards his mother. Legacies of his mother's trauma were still being activated in his life. In a back-and-forth process, we explored the helplessness he had felt repeatedly at the injustices his mother had suffered and the awful grief he had had to keep under wraps when he lost her.

> It was the loss of a total way of life, and of a set of values about the worth of people, about being relaxed and about seeing life as an adventure.

I was hearing a reflection of the lifestyle and values he had told me about at the beginning of the session, which he had enjoyed with his mother and which, until recently, he and Angela had been establishing together. The story Clem was telling both in his body and through his mind was revealing his absent but implicit determination that the traumas and stresses of his early life would not have the last word (White, 2006). The knowledge that his body was providing about exactly how the past was putting the present in danger was liberating. Clem was clear about which he preferred.

The Magic Loom at work with Clem

In this first therapy conversation with Clem, the mind related space was opened and Clem wove in some shining threads representing his positive relational experience with Angela. Then as his intensely felt complaint towards her was linked with a bodily sensation via the space-making questions asked by the co-Weaver, an image arrived. A body narrative was woven in with the strongly textured thread of metaphor and the Co-weaver opened narrative space so that Clem could weave in the meanings related to what he was exploring. When Clem's body signalled a change in his sensations, he was again able to listen to his body and to his grief as the Co-weaver gave him that space. New threads of information could in turn be explored using the space provided for reflection. Clem was able to embroider a brightly threaded section and to link the early days of beneficence with his mother with hopeful times in the present. He attached a series of strong markers as he wove through the space opened up for mind-led exploration and arrived at new understandings about the nature of triggering and its effects on his most intimate relationship.

Angela deepens her understanding of over-reactivity

As our session started I asked Angela what she meant by the over-reactivity she was talking about.

> *A couple of such events had happened recently. One occurred when Clem was really unwell. As Angela tried to look after him it was as if his importance grew. She found herself feeling totally diminished by this and overwhelmed that he needed her attention.*

> *She recounted what she described as similarly "right over the top" behaviour on a second occasion. She had just returned from her parent's place. As Clem greeted her he seemed really happy. He shared his enjoyment about a whole lot of things he had achieved on their land while she was away. She found herself being totally affronted. She was furious and just wanted to turn her back and walk away from him.*

Angela was talking about automatic reactivity, so I introduced the idea of listening to her sensations. She scrutinised both the situations she had described, recalling how her body had felt each time. On both these occasions Angela identified a tightness in her chest and I couldn't help but note the similarity to the way Clem's body had caught his attention. Yet sensations in the chest, as I later reflected, cued a totally unique set of historical circumstances for each partner.

In response to my request, Angela focused mindfully on the most recent experience of over-reaction and the following memory came into her head.

> *She said that she could see herself at four or five. She was actively trying to make herself sick*

171

because she felt "so left out". Such episodes of "pretending to be sick" were a bit of a theme throughout her childhood.

We began to explore more of her history.

She had the perception or belief that her mother and her older sister were "a tight unit". She was always being told that she would be able to do certain things "when you get older". It seemed to her that she was always excluded from the exciting things. She formed the opinion that her sister, with her very strong personality, was definitely the favourite. In contrast, she felt as if she had to continually vie for her mother's attention.

As I asked what it was like to have her body pinpoint her 'left-out-ness', Angela was also intrigued that what had happened so long ago could turn up now and start to spoil the relationship with Clem which meant so much to her. She talked for some time about the dominance of the narrative of left-out-ness and about the anxiety which had the capacity to go on stressing her in such ways.

The Magic Loom at work with Angela

In this excerpt, the Co-weaver responded to Angela's distress at her over-reactivity by giving her space to weave new awareness through her bodily sensations. A couple of relevant body narratives from childhood emerged enabling her, with the co-Weaver doing her opening work alongside her, to then weave in the brighter threads of understanding she needed. When encouraged to reflect on her somatic experiences, Angela chose a thread with darkly textured but strong colours and recognised how the impacts of the prolonged stress in her childhood had continued to affect her and had recently been the factor which had been threatening her relationship with Clem.

Angela and Clem become newly aware of each other

When they finally came to therapy together, Clem and Angela were able to review the work each had been doing. It was clear that the body-focused narrative therapy exploration with each partner had given both partners an experiential understanding of the origins of their reactivity and the empowering knowledge that the past was being triggered by their present dynamics as a couple. It made complete sense to them both. Their personal reactivity had provided a window on what had deeply affected them in childhood. They each recognised that bodily sensation carried important stories.

As our conversations had continued, both Clem and Angela had responded in particular to the practice of restructuring their bodies, which they found could bring calming relief. I turned my curiosity to ask each of them about sensory activities that each had experienced as calming. Between them, gardening and cooking, building things and listening to music figured largely. Along with movement, they each then experimented by focusing on their senses and they found this practice could settle arousal and help keep them in the present.

Each of them had an innate inner knowledge or wisdom already. It only needed to be noticed and named so that it could come to be more intentionally utilised. I also enquired about other concentrated activities they found soothing and Angela and Clem talked separately about how art activities for one and electronics for the other took them into a different kind of zone. Both could recall times in the past when they had used these kinds of activities to manage stress.

Rothschild (2000) calls these kinds of tasks that require a lot of concentration, oasis activities, suggesting that engaging in such activities can bring balance and refreshment into a person's lifestyle when old trauma is continuing to cause harm.

Both Clem and Angela had earlier shared with me some of the hopes and dreams they had had for their partnership. They had each described how important it was to them to be "growing people". As our conversations continued, there were expressions of real satisfaction and joy as each experienced her or his own cherished growth.

I enquired about what they were now doing differently. They shared that they were refusing to waste time on a blame game that could easily take hold and escalate. They were learning to give each other space.

As I reflected later, it was obvious that, for Clem, traumatic events and griefs had never been resolved. He had been unsupported during vulnerable childhood grief and unfortunate circumstances. Yet the same was true of the longstanding stresses that Angela had experienced in her childhood. Both felt confounded when they were assaulted by sensations and emotions that failed to make sense and which had them so upset and conflicted. Their relationship with each other was being affected because of the way their brain architecture had set itself up in response to early threat, alarm and grief for one of them, and the prolonged nature of stress in and throughout childhood for the other. Both had experienced isolation.

Co-theorists

Helping this couple focus attention on their bodies had them dusting off the cobwebs and making sense of factors that had been below the level of conscious awareness. They showed me that when the therapy conversation is holistic and when self-care starts with the body, the person's own body can help her constitute objectivity and peacefulness for the mind.

This therapy journey wasn't a long one, because Angela and Clem were about to move to a new location. Nonetheless they felt confident that they had established a new freedom to pursue the lifestyle together that both wanted. A new realistic relationship narrative was emerging for them. In coming separately for the early conversations, they had demonstrated to me the importance of

173

working individually when each is triggering the other. Once each person finds effective ways to master the triggers happening within the dynamics of the relationship, they are ready to do some work together.

Later feedback

About twelve months after their short time in therapy, I spoke separately to Clem and to Angela by phone. They separately reported that the changes they had made during our therapy conversations were being sustained.

> *Angela was keen to talk about how she was generating beneficial changes with Clem, and that her relationship with her mother was also in a process of change. As a result of being able to calm what had been a repeated experience of arousal in her nervous system, she had been able to leave behind the old story of 'left-out-ness'. As a direct result of this, she was finding that she could appreciate her mother better in the here and now. She was looking at her with new eyes and when her mother responded with mutuality, she was able to receive her love, her respect and her support. For the first time she was experiencing some of her mother's closeness and warmth.*

I was hearing that resolving early trauma or prolonged stress, and working on removing the power of the past to go on damaging the life of an individual, can bring about change within the most intimate of relationships. It can also spread out to encompass and bring healing within other significant relationships.

Anthony and Elizabeth make sense of their relational conflict

This couple came for therapy because of conflicts they couldn't resolve. The conversation went back and forth, as, in a narrative vein, I asked them to each describe some of the strengths of their relationship. The ensuing discussion proved to be a positive and fruitful foundation for what came next.

> *Anthony clarified that they were also in a business together and that this was the context where conflicts and challenges were blocking their progress. They felt they needed help with communication as they had both had poor role models.*

I again sought some details of the way they did business together that they might describe as strengths. Once again, the strong values they described reminded them that they had many elements of an effective partnership. I had the opportunity to notice and name what I had heard. This narrative approach meant that if early trauma was to be found in their stories, they would be clear about the values and practices to which they were dedicated. They would be holding these in the forefront of their minds.

However, they had come with a problem and soon it was defined. It was at times of decision making and when doubts or concerns arose that they seemed to spin into frustration and mounting

CHAPTER 11 BODY-FOCUSED NARRATIVE THERAPY WITH COUPLES

resentment. Anthony described a recent argument with Elizabeth when he just blew up.

I didn't feel as if I was being heard. It clicked me into a negative headspace. When that happens, I'm bombarded with all sorts of thoughts. My shoulders and neck and back hurt. Then I get headaches, a sort of hypochondria. All I feel like doing is clamming up.

Hearing Anthony describe these tell-tale body sensations, I asked Elizabeth if she would be willing to be a witness to a part of the conversation that would put the focus on Anthony.

This is a helpful narrative approach for work with couples, and the witness who becomes an audience for the other can provide a resonating voice alongside the therapist. Dominantly negative ways of describing a partner can be laid aside as the witness take up an important and hopefully more objective role. Elizabeth was happy to take it on.

Sensing the subjugating impacts of trauma, I asked Anthony if he could once more imagine himself back in the argument with Elizabeth. I asked him to recall the situation with his body that he had described: how he had felt assaulted by neck and shoulder tension, the headiness and a sense that his mouth was closed. I asked him if there was an image that went with what his body was expressing. His reply was swift.

I can see myself. I am standing up to my father. I had been going to the gym, so I could get strong enough. I wanted to show him! I was in his face but then I didn't have to do anything else. He knew I was strong and determined. I was sick of his violence. Mum had been bashed for years and the old man regularly had a go at all three of us kids as well. It was alcohol abuse. My father drank and drank. He didn't care. I just remember I felt absolutely powerless for my whole life. I have to say, the fighting came from both sides.

At this he launched into another memory.

I remember getting woken up at two in the morning. Mum was in the kitchen. She had a pot of water boiling on the stove. She was going to pour it over Dad! I wanted to do it with her. I was seven or eight. But then it stopped. She didn't go through with it.

In line with narrative exploration, I asked Anthony to talk more about his mother.

Although she retaliated against the violence, she was different from Dad. She was completely approachable. You could sit down and talk to her. She had good morals and values. She sort of rose above the abuse.

As I expressed my curiosity about how she did this, Anthony described what happened when he and his siblings got home from school in the afternoons, how they always sat around with mum and told stories. There was a lot of laughter. He continued with greater intensity in his voice.

That's why I feel so ripped off! My mother died. She got motor neurone disease. Life in my teen years just got worse and worse.

175

We sat in the sadness for a moment. His grief was something we would take up again, in a later conversation. After a while Anthony again took up his story.

It wasn't until I was nineteen. That was the day that flew into my mind when you asked for an image. I literally stood up to my father. Physically he could see that I could beat him if it came to a fight. From that day on, the violence towards us kids stopped. But that was years after mum died.

Acts of resistance and reflection from a narrative stance

I asked Anthony what effect he thought his mother's stories, her laughter, her good values, even her act of boiling up the water but then deciding against tipping it over his father had had on him.

It had taught him the value of having a warm loving family. Also, he always puts a high value on safety. It's why if he sees situations of domestic violence in his work [which has him entering the homes of people he works for], he has a habit of quickly stepping into the role of the knight in shining armour. Anthony described how he had learned to be able to hold back on his own power and never to give in to violence. He knows how to restrain himself.

When I asked him how he viewed these attributes of his, Anthony said that he was pleased with the values he had chosen. He was especially happy at always being able to modify his rage.

I asked Anthony if he was aware of ways he had that helped to calm himself when he became upset. He had been recognising the benefits of spending time in his shed doing physical work. It always helped him calm down. Movement of any sort was useful.

I invited him to experiment with a strategy called body re-structuring and we stood up together. I asked Anthony to recall again the moment when he blew up in the argument with his wife. I asked him to consciously notice how his feet gripped the ground and then to practise tightening his thigh muscles.

Anthony reported that his spine became straighter and his chin and his head came up. This kind of stance was making him feel solid instead of sick.

I asked about his breath.

It seemed to have settled back to natural instead of being rushed and tight. Change happened quickly. He said he felt more relaxed already.

Simply restructuring and feeling his body's musculature in these simple ways helped Anthony to calm his triggered arousal himself (Rothschild, 2000).

We were coming close to the end of the conversation. We discussed together what action Anthony thought he might take if he and Elizabeth got into the same impasse again.

Anthony said that he knew he wouldn't be able to speak but he might be able to make a signal, a time out 'T' sign with his hands, which he demonstrated. This could be a way of letting Elizabeth know that he needed time out to calm himself down and that she didn't need to take it personally.

I asked if Anthony thought it was any wonder after the years of family violence that he could still get so wound up. He said, "No. It's no wonder I feel like this!"

I asked him if he could remind himself of this whenever he felt stirred up, like a sort of mantra and I saw Anthony relax in his seat.

> *That would be great. I think it would help me separate the present from the past. It is no wonder I react. Now I know why, I might still need some time out. But I'm pretty quick. I think I could do it. I can. I can get on top of it.*

I drew Elizabeth back into the conversation asking her what it had been like to witness Anthony's stories and the process of listening to his body and the images and memories it stored. She said that it opened her heart up to him. It had always made her sad to think about what he had gone through as a child. It had always touched her.

> *Her respect for Anthony had gone even higher as she listened to what he had said during the session. She had known for a while that it was the past that had its ways of messing them up. It kept intruding, but she hadn't known how it did that. Now she could understand more about what was going on. She felt very hopeful because of Anthony's good values. She described some of the ways he lived them out. He was a very loyal person and she trusted him to work on his way of reacting to things.*

It was interesting to hear Elizabeth become a mirror as she talked about Anthony's values. There was a chance for him to experience this resonance.

From her angle, Elizabeth said that she had learnt that she could take greater care to listen calmly to Anthony's points of view, rather than getting triggered by them herself and allowing conflicts to escalate out of control.

Anthony seemed to have a natural awareness of his body and its sensations. I wondered if it was because he hadn't been educated into a Western mindset, as he came to Australia as an adult. As the story demonstrates, he was amazingly quick not only to grow in awareness of his body's signals and his triggered behaviours, but also to begin to utilise the body strategies that were helpful to him.

Later feedback

The depth of developmental trauma in Anthony's past and the years of impotent rage had been taking its toll on more than his relationship with Elizabeth. Not long after the therapy conversations, he suddenly found himself in a medical crisis. Part of his bowel had to be removed because it had become 'dead'. Despite numerous tests, the doctors had no medical explanation for this.

When I caught up with him and Elizabeth a couple of months afterwards, there was excitement in the air. Anthony had visited a practitioner educated in Chinese medicine, who understood about psychosomatic illness. He considered that Anthony was the expert on his own life and that his body held truth for him.

As a result of this practitioner's investigative questions, Anthony's highly anxious stomach was pinpointed as perhaps his most sensitive body signal. It managed to let him know loud and clear that he was being triggered. It was as if his stomach first set off a volcanic eruption of activity in his mind, and then Anthony's thinking would go into a whirl.

What he prescribed was a different way of reinforcing Anthony's awareness of its signalling. He requested that Anthony keep a record each time he noticed his stomach acting up. When it happened, he was to ask himself about any stress he had experienced in the immediate or recent past and to make the links. Anthony said:

> *What I've realised is that it's not all about the science. It's about me. I'm learning to be really aware of my own body. I'm getting tuned into it.*

This practitioner also provided another body strategy. It was a quality of deep rhythmic massage, which set out to release the high level of constriction present in Anthony's internal organs (Masarik-Williams, Polizzi, & Punshon, 2016). After only three sessions much of this constriction was released, and after only the first massage session, his chronic sleep difficulties seemed to disappear. Being able to get a full night's sleep was having amazing benefits.

Both Elizabeth and Anthony talked about how awareness of his body had helped Anthony better manage the rage that had been an almost daily phenomenon. Its emotional and verbal expressions in the past had sometimes been frightening, even though they never led to actual physical violence. Now, for example, at family meals it no longer erupted to spoil the liveliness and enjoyment.

Anthony told a similar before and after account of his rage.

> *He described how being treated with contempt in any way by a tradesman would have had him fuming and then ranting and raving in his mind for hours. Only that week, something of this kind had occurred, but in complete contrast he had found himself responding to it with humour. Then, in contrast to the past, the encounter and the rage it triggered was over.*

Anthony's action patterns and behaviours were lining up with the good values he so greatly preferred. As a range of neuroscientists and therapists suggest, it seemed to me that Anthony was providing lived experience of the benefits of including a person's internal sensory experience, body reactivity and body narratives in therapy in order to truly resolve past trauma (Masarik-Williams, Polizzi, Punshon, 2016; Ogden, 2015; Porges, 2011; Schore, 2003; van der Kolk, 2006).

Anthony also told me about some unexpected validation that the massage practitioner gave him about both the strength of his body and of his intelligence. Earlier in my conversations with him, he had told me about the time in his adolescence when his father refused to sign papers that would have allowed him to represent his country at the Olympics!

Now, he said that as a result of the personal validation of this male professional, this old disappointment was losing its power over him. He talked about now being able to imagine a world of new opportunity and challenge and a very different kind of future.

The personal validation of a community-minded professional was providing resonance for Anthony. This reminded me of the importance of the village or the wider community in helping a survivor of prolonged family violence to be able to not only recover but also to be able to build an alternative narrative.

The Magic Loom at work with Anthony and Elizabeth

Anthony initially began to weave through the body space, drawing attention to his body's strong reactivity during a marital argument. The Co-weaver as a result made this reactivity the focus, and asked Elizabeth to take up the role of witness. She hoped Anthony might experience Elizabeth's added support as he wove his personal fabric.

The Co-weaver helped Anthony thicken the threads he was weaving through the space given for body awareness. Then she opened the complementary space for him to reflect. He began to use his shuttle, powerfully picking up threads of different, sometimes dark, colour as he made sense of his childhood history of family violence and grief. The Co-weaver kept the mind-focused space open and Anthony chose a shining thread to make a strong contrast as he explored precious values he had picked up from his mother.

As the Co-weaver opened space for his body, Anthony used strong layers of threads when he discovered that he could re-structure his body to settle unwelcome arousal. Inviting Anthony to weave by giving space to his body again allowed him to add a glittering thread marking an 'aha moment' when he understood how present dynamics in the marriage/business partnership had routinely been triggering somatic impacts and unhelpful behaviours. The past was still in play. This was pivotal. Anthony wove new threads through both spaces, perhaps adding a marker to his fabric that meant the important stand he was making was not going to be forgotten. He was explicit about his intention to embody an alternative narrative.

Elizabeth was given the opportunity to briefly weave her own threads of experience and understanding through both body and mind spaces. She wove in her observations as a witness. She reported finding some new threads of understanding of her own that chimed in with what she was seeing in Anthony. She was already entertaining the idea that she could begin to weave her own life fabric differently. She was clearly being transported as a result of what she has witnessed.

Chapter 12
Body-focused Narrative Therapy with Children, Adolescents and Families

When we are excited, and our excitement is accepted and supported, we develop attitudes that expand our boundaries. We reach out …. Stanley Keleman

As a body-focused narrative approach helps a person who has experienced early developmental trauma to learn to trust her body again, it can be a particularly helpful approach for a child or young person. Healing the effects of trauma through finding the language for what she is holding in her body can help to her to rebuild her self-confidence, so she is better resourced for making life-enhancing decisions as she faces the challenges of adolescence and early adulthood.

Amy builds her own safe boundaries

Sixteen-year-old Amy came for help some weeks after a stressful event had occurred in her life. Her mother and step-father were worried about her, and Amy herself also recognised that she needed some help. She seemed stuck. She wasn't getting over what had happened. She was having difficulty functioning. In fact, she seemed to be reacting in an over-emotional way to everything.

> *Amy told how during a sleepover party, she fell asleep late at night on one of the beds. Others were asleep on the floor on either side of her bed. In the morning, she was distressed to discover her jeans had been undone. A friend told her that one of the boys had been all over her and*

fumbling her while she slept. After a couple of weeks Amy was still feeling shut down, extremely scattered and wanting to sleep all the time. She was doing her best to keep her mind off what had happened or might have happened. She found herself wanting to keep on the move all the time. She couldn't focus on her school work and was worried about getting behind.

It was clear that Amy was struggling emotionally, but it was unclear whether it was the presenting story that was the major issue or if there was more. I sensed that what Amy needed most at this stage was to be fully heard.

She told me that she had confronted the boy in question. She felt a bit confused by his denial of the touching. But she said that in the end the event at the party didn't seem such a big deal. Everybody had been drinking that night. Nothing really sinister had happened to her. She wasn't interested in taking allegations any further.

When Amy raised the issue of how much alcohol had been imbibed, she was ready to engage in a narrative-style exploration about what she was perceiving more clearly to be problems associated with the use of alcohol and drugs in youth society. She expressed a great deal of relief as the first conversation came to an end.

The next week when Amy arrived it was her inability to function properly that continued to be her worry.

She began the conversation by describing a blow up that she had with her mother. She couldn't understand why her rage over "nothing much at all" had been so extreme. It was particularly hard for her to understand, because in dealing with the incident at the party she had been feeling incredibly supported by both her mum and her step-dad.

I asked if we could focus on the incident with her mother. Introducing the body scaffold, I asked Amy to describe her sensations right at the moment the rage surfaced. She said she had found herself grinding her teeth. Her fists were clenching and unclenching.

I was so angry, I just wanted to throw, smash and rip. Then I got sad and there was a lump in my throat.

Without further prompting she began talking about an incident that had taken place when she was twelve.

She had been staying at her father's place. Her father had an argument with his girlfriend and during it he hit the girlfriend and threw her mobile phone across the room. Amy described how traumatised and shocked she had been. The girlfriend had a new baby and Amy remembered snatching the baby up and running up to her room. She managed to shut the door and she pushed the wardrobe up against it. She said that she was panicking and finding it hard to breathe. She stayed there for a long time keeping the baby safe. Evidently the girlfriend called the police. It wasn't till they arrived that Amy ventured back downstairs. She sat on the stairs, and although she was crying, she was able to overhear what was happening and every word that was said. She described how her father "talked his way out of the whole thing".

At this her anger erupted.

I just hated it; the way he could rewrite history. He's so good at that and it confuses me. At other times he used to be so good at calming me down when I was in a state. When I heard him talk himself out of the assault that night, it's, like, it took my breath away. Luckily Mum and my step-dad came and got me immediately. They agreed that I didn't have to go back to Dad's. I haven't been back there since it happened.

I asked Amy to think a bit more about her history with her father.

She shared about some good times, but also about how they were often spoiled. Then she recalled that the best thing about being with her dad was that she was often able to be with the rest of his family.

She talked a lot about the wider family and I asked her about her choices.

She was forming the opinion that she could choose against a family relationship that did her harm and in favour of others that were good for her.

I asked Amy to think about exactly what factors keep her safe.

She was coming to the conclusion that it was about having strong boundaries. This related to her father. He often caused her confusion and fear. Being alone with him didn't feel safe. She said that occasionally she could talk to him on the phone, but she didn't want to be in a situation where he was in control of her.

I asked her about where her trust could safely be placed.

Amy shared about the family she lived with, but also a lot about her extended family on her father's side. She felt they were all people she could really trust. They had integrity. She gave specific examples of this.

I was hearing the inner wisdom of this young girl as she sifted her relationships, and, in narrative terms, 're-membered' her life. She wanted to be surrounded by healthy influencers.

It was important to explore whether Amy had ways of calming herself that had proved helpful in the past. This narrative conversation led into to a longer conversation about stress and trauma and its impacts.

Amy talked about music and art. Music is a big thing for her and it always made her feel good.

I asked Amy about any similarities she could notice about her emotions after the party event and how she had felt when her father hit his girlfriend.

Amy felt they brought feelings to the surface that were very similar.

I helped her to again focus on the rage that had erupted with her mother that week because it was so recent and accessible to memory.

As she remembered the teeth grinding and the way her fists were clenching and unclenching, and then got in touch with wanting to throw, smash and rip and finally the sadness experienced as a lump in her throat, Amy was able to pay attention to her breathing in a similar way to her patterns when she prepares to sing in public. She found she could settle the intense arousal down quite quickly.

Amy again took up my question about similarities between her two stressful experiences.

She could now see that the recent event had taken her back to the confusion and the powerlessness she had felt when her dad was so violent and so two-faced. Her panic had kept on recycling. After the recent events she hadn't known if she could trust the boy's version of events. Had someone been lying? She was also understanding the way even a minor frustration with her mother could suddenly set her panic going. She was eager to find strategies to manage it. Otherwise it could take over.

From this time on, I worked with Amy so that she could practice settling arousal and its over-reactive symptoms. She did a lot of work noticing her breathing and the body signals of anger, which she was now more aware of in her body system. She really hated being at the mercy of overwhelming anxiety and those sudden bursts of emotion she hadn't had the power to control.

Gradually life settled down. Amy reported that she was doing her homework again. She could concentrate well, and her friendships were thriving. She told me how she had changed her friendship group and was establishing new friendships with people who were closer to her in what she thought mattered in life.

I led her in an enquiry about her values and soon noticed that the values she had articulated were guiding the way she was putting her boundaries in place. She felt she was moving forward. There was a lot of music going on and Amy could lose herself in it. She was preparing for a gig as the lead singer with her band. Her step-dad was helping her with organising the sound equipment. She was so grateful to him and to her mum.

In narrative and somatic terms, Amy seemed to be embodying a new narrative. She was feeling as if she had been able to put the past behind her. It was no wonder she had had such a long, drawn-out reaction. But now she had got herself back.

As I reflected on Amy's process I couldn't help noticing the importance of breath. Her father's behaviour "took her breath away" and her alternative story took shape as she modulated intense sensations, emotions and behavioural impulses by focusing on her breathing in an intentional way that was healthy and already familiar to her.

CHAPTER 12 BODY-FOCUSED NARRATIVE THERAPY WITH CHILDREN, ADOLESCENTS AND FAMILIES

The Magic Loom at work with Amy

In the first conversation the lingering effects of a stressful event were obvious and the Co-weaver gave Amy the space in her enquiry to help her make her understanding visible and to thicken threads of trust. When, at the start of the second conversation, Amy described extreme over-reactivity over a minor conflict with her mother, the Co-weaver opened space for Amy's body and the memory of a triggered early trauma was cued. Amy wove into her fabric some entirely new threads, tying some together to mark her new awareness. Then, threads of understanding were also woven in as a result of a thorough contextual mind-opening exploration. The discovery of a triggering dynamic of deceit warranted a strongly textured section. Through the narrative mind space, Amy was able to weave in threads denoting her values and she discovered these were diametrically opposed to the dishonesty she had found in both the present and the past dynamics. The Co-weaver opened space to shift enquiry so Amy could also begin to take in the witness of nourishing supporters in her life. Thereafter, the weaving moved rapidly between the mind and body, so that narrative exploration and body-based calming strategies could be mindfully explored and practised. Amy was quietly weaving new internal trust into her fabric, and this showed up in the changes she began to make in her friendship circle. Her newly woven fabric bore witness to her re-authored narrative that revealed her intention to both keep herself safe relationally and to embody the values she prefers.

Heidi writes her own counter-document

Fifteen-year-old Heidi's mother had sent her to have some therapy conversations because she seemed to be sabotaging her own happiness. She handled conflict with her siblings poorly.

In our discussion, Heidi did some thinking about her life on the home front. I asked her whether she agreed with her mother's idea of self-sabotage. If so, what did it look like?

> She had said that perhaps her mother had a point. When her brother or sister upset her, she could really fly off the handle.

This prompted me to ask about the anger and its tactics.

> Heidi began to talk about how sometimes the anger made her smoulder inside (sort of in a sulk), then it would have her setting her mind at finding ways to get back on the others. She often did it by pestering them till they wouldn't take it anymore.

Heidi appeared to be identified with this pattern of behaviour. I asked her if it had a name and after a bit of thought, she came up with the name 'the push and pull problem'.

I thought that researching another landscape might be helpful, so I enquired if this push and pull problem ever turned up at school, and if it did, could she describe how she handled it.

> *Heidi said it didn't turn up as much as it did at home. However, she remembered a recent argument with a friend. She recalled that she had taken off and gone for a walk. She found herself looking for birds with which she was familiar. After a while she was okay, and she returned to her group.*

I asked Heidi what it was like to see the way she had used her own power to get herself back so that push and pull problem didn't have the last say.

> *She seemed surprised that she had done this. It felt good.*

We had a conversation about other ways she might be able to win if there was a battle with push and pull, especially at home.

Here is what she wrote as the upshot of this part of our conversation.

- The minute trouble starts I can go for a walk. I love nature. I can notice things like the types of birds I see.
- I can slow my breathing down.
- If I can stop the push and pull of anger at school, I can do it at home as well.
- Push and pull (sulking and getting my own back) keeps sabotaging me.
- I can be in charge instead of the old pattern.
- Maybe I can talk to mum or ring a friend.

In this conversation with Heidi, I had made use of several narrative approaches: calling on witnesses, the practice of externalising, and seeking out detail from arenas other than the problem-saturated one. I also drew Heidi into narrative therapy's documenting practice. I was fascinated at how intuitively Heidi turned to her body to find ways to put the brakes on an arousal pattern that could routinely sabotage her life. Narrative approaches brought body strategies to light for her.

Levine (1997) tells the story of a group of children who were kidnapped and then imprisoned in an underground bunker. One child was able to minimise the traumatic impact of what happened because he actively mobilised his body to dig his way out. The outcomes for this boy contrasted strongly with those of others in the group who remained passive. This story helped to convince researchers that sometimes traumatic energy needs to be discharged. When it remains undischarged it continues to burden the nervous system into the future.

I knew a little about the family violence Heidi had witnessed all her life, and now I was seeing that she could begin to discharge arousing emotions that might be linked to traumatic impacts as simply as by intentionally going for a walk and watching out for the birds she loved.

At the end of our conversation, Heidi took up the suggestion that she write down some things she didn't want to forget from what we had discussed.

CHAPTER 12 BODY-FOCUSED NARRATIVE THERAPY WITH CHILDREN, ADOLESCENTS AND FAMILIES

In addition to her list of strategies above, she also wrote the following list of her qualities, which had arisen as I asked her how some of her friends and teachers would describe her. She wrote:

- I am good at making friends and at keeping them
- I know how to make up after a fight
- I have the capacity to put something I want aside because I don't want to lose a relationship
- I like learning new things
- I like to discover things, e.g., science
- I enjoy interacting with my teachers
- I have a good sense of humour
- I am flexible
- I can cope with major change.

The Magic Loom at work with Heidi

This conversation with an adolescent involved a different type of weaving. Early trauma while implicit was never explicitly identified in the therapy conversation. When the Co-weaver opened space for Heidi to consider her own body-based calming strategy in the territory of school, this became the foundation for mind-opening curiosity and co-research. The Co-weaver could then help Heidi find ways to use both her reflective and her recording capacities to transfer body –based calming strategies from one territory of her life into another.

Mindy provides holistic support for her children

This story illustrates how body-focused narrative approaches can be transmitted from a therapist to a parent who, having found ways to combat some of the inroads of early trauma in her own life, is in a good position to support her children to do the same. Narrative therapists are interested in extending therapeutic benefits in this open-ended way.

Mindy had discovered that her young son Larry was being bullied at school. She had visited the school, and the teachers were working to help him in that environment. However, Larry's behaviour at home was causing trouble.

Together Mindy and I explored the nature of the problems.

> Mindy articulated her sense that the bullying was possibly having a triggering effect on her young son's nervous system, because all his life had been lived in a context (at home) that had been characterised by bullying and violence. Perhaps this complexity was magnifying his emotions and his feelings of helplessness and this was resulting in behaviours of his own that went out of control.

187

THE MAGIC LOOM PART TWO - THE PRACTICE

Mindy had worked on her own fears using the narrative philosophy of externalisation and we discussed this kind of process in some detail.

When she returned the next week, Mindy described the way Larry would run around the house, refusing food, and shouting and hitting out at anyone who got in his way. She reported having to stay calm herself so that eventually she could get him to sit down and talk. Together they had eventually found a name for what was going on. They called it the "gallop behaviour".

Larry was then able to think about the effects of the behaviour. It was causing disruption to everyone in the family. When she got him talking about how it was affecting him she invited Larry to remember how things had been before the gallop behaviour started. He came to the conclusion that he preferred the more peaceful and cooperative way of being that he could definitely remember. In fact, he hated the gallop behaviour. It was just that, once it started he felt like he just couldn't stop.

Mindy was using classic narrative approaches with her son. She told me that she could understand where he was coming from, having been through it herself. We then discussed some of the body strategies that had helped her and ways she might encourage Larry to set up his own experiments.

Mindy started by helping Larry to notice his breathing. She taught him to breathe deeply. It was a strategy that related well to the family practice of music, especially to singing or blowing a wind instrument. Mindy knew from her own experience how it had helped her to settle her own nervous system arousal. She talked to Larry about the idea that he was losing himself in the times of gallop behaviour. She encouraged him to find ways to get himself back. The strategies they explored included going for a walk outside, having a drink of water or taking refuge in his own room where he could punch a pillow.

Mindy said that Larry's motivation grew and sometimes he managed to discover his own unique strategies of calming or grounding himself. One day she found him, for example, gazing at a letter of appreciation his teacher had taken the time to write for him. He said that reading it made him feel better. Sometimes concentrating on a project in his room or playing his trombone or pounding on the drums also helped.

Things improved. Mindy worked at being consistent over time and the gallop behaviour, along with Larry's sense of powerlessness ebbed away. She saw new friendships develop for Larry at school. There were improvements both at home and in the classroom. Mindy reported that she saw her eight-year-old become again the loving and happy boy he much preferred to be.

When I saw Mindy quite some time after the upheaval of a family move, which also entailed moving schools, she related that Larry's aggressive behaviours were galloping again. She was faced with an ongoing challenge. But she recognised that she had experienced this kind of repetitive cycle in her own journey. She understood the importance of reinforcement. Old neural mechanisms aren't easy to change. She also reported again the importance of staying calm herself and of consistently putting boundaries in place that limited the aggression.

188

The tree meditation

Rothschild's (2010, pp. 135–140) tree meditation is a strategy that many parents, like Mindy, have found helpful for a child who is experiencing bullying.

Perhaps its benefits lie in the fact that the parent kneels in front of the child and gently holds the tops of her feet, while engaging her meditatively in conversation about the qualities of a well-rooted tree. The child is experiencing this family support in a very tangible and embodied way. It is the kind of touch that is safe and anchoring. When the child strengthens her thigh muscles in line with feeling the strength of the tree trunk, and takes into herself the felt sense of rootedness as her parent's hands hold the tops of her feet, she may develop the somatic felt sense of rootedness. She is using her imagination and engaging mind and body with the metaphor.

The tree can be explored in a multifaceted way. It can move and sway with the onslaught of a big wind without losing its grip on the earth. Its roots can be pictured reaching as deep and as wide as its canopy stretches into the sky. Its strong tall trunk provides a sense of solidity, which matches her sensations, standing tall with strength in her muscle-toned thighs. The sense of being like a tree is on the way to becoming experiential because the mindful meditation invites complexity. The child develops a body experience of feeling grounded. With the twin supports of sensation and image, being like a tree is easy to remember and to summon at will. The child can be invited to talk about how her rooted strength like a tree might be of help if a bully turns up.

This is a different way to raise awareness of the body. Like all somatic experiencing, it tends to aid and accelerate cognitive process. In terms of language and imagination, it draws on a child's strengths.

An audience for a teenager

Just prior to an interstate move away from the family home, there was a different problem to solve. Mindy was concerned for her teenager, Becky, who needed support for more than one reason.

Rather than tackling the problem alone, she decided to give her daughter an audience. She called a meeting between herself and the other young women in the family. Mindy told me that there was a clear sense around the caring circle of women that the respectful and trusting values she had been modelling were resonating within her family. There was a genuine sense of collaboration.

I reflected that Mindy had moved away from the territory of isolation, in which negative internal processes and labels like 'failure' had dominated her story. Since starting at university, she had taken up a more socially interactive model.

She told me how impressed she was with the surprising depth and hopefulness that arose from the time of communal storytelling she had instigated. Her teenager let go of defensiveness and was visibly touched by being heard and supported. The process was able to help her move forward.

Mindy was showing me as she shared more of the details, just how a parent can make use of an array of narrative and body-focused strategies with the collegial therapist at one step removed. She could pass on her own experience-near discoveries, so that the impacts of prolonged stress and trauma on her children could begin to give way to a hopeful re-authoring of life narratives.

The Magic Loom at work with Mindy, Larry and Becky

Mindy became the Co-weaver herself when she opened space for her eight-year-old, with his already close connection to her, to find a name for a problem. Larry explored the effects on himself and others of the "gallop behaviour" in an externalising way, and then wove in a very strong thread as he took a stand and named his own alternative preference. When Mindy, as Co-weaver, opened space for his body Larry experimented weaving into his own tapestry some of the best ways he knew to defeat the gallop behaviour and to get himself back. Mindy enabled Larry to find positive threads for his life fabric by involving herself with his school.

It was clear that as she took up her role with Larry and then later with Becky, Mindy's fabric had been woven clear and strong. She was embodying her own new narrative and a set of values that were community-inclusive. When she gathered an audience for Becky she found that family members were tuning in to her. She had moved herself out of isolation. Providing her teenage daughter with an audience gave Becky space to experience the attunement and the resonancing that comes with a respectful audience. She too could begin to weave her way out of isolation.

Owen finds empowerment and connection

Some months after her own therapy conversations came to an end, Pearl returned to talk about her concerns for her oldest child, Owen, who was nine years old. She described some struggles she was having in her role as a single mum, particularly towards the end of each day. Owen had a way of collapsing and refusing to take on any share of the family responsibilities. Then he would become angry and dig his heels in. After some discussion, we agreed to include Owen in some conversations on his own and with both his parents present.

In one of the conversations that resulted I asked Owen about whether there were any problems he was facing. He immediately talked about getting angry.

I wanted him to be able to be more specific, so I first enquired about where he was when 'the anger' usually arrived. I also wanted Owen to understand that his anger didn't define him. It could be externalised and looked at more easily.

Owen was able to locate some specifics. It sometimes arrived at home and sometimes at soccer.

CHAPTER 12 BODY-FOCUSED NARRATIVE THERAPY WITH CHILDREN, ADOLESCENTS AND FAMILIES

I asked him about the idea of giving the anger a name, and Owen said that sometimes it was a bit like "a raging beast".

I expressed my curiosity, asking if he had found any ways to deal with this raging beast.

> Owen started talking about soccer. He said that when it came along in the middle of a soccer game, what he had to do was concentrate on his part of the play. If he did that he could get rid of it.

I enquired about how doing this made him feel.

> Owen expressed some pleasure and surprise that he had worked this out. He went on to say that sometimes the angry beast also turned up when his dad put him on a wave at the surf and he got thrown off. The beast disappeared when he noticed that he was secretly enjoying the battle with the waves. Right at that moment he really wanted his dad to keep on helping him to keep going.

I asked him to say more about the secret enjoyment.

> Owen liked that it was something only he knew about.

I wondered aloud whether there was also a secret way of beating the angry beast, for instance, when it turned up with his mother.

> Owen said that he didn't like it turning up with his mum because it made her sad. He didn't know any secret about this.

I suggested that we reflect a bit about more about his knowing about how to beat the beast at soccer.

> Owen said that in soccer winning or losing wasn't the main thing but trying hard was. He had some ideas about what it means to him to be a good team member. This was where getting the beast out of the way was important, so he could pull his weight for the team.

We talked some more about the trying hard and being a good team member.

> Owen said it made him feel good.

When I asked what it was like to have all this secret know-how about how to get the beast out of the way.

> Owen said he really liked that.

I asked him if his know how about beasts at soccer and in the surf could be of help at home.

> Owen said he would have to think about it.

Owen was showing me the inner wisdom of a young child who knew more than he thought he knew (White, 2004) and reinforced the benefits of narrative curiosity about different territories and inner wisdom.

191

THE MAGIC LOOM PART TWO - THE PRACTICE

In a different conversation one day, when both his parents had come along, Owen became interested in beating another beast. After some discussion as a group, the name 'the collapse thingy' seemed to everyone to be the best way to describe the phenomenon.

Owen had a sense that this thingy often seemed to take over.

His mum had reported that it was as if Owen suddenly became exhausted. He "couldn't manage another thing" even if he had just been tearing about outside full of energy, and he could immediately perk up if friends arrived. Both his mum and dad had seen this thingy at work, and it was nearly always in the family arena.

As the collapse thingy had been described in very physical terms, I asked Owen if he would mind if everyone had a go at working out what it looked and felt like.

With his agreement we all practised taking on the body shape (configuration) of collapse. Owen sat in the chair and draped himself over it. His parents also let their bodies slump. I joined in. Then everyone tried out how it felt to do the opposite.

Owen sat up very straight. He lifted his chin up and straightened his shoulders.

Everyone in the room did this experiment a few times, trying to notice how the ground felt under our feet when we sat with straight backs and pushed our feet onto the floor.

Then we stood up to practise the feel of the collapse thingy. We noticed what it felt like to tighten up our thigh muscles and we thought about how our feelings changed when we changed our bodies away from a slump.

Owen didn't have much to say but he seemed intrigued.

Ogden (2016) describes the way unhelpful body patterns can arise early. Because of the body's own wisdom, she claims that a little change can change everything. Pearl gave me some feedback.

Owen was enjoying re-structuring his body whenever Pearl prompted him, particularly when the collapse thingy seemed to be taking over. He seemed to become very engaged by his new power.

Pearl said she had also helped him to experiment with movement as a strategy that Owen could choose himself at any moment. He could go outside and run right around the house. Doing this seemed to make a difference. The collapse thingy was losing its power.

Calling on witnesses

In a later conversation with Owen and his mum, I suggested that it might be interesting to call on witnesses to Owen's life. I asked him if he could help me make a list of people who knew a bit about him and who might like to be of help. The following letter (Morgan, 2006) ended up going to two of

192

CHAPTER 12 BODY-FOCUSED NARRATIVE THERAPY WITH CHILDREN, ADOLESCENTS AND FAMILIES

his grandparents, a beloved pre-school teacher and a neighbour as well as to an elderly gentleman who had once helped Owen do some woodwork, which he had really enjoyed.

> *I have been meeting with Owen and his mum and dad to help with some problems they are facing together. Owen says that you are an important person in his life, so we are asking for your input.*

> *I have heard some interesting things about Owen and what he stands for and I'm curious to discover more details about these things. I'd be keen to hear anything you know about Owen's commitments for his life, for example:*

> - *Which commitments catch your attention?*
> - *What images come into your mind?*
> - *Why do you think this has struck a chord for you?*
> - *Is there a little story of Owen that gives evidence of his commitments?*
> - *When did you witness these things?*
> - *How has knowing that Owen stands for these things contributed to your life?*
> - *How has knowing Owen changed you? What might you do differently as a result of knowing these stories for example? What has thinking of these stories reminded you of?*

> *I hope you are willing to help out with this. If you could send me just some rough notes as soon as you can, we will read them out to Owen during another of our sessions and ask him and his mum and dad some questions about their reactions.*

I am including verbatim part of just one of the very helpful emails and letters that came in response. This one was from his pre-school teacher.

> *When I think of you, Owen, two words always come to mind: respectful and wise. You were always respectful to everyone you encountered, and you showed wisdom that inspired myself and others to be the best they could be.*

> *I remember one particular day when we were all playing in the hall with Lego and other construction toys. Do you remember the Lego bikes we had Owen? We only had two bikes and all the boys wanted to use them. You were playing with one bike and another boy wanted it and tried to take it from you. You looked him in the eye and said something like this. "No, I'm using it, but I'll give it to you when I've finished with it." True to your word, a few minutes later you gave it to the other boy. I thought that was so respectful and fair of you. I felt proud of you.*

> *You were often the 'voice of reason' among the boys back in the day, Owen. One day you came and sat beside me in the sandpit. You said, they're playing with sticks around there, someone might get hurt … You understood that it wasn't safe.*

> *All the children admired your sense of justice and your desire for everyone to get along. The truth is, Owen, when you were away sometimes on holiday, someone would always ask, "When is Owen getting back?" Your friends looked to you for leadership and you never let*

193

them down ... I remember your kindness you showed younger children, especially your little sister, and the pride you showed when you conquered a new skill like writing your name or jumping from the high beam ...

You made a huge contribution to the preschool community, Owen, and I'm glad I had the privilege to watch that part of your life unfold. You always made me feel that, with kids like you around, the world would be in great hands.

The other responses were also detailed and provided stories of similar interest. When these were read aloud, Owen and his parents reminisced about things they either hadn't thought about or hadn't remembered for a long time. Sometimes the memories had them laughing uproariously together. While he had few words to describe his feelings about them, Owen's body language expressed his delight at what the witnesses had to say about his life. He was, I observed, experiencing the sense of being surrounded and supported.

Certificates

At the end of the therapy conversations, the letters were included with a certificate in a folder as a record of his qualities, which also included a description of Owen's ability to "beat raging beasts and thingies". He could continue to refer to this documentation long after our conversations came to an end.

In a collaboration with Michael White about narrative therapy with children and their families, Alice Morgan (2006) says:

As families and children have told me of the many positive ways that audiencing practices have contributed to their lives ... I now make sure that finding an audience is one thing that doesn't get missed (p. 108).

The narrative idea of providing an audience is a practice that brings body and mind approaches together. It allows the child to have a lived experience of both body attunement and resonance.

Pearl gave me the following feedback.

I felt there was a shift in Owen's attitude after the time we all spent in therapy and shared the letters written about him and for him. Firstly, he seemed to have more awareness of how much he is loved. Not only by myself and his father, who were both present, but by all who shared their thoughts and feelings by email and mail.

Owen seemed to find life more manageable after these sessions. The difficult behaviour I had been experiencing with him prior to our shared conversations lessened. I felt he was less worked up by situations and was better able to control himself. I think he felt more safe and in turn felt more settled.

CHAPTER 12 BODY-FOCUSED NARRATIVE THERAPY WITH CHILDREN, ADOLESCENTS AND FAMILIES

A few months later this work again became important for Pearl and Owen. Night time fears, which Owen had struggled with for a long time, seemed to be escalating. He was hearing scary voices. Pearl and I talked about the phenomenon of dissociation. Perhaps memories not available cognitively were being triggered at night and anxious imaginings were causing his anxiety (autonomic nervous system arousal).

As I helped Pearl reflect on the calming body strategies she had learnt to put into practice in her own life, she began to help Owen further. She practised the body restructure and other movement strategies with Owen. She could refer to his folder and remind him of his confidence, his bravery and his humour, and his secret ability to beat troubling emotions. Together and separately, even sometimes secretly, effective ways to manage arousal in the primitive parts of Owen's brain were becoming part of his own bag of resources. Soon she communicated her sense that Owen was learning to soothe himself and responding well to the idea that he could easily get himself back. His night time fears had subsided.

It was clear to me that the way Pearl had changed her own life narrative, partly by understanding the roots of her own traumatic fear and rage was now helping her to understand and help her son in his responses to stress. Moreover, it was happening while he was still young. She was finding a way she could help him change his storying pattern. Endless unconscious triggering and entrenched negative dominance might be brought to an end instead of plaguing him into adulthood.

The Magic Loom at work with Owen

Owen's mind was engaged when he was invited to externalise a problem he was having with the emotion of anger. Exploring different territories, particularly his favoured soccer zone, enabled him to begin to weave a re-authoring process, nimbly transferring wisdom from one zone into another.

The second conversation concerned a body problem, which was again externalised and given a name. Owen was accompanied by his parents who joined him in a playful body-restructuring game. This too had re-authoring potential and it could take place because space had been provided for him to become aware of his body. Owen began to weave into one fabric what his body was doing with what he was saying and thinking.

The Co-weaver called on witnesses to Owen's life by sending a letter, which set the parameters of both mind and body and their inter-weavings. When Owen and his parents received and shared the witness statements about Owen's life, they participated in both the weaving in of the sense of bodily attunement and the possibility that Owen in particular could experience resonance and weave it through the reflective mind space.

> Weaving using body awareness became a priority for Owen when he was later experiencing night time terrors. His mother became his Co-weaver and helped him by opening space in which he could use his body resources and weave calm into the fabric of his life to counter some early very influential fears.

Carly discovers a sense of significance and equality

Carly's mum and dad were worried. They reported that Carly seemed to have a growing tendency to get extremely upset over many things. Her angry outbursts and super-sensitivity seemed excessive. I suggested that I introduce Carly and her sister to some sand-play and engage in some conversations with them both in that context.

When the two girls were introduced they were eager to take a turn at playing in the sand tray while their mum did some shopping. Carly's older sister enacted her story with houses, pets and happy people. There were gardens and fences and pets. She had chosen symbols of security and peace. In contrast, Carly engaged more actively, depicting several scenes where wild creatures were prowling. In another scene an angry girl with red hair got dragged out of the way.

Sand-tray work

Carly's mother had described how her own anxieties and anger often overflowed onto her children. She was finding an alternative story of her own, and experiencing what it is like to be free of the triggering repercussions of early trauma.

It is my reflection that even young children can be helped to dampen down legacies of trauma that may be having a dysregulating impact on their behaviour. Sand-play is body based, and it provides a set of safe boundaries within which a child can express and digest runaway emotions and manage unhelpful behavioural impulses (Miller & Boe, 1990).

Lobovits, Epston and Freeman (2000) describe the difficulty children have finding their words when they are emotionally caught up in a problem. The problem shows up in their body language, their facial expression or posture and/or their way of moving and in their behaviour, and they need to be helped to bring the somatic into their awareness. The authors suggest that activities that don't need words, but which demonstrate an adult's acceptance of the child may be the best means of communicating with them at such times.

People of all ages, but especially children, seem to relish creative and symbolic ways of working things out. The sand-play approach relies on the therapist being a respectful presence who attends to the child, while mostly staying out of the way of her process. This kind of attuned and supportive embodied presence has much in common with the interpersonal and collegial stance of narrative practice.

CHAPTER 12 BODY-FOCUSED NARRATIVE THERAPY WITH CHILDREN, ADOLESCENTS AND FAMILIES

Carly obviously enjoyed the sand tray time, but it wasn't something she wanted to talk about during the rest of our time together. As we conversed about school I gave her a page full of stickers asking her to pick a couple that she felt would help me to get to know her better.

Carly chose a sticker with the word 'sensitive' as the descriptor. I recalled that the word had been used of Carly by her parents and that she had (likely) heard it applied to herself.

I asked her what she thought were the best things about this word. Though she seemed surprised at the question she soon had something to say.

> She was the kind who noticed when someone was upset and who went over and helped them. She could be quick to help someone else at school and sometimes at home. Being sensitive meant she was a good help to mum in the kitchen because she had the best sense of smell and taste in the family.

I asked her whether there were other things that sensitive had to say. She talked about getting upset. I asked her for an example and very quickly she had a response.

> She described how she gets scared and starts screaming at circus when the swing goes too high. She said that sometimes she also gets very angry. She feels like hitting people and sometimes she does.

This concentrated our minds on the way sensitive can team up with angry, and have a person lashing out. I asked whether we could give this combination a nickname. Carly decided to call this sensitive-angry combination 'the blow-up monster'. I asked Carly how the blow-up monster affected the family as well as Carly herself.

> Carly said it upset everyone and it made her feel especially bad.

I wondered if she had ever found any ways of getting the blow-up monster off her back.

> She replied that she could do it by going to her room and lying on her bed and reading a book.

I was curious about how she had worked that out?

> She said it had just happened by accident.

I said it sounded as if there were times when she really felt determined to put up a fight against the blow-up monster's power. It may have happened by accident the first time, but I asked her how she thought it had been able to continue. Was it somebody else who made her do it?

> Carly said she just did it herself.

I asked her what it was like to notice the way she took herself to her room on purpose and opened her book?

> She was happy.

197

THE MAGIC LOOM PART TWO - THE PRACTICE

I asked if perhaps we could search together for some other ways of pushing the blow-up monster away that might be worth trying. Were there other things she thought she might be able to do on purpose? Carly immediately began to come up with ideas.

She knew she could do it by playing with the dog. He was so soft and cuddly. Also, she could take him out for a run in the garden.

We talked more about the garden.

Carly told me about the tree house. That was a good place she could go to if she wanted to get away and get herself feeling better.

A witness ceremony

A couple of weeks later, Carly's parents and her older sister came for a conversation and all took turns at becoming an audience for each other. I initiated a narrative externalising practice, which at the same time provided each of them with an embodied and resonating audience.

Each family member took turns naming a problem she or he thought was interfering with how they wanted life to be. They had fun finding appropriate names. The father came up with the name Grumpy Bear.

Everyone talked constructively and made new discoveries. When Carly's turn came, it was significant for her to have her struggles with the blow-up monster witnessed in this way. She talked easily. I could feel how helpful Carly found this democratic and intersubjective family process. Not only was she no longer feeling stuck with a negative label that she couldn't escape, but like everyone else in her family she was able to talk about the various body-based ways she had found to get herself back when problems like a too sensitive factor or the blow-up monster had its effects.

Morgan (in Morgan & White, 2006) says that:

I think of resonance as being a bit like sound waves emanating from a central point and bouncing back and forth as they touch on other objects. Each time they bounce or touch something else they grow stronger or are more easily heard or recognised (p. 111).

This narrative therapist is describing resonance in very physical terms. I found myself thinking back to the resonance I had observed in the interactions between Pearl and Henry and their son Owen. Resonance was further extended as witness statements about Owen were read out, even though the writers weren't present in the therapy room. It was as if a sense of embodied presence was mediated by the documents that were read.

Now I was seeing the same kinds of resonances happening between Carly and the rest of her family as they told their stories and each of their narratives was witnessed directly. For Carly, the sand-play and previous body-focused narrative conversations gave her both the language for and the experience of a story alternative to the one dominant in both her own and her family's lore.

The Magic Loom at work with Carly and her family

In the first conversation, the Co-weaver used sand play to open space for body expressivity for six-year-old Carly and her sister. They both took up the shuttle and wove threads of different colour displaying a sense of emotional safety and some behavioural containment.

The Co-weaver explored the word 'sensitive' with Carly and the opening for thoughtful reflection allowed her to notice its effects. An externalising conversation ensued. In a continued narrative exploration about ways of getting 'the blow-up monster' off her back, Carly wove into the picture some of her own bodily wisdom. Then, as the Co-author asked her what this experience had been like for her, she was again able to use her mind and to weave brightness into her personal fabric. She solidified her ideas about a way forward.

A conversation with Carly's whole family built on the personal one. Primarily opening the conversational space to allow reflections of the mind, the Co-weaver embarked on a more general externalising conversation. Carly was helped, in an implicit embodied engagement, to feel the attuned and resonating impacts of a fully involved audience. She was able to weave a stronger fabric more confidently as a result of this embodied and interpersonal mind-opening narrative approach. She was no doubt benefiting also from the egalitarian nature of the exercise.

Conclusion

The imaginative application of the narrative mode ... strives to put timeless miracle into the particularities of experience. Jerome Bruner

The interpersonal and collegial conversational approach of the narrative therapist undergirds this model and narrative therapy's many other approaches are essential to it. Including a person's body means that several other key threads are woven together with narrative approaches and with each other to create the beautiful and enduring effect of the body-focused narrative approach.

In this conclusion, I explain the main factors, and then, appropriate to the values of this approach, I leave the final word to someone whose voice is often not empowered in our society.

Features of the model

While each feature is effective in its own right, this model owes its transformative power to the synthesis of all of them.

Listening to the body

In exploring the body, the body-focused narrative therapist is simply learning to listen to another voice. She is bringing her attention to a different suite of narratives, those of the body. She comes alongside the other participant in the conversation, bringing with her a readiness to learn to listen to that different voice. She can then help the person to apply her attentive curiosity to any frightening or confusing body signals and then to the narratives cued by her body which have not usually been considered before.

Trauma memories held in the body

Neuroscientists inform us that unresolved aspects of trauma become hidden within a person's somatic memory (van der Kolk, 2006). These memories are not cognitively or narratively retrievable, because at the time of the original trauma, the immediate hormonal impacts on the traumatised child's brain prevented vital neural signals from reaching the higher, sense-making parts of the brain (Perry, 1997; van der Kolk, 2006). The trauma is remembered, not by her rational mind but by her body.

Therefore, when the therapist raises a person's awareness of her body and its narratives, she is helping to make explicit and visible to the person what has long remained implicit and hidden. As a result, the person is enabled to immediately begin to resolve and make sense of both trauma stimuli and traumatic impacts (Rothschild, 2000; van der Kolk, 2006, 2017). It's as if her body gives her back her voice and her mind.

The nature of triggering

Neuroscientists (e.g., Mason, 2014) have also discovered that the brain associates later stress in a person's life with early trauma. The unresolved or undigested trauma memories held in the body are often triggered in the person's ongoing life, and they have the effect of impacting her again with intense and sensory traumatic experience. The person has little way of knowing what her triggered experience signifies. It's as if she is chained to the past without a key to unlock the chains. Fear may negatively cramp her life.

Reactivity in the present is the key indicator

Investigating a person's extreme reactivity while they are having a triggering experience (Damasio, 2000) is the key that unlocks the door to the past. This kind of investigation provides the person with a way of accepting rather than shunning her body.

The therapist invites the person to look inward, which van der Kolk (2006, 2017) claims is of primary importance if a person is to put the trauma behind her. The person's brain has been making automatic associations with the past, but the body-focused narrative therapist uses her curiosity to help the person address the present. She seeks to help her investigate the sensations that are at the heart of her experience of somatic triggering.

Within an explorative narrative-style conversation, the person can immediately begin to change her attitude towards her internal somatic sensations. As these are respected by the therapist, she can gradually accept them herself, instead of instinctively pushing them away or ignoring them. An important narrative approach sees the therapist, throughout the conversation, repeating the questions that encourage the person to reflect on her own experience of what her body is telling her. She uses what narrative practitioners call experience of experience questions.

The focus is on the present

While it takes up an exploration of the person's context and history, this approach is pursued, sometimes in some detail, only as a springboard for the person to find her own preferred ways to move forward and away from any negatively dominant story. The therapeutic direction is always towards a more enlivening present and future. So too the body-focused approach. It is the person's sensations in the present that are given attention, and from there a historical exploration can be undertaken so that the person can generate a better way of living both in the present and into the future.

Intense sensations cue trauma memory

The body-awareness-raising practice that is the *modus operandi* of this integrated methodology has been shown to cue traumatic memory convincingly. Its effectiveness is supported by the theory of somatic markers (Damasio, 2000). The lived evidence presented in the case material supports the idea that triggered sensations cue the kind of memory that is both genuine and of relevance to the person's early trauma. For the cohort whose stories are documented, the idiosyncratic narratives cued by each person's body have proven to be safe to explore. Setting out to explore body-cued narratives has not re-traumatised these people.

The practice of concentrating a person's attention on the intensely aroused somatic sensation/s that most caught her attention at the time of a triggered moment/event fits with the neurological idea (Siegel, 2010) that healing and integration can occur when a person is enabled to re-encounter the intense neural firing of original traumatic stimuli.

I suggest that the intensity of a person's reactivity relates to the levels of anxiety or terror that originally left her traumatised as a child. The same strong affect (emotional presentation) shows up at the centre of the triggered experience. In drawing the person's attention to her body sensations, rather than to her emotions or affect, the therapeutic aim is to awaken the person's curiosity. Focusing on her sensations may help distract (turn) the person from the emotional impacts of terror and intensity. She discovers that the sensations she is feeling in specific places in her body have something important to tell her. She is looking in an alternative direction. Her body's own wisdom provides a way forward. Her respect for her body increases.

Attending to the body increases ability to focus

One of the major effects of early trauma is said to be a difficulty with attending or focusing (van der Kolk, 2017). A surprise finding from an overview of the therapy conversations that have been presented is that attending to the body didn't create difficulties for the participants. They felt safe to explore the narratives that arrived. It appears that the body awareness in direct relation to problematic triggered sensations so captures a person's attention, it's as if she is immediately given an inoculation against fear.

Externalising the trauma problem

The externalising philosophy of narrative approaches is particularly important for the body-focused narrative approach. Simply putting the focus on a person's body helps her externalise the trauma, so that she can start to recognise that she is not the problem. The metaphor of the body as the first responder to early traumatising experience provides the seeds of an alternative view of the body. As the person discovers that in its very reactivity her body is signalling to her, helping her to, as it were, find a safe way across the minefield of the trauma, her attitude towards it is likely to change. When the person's reactivity, which shows up in her sensations, is the factor that cues a relevant trauma memory, the trauma survivor may quickly conclude that her body is of help to her: it was never the problem.

Externalising trauma and its impacts from within the person steers her away from self-blame and away from the continued internalisation of a spoiled identity (White, 2007). As she shifts blame away from herself, and as the body-focused conversation continues, the survivor is helped one step at a time to establish a new narrative, which starts with her fresh respect for her body.

The role of therapeutic curiosity

The body-focused narrative therapist applies her customary curious and investigatory approach to the narratives and wisdom of the person's body. She always does her best to phrase her questions in an open-ended way. The reader may have observed (in the case studies) how the therapist's open curiosity towards the body influenced her conversational partner. The attitude of open-ended curiosity can be thought of as a pre-cursor to the receptivity that Siegel (2010) describes as a crucial state of mind to enable a person to effectively put the impacts of trauma behind her. It allows her to make profound changes in her brain.

Meaning making that changes neural networks

Once memories are cued, the body-focused narrative therapist sets the direction of the enquiry so that the person immediately begins making meaning of the past. As the case studies demonstrate, agency quickly arrives. Open-ended narrative exploration helps the person make such sense of the memories that she can move beyond them, away from what narrative practitioners might describe as a less-than-well-supported performance of identity.

Neuroscientists might say that once memories are set free from their somatic clouding, the therapist helps the person to make use of the higher regions of her brain by using her words and her reflective processes. The child's traumatic experience led to fragmentation: intense emotion and sensation became separated from sense-making. No one helped the child at the time to make sense of intensely traumatising events or to understand that what happened was not her fault. Unhelpful schemas may have taken root within her autobiographical memory (Scaer, 2014). Her body has continued to hold within it undigested emotional and somatic frenzy (Levine, 1997).

The body-focused narrative therapist supports a mind-body partnership. The model not only helps the person recover unlinked material from her implicit somatic memory, but, having made it conscious and explicit, it then helps her to explore and to make useful meaning from it.

A protocol of mindfulness

Neuroscientists consider that a protocol of mindfulness is essential for a therapy to help a person to fully integrate unwieldy trauma material into her life autobiography (Siegel, 2000). This protocol is central to the body-focused narrative approach.

Different words are sometimes used to describe mindfulness. What may be novel in this methodology is that mindfulness is used to directly address sensations. A person's sensations, rather than her emotions or thoughts, provide a tangible or concrete focus on which she can easily fasten her attention. As well as noticing sensations in a mindful manner, the conversational participant can examine her attitudes of mind towards her sensations, and can consider exchanging attitudes that are routinely judgmental or dismissive for kinder ones.

The emphasis on kindness often carves out an exception to the norm, and this clearly becomes pivotal. The case studies provide evidence that as a person learns to address her sensations with greater compassion, this kindness can generalise further. Offering her sensations greater kindness and acceptance helps her to renegotiate the esteem in which she holds herself in general, and she is likely to begin to perform an entirely new sense of identity. She is encouraged to find soothing practices within her own life experience or to experiment mindfully with a wide range of body strategies in order to modulate the reactivity with which she is struggling. This is one of the ways in which the therapy model is integrally and repeatedly providing the early trauma survivor with the opportunity to use her own mindful capacity to bring about changes to her brain (Doidge, 2015).

Body and mind narratives are interwoven

In this model, the language-based conversational scaffolding familiar in narrative practice always ushers the body into the therapy conversation. It provides a good template for how to help the person to listen to her body. The metaphor of weaving describes how seamlessly the conversation can be scaffolded so that the body can easily be moved into the forefront or into the background of each therapy conversation. A body narrative relevant to her early trauma is often cued by a person's body, and a language focus is immediately scaffolded in once again so that the trauma story can be meaningfully explored. Later the body-focused conversational scaffolding enables the person to explore the many resources of the body, which can be of help to her in modulating trauma's most intensely arousing or dissociative impacts (van der Kolk, 2006). In some instances traumatic arousal is so overwhelming in a life that the exploration of calming body resources needs to be given primary importance.

Integrating mind and body experience

When the therapist shines a light on the way a person can calm intense impacts of trauma (her triggered sensations) using the resources of her body, this expands curiosity and opens the person to a great deal of experimentation. She can investigate her own wise and familiar resources, but also trial less familiar ones in order to gain mastery over the triggering experiences that have been re-traumatising her. In this way, she can explore the resources and the wisdom of her body to complement those of her mind.

The third phase of the body scaffolding then helps the person distance herself even further from trauma's uncomfortable impacts. Measuring the intensity of her sensations before and after applying a body resource, exploring metaphor, making use of a mantra or practising meditation are all activities through which she can engage her body and her mind almost concurrently. All this exploration is likely to help her increase the mind-body flexibility that is characteristic of good internal regulation and to make it possible for her to build a more life-affirming self-narrative.

Unique contexts of trauma emphasised

The injury of early trauma is always unique to the developmental stage, personality and family context of each child. Scientific findings emphasise the importance of helping each person explore her own context (Perry, 1997; van der Kolk, 2006). The therapist needs somehow to reach the person's body in a way that relates to the original injury, so that the particularised context is addressed (Hanson, 2017; Siegel, 2010). I maintain that the way a body narrative is cued in this model makes this possible. Evidence for the usefulness of sensations is borne out in the case material.

De-centred narrative approaches put as much emphasis on context as the science does. The narrative practitioner is trained to always help a person explore the context and history of the narratives which are personal to herself and to her circumstances.

Exploring responses to trauma as the catalyst for change

The body-cued narratives display how and why a dominant story developed. Becoming aware of just how the early trauma caused her to internalise negative identity conclusions can allow a person to bifurcate (head off in a different direction). When a child's responses (the second story of trauma) are also made visible within her resurrected narratives, these responses can go a long way to alter her perception of herself. Attending to the second story of trauma has been long recognised by narrative practitioners as agentive. Some neuroscientists (e.g., Meares, 2016) suggest that too often the nature of the trauma itself has unhelpfully preoccupied both the survivor and the therapist. Instead, when a person is helped to examine her body narrative and her responses within that story, and is then helped to scrutinise her life values, she discovers a story of consistency over time that is immediately enlivening (White, 2011).

CONCLUSION

Exceptions become pivotal

Narrative practitioners are alert for news of difference and for moments that are pivotal. The evidence of the case studies is that when a person becomes aware of her recently aroused sensations, and a body narrative is cued, she is immediately turned away from the subjugating power of the trauma. She is quickly able to use the research capacity of her mind to begin to make sense of what was hidden before. The narrative approach helps her to use her body's wisdom, and she very quickly pivots towards making peace with extremely disruptive internal sensations (van der Kolk, 2006). Narratively she has begun a re-authoring process. Exceptions lead to the construction of a preferred alternative narrative.

Cultivating dual awareness and greater internal unity

Almost every adult contributor to this book highlighted ways in which her feelings of isolation contributed to her sense of trauma. As the holistic process pivoted a participant away from her earlier entrenched self-blame and disgust, it often turned her in the direction of a healing dual-awareness (Rothschild, 2000). Her body-cued memory invited each person to observe her earlier experience. We saw repeatedly how this led to an experience of greater internal unity. One part of herself was no longer fighting or judging another part.

Hannah talked of a different split. She felt intellectually strong but powerless when it came to the emotional reactivity she experienced. It was as if her mind and her body were at odds with each other. Dual awareness helped heal this too. With greater self-understanding and the modulation of emotional intensity, intellect and emotion also came together. Body-focused narrative approaches made the exploration possible. Like others, she learned to apply a similar kindness to her child-self as she regularly gave her own children.

Relational approaches reduce isolation

Narrative approaches help a person to explore and helpfully recognise the influence of significant witnesses to her life. The provision of a resonating audience can have an intensely healing impact. Such interpersonal approaches equate with the somatic concept of anchoring (Rothschild, 2000). By inviting a person simply to talk about a person whose presence has proved calming or enlivening in the past, the person's imaginative resources help her to modulate her triggered distress and reactivity. These relational approaches all play a part in helping the person to move away from the isolation that trauma has regularly reinforced. When she explores the significance of the effect she has had on others in her past, her agency increases as well.

Empathy is required for healing

It is only in a safe environment or a safe therapy relationship that a person is likely to find healing or to be able to resolve complex developmental trauma (Perry, 1999). Therapy becomes a healing experience when the person feels truly connected to the therapist by genuine empathy. The relationship needs to approximate to the healthy attachment relationship that every infant needs at the start of life (Schore, 2003). Siegel (2010) considers that when this occurs, the survivor learns to feel that she is no longer alone, and develops the sense that she exists in the mind of the therapist.

Attunement creates safety

In this book, I have evidenced congruency between narrative and somatic approaches to therapy in regard to the provision of safety. Both types of therapy, as discussed earlier, have a de-centred approach that puts the person seeking therapy at the centre. They engage with respectful and close collegiality and offer intersubjective space in which the survivor experiences genuine equality and the sense that she is regarded as the expert on her own life and body.

In the body-focused narrative therapy model, weight is given to the fact that there are always at least two bodies in the room, and that communication through body-language may be even more important than the words spoken. When a person senses that the therapist is tuned in to her body (psychobiological attunement), her implicit sense of safety is enhanced. Then as the therapist scaffolds her enquiry in the direction of the wisdom of the survivor's body, the sense of respect for her body grows. White (2011) highlights the importance of the provision of healing resonance within the collegial conversation. So that the person will pick up the resonances, he counsels the therapist to continuously orient herself towards the person: to her narrative-telling, her ideas, her values, her initiatives and her responses.

Identity construction reviewed

Some trauma therapies seem to ignore the impacts of trauma on a person's identity. This is an important theme of every narrative re-authoring process. As the case conversations make plain, investigations of the body contribute positively to fulfilling the therapeutic task to which White (2006) draws attention:

> When traumatic memories intrude into everyday consciousness ... this uncoupling of consciousness contributes to a dismantling of a familiar sense of self that has continuity across time ... the primary therapeutic task is the reinvigoration and redevelopment of the memory system called the stream of consciousness, in the instatement/reinstatement of a 'sense of myself' (p. 75).

The contributors in the case studies made various changes in identity construction as a consequence of coming to accept the wisdom of their bodies. Narrative philosophy reinforces that identity is a social construction. As isolation is diminished, trauma's impacts are simultaneously defeated, and identity development is freed up. This has a great deal in common with the understandings of the polyvagal theory, which links nervous system processes with behaviour and relationship development (Porges, 2011).

Kinaesthetic and vestibular systems contribute to recovery

Perry (1999) contends that addressing early brain dysregulation by using repetitive somatic intervention can help the brain become more regulated from the implicit bottom up. In a small number of the documented therapy conversations, I extended the model's body focus to include a rocking intervention. Each survivor, who engaged relationally while also listening respectfully to the kinaesthetic or vestibular systems of her body, went on to describe a corresponding healing thrust in cognitive, behavioural, emotional and relational directions that is not easy to dismiss.

Survivors initiate re-authoring

I have described how often I have been surprised at the speedy responses made by the conversational participants with whom I've worked. When the person begins to become more aware of her sensations, she often starts to initiate re-authoring processes and to actively move herself forward in regulating, resolving and transformative directions. Sometimes the initiatives relate to her associations and relational influences. She is choosing to nourish a new and developing sense of self, and does so by making changes in her relationship web. In these different ways, she demonstrates outcomes that authors such as van der Kolk (2006) suggest a therapist can expect if a person is helped to look inward with safety. The initiative taking, particularly in social behaviour, is also exactly what Porges (2004) predicts as spontaneous because it is "a natural emergent property of the better cortical regulation of the brainstem structures involved in the Social Engagement System of the nervous system" (p. 24).

The body-focused narrative therapist is always at hand to help the person notice and consolidate the stands she is taking. She helps the person to continue to explore and to thicken even further her new identity and narrative formulations. Her initiative taking and the stands she prefers to make arguably indicate that she has already moved away from the fight, flight or freeze mobilising and immobilising extremes of the more primitive parts of her brain and nervous system, and that she is functioning according to her more highly evolved social engagement biology (Porges, 2011). She is setting herself free from trauma's dysregulating impacts and is both re-authoring the narrative she prefers to live out of and experimenting with embodying a new life narrative in the world she inhabits.

Weaving a rich fabric of newness is the healing potential of the body-focused narrative approach.

Philip advocates for the model

Like other participants whose stories have been woven through this book, Philip, a homeless man, has become an advocate for the body-based narrative therapy model described in this book. This is his story.

> *One day recently, he became extremely overwhelmed and anxious. He knew the feeling well. A guy had pushed and shoved him when he was standing in a food queue and minding his own business. He had not invited the aggression in any way. Once he escaped from the line and felt*

safer, he took stock of his body. He remembered how it had sort of collapsed in on itself. He noticed how his chest was hunched and his shoulders slumped. His back ached. His jaw was tight.

Philip took action. He straightened up his spine. His ribcage lifted and his breathing, which had become quite shallow, began to slow down and to deepen. He took some deep breaths. Already he felt better. He lifted his chin higher and noticed that he wasn't holding his jaw so tight. He deliberately put his shoulders back and felt his chest expanding even further. His legs no longer felt like jelly, his stomach wasn't churning.

Tightening his thigh muscles, Philip remembered a meditation we had focused on one day. He moved his legs about thirty centimetres apart and pushed his feet onto the ground like a well-rooted tree. As he dwelt on that image he could feel his resilience returning and strength flowing back. No wind could uproot his tree. Over a couple of hours, he returned to this stance several times and was delighted that the anxiety wasn't taking hold as it usually did.

Reflecting on the incident later still, he realised that it had triggered memories of how his father used to beat him when he was drunk. Philip never did anything to bring these beatings on, just as he hadn't invited the guy in the queue to attack him. He just happened to be the one who was there. Now he repeated a self-nurturing mantra he had made his own. "No wonder I felt like I did! When that guy pushed and shoved me today, it took me back to when I was very young and completely powerless against my father. It was tough being me when I was little. I never deserved what Dad shovelled out."

Now he felt confidence flow in. He hadn't over-reacted. He knew to keep out of that fellow's way in future. He was obviously a person with some problems of his own!

Philip realised that he was feeling freer. He was mastering his triggers. They didn't overwhelm him like they used to. He knew how to clarify their meanings and to put them into the past where they belonged. He experienced a sense of mastery and empowerment. He found he could let the incident go. He didn't have to keep mulling on it, over and over. Like his childhood trauma, it was in the past.

References

Amanti, M., & Gallese, V. (2014). *The birth of intersubjectivity: Psychodynamics, neurobiology, and the self.* New York, NY: W. W. Norton.

Amini, F., Lewis, T., Lannon, R., Louie, A., Baumbacher, G., McGuinness, T., & Schiff, E. Z. (1996). Affect, attachment, memory: contributions toward psychobiologic integration. *Psychiatry, 59*(3), 213–39.

Australian Childhood Foundation. (2011). *Polyvagal theory and its implications for traumatised students.* Smart Discussion Paper 18.

Australian College of Contemporary Somatic Psychotherapy. (2017). *Contemporary somatic psychotherapy.* Retrieved from **www.somaticpsychotherapy.com.au**

Barlow, J. (*n. d.*). *Workshops.* Australian Institute for Contemporary Somatic Psychotherapy. Retrieved from **www.somaticpsychotherapy.com.au/index.php?option=com_content&task=view&id=43&itemid=39**

Beebe, B., Knoblauch, S., Rustin, J., & Sorter, D. (2005). *Forms of intersubjectivity in infant research and adult treatment.* New York, NY: Other Press.

Berne, E. (1961). *Transactional analysis in psychotherapy.* New York, NY: Grove.

Berntsen, D. (2009). *Involuntary autobiographical memories: An introduction to the unbidden past.* Cambridge, England: Cambridge University Press.

Bogdan, G. (1986). Do families really need problems? *Family Therapy Networker, 10,* 30–35.

Bower, G. H., & Sivers, H. (1998). Cognitive impact of traumatic events. *Development and Psychopathology, 10*(4), 625–653.

Bowlby, J. (1988). *A secure base: Clinical applications of attachment theory.* Abingdon, England: Routledge.

Bruner, J. (1986). *Actual minds, possible worlds.* Cambridge, MA: Harvard University Press.

Cambridge Body Psychotherapy Centre. (*n.d.*). *Training in body psychotherapy.* Retrieved from **www.cbpc.org.uk/bodytrain.htm**

Caplis, C. F. (2014). *Feasibility and perceived efficacy of the neurosequential model of therapeutics.* Keene, NH: Antioch University Press.

Chitty, J. (2013). *Dancing with yin and yang: Ancient wisdom, modern psychotherapy and Randolph Stone's polarity therapy.* Boulder, CO: Polarity Press.

Condon, W. (1975) Multiple Responses to Sound in Dysfunctional Children. *Journal of Autism and Childhood Schizophrenia,* Vol.5, No.1.

Damasio, A. R. (1994). *Descartes' error: Emotion, reason and the human brain.* New York, NY: Putnam.

Damasio, A. R. (1999). *The feeling of what happens: Body and emotion in the making of consciousness.* London, England: Vintage Books.

Damasio, A. R., Damasio, H., Bechara, A., & Tranel, A. R. (1997). Deciding advantageously before knowing the advantageous strategy. *Science, 275,* 1293–1294.

Denborough, D. (2007). The team of life approach. Retrieved from **http://dulwichcentre.com.au/team-of-life/**

Denborough, D. (2014). Recent developments in narrative responses to social suffering. Retrieved from **www.dulwichcentre.com.au**

Doidge, N. (2015). *The brain's way of healing: Stories of remarkable recoveries and discoveries.* Melbourne, Australia: Scribe Publications.

Duval, J., & Béres, L. (2011). *Innovations in narrative therapy: Connecting practice, training, and research.* New York, NY: W. W. Norton.

Epston, D., Freeman, J., & Lobovits, D. (1997). *Playful approaches to serious problems: Narrative therapy with children and their families.* New York, NY: W.W. Norton.

Epston, D. (2000). *The history of the archives of Resistance-Anti-anorexia/Anti-bulimia.* Retrieved from **http://www.narrativeapproaches.com/%20folder/history.htm** You will find this reference in **Our archives** at top of page labelled **Narrative approaches** if **page not found** comes up. Epston, D. (2000).

Fisher, R. M. (2001). Working experientially and somatically with couples. In B. J. Brothers (Ed.), *Couples and body therapy* (pp. 91–106). Binghamton, NY: The Haworth Press.

Fivush, R. (2011). The development of autobiographical memory. *Annual Review of Psychology, 62,* 559–582.

Ford, C. W. (1993). *Compassionate touch: The body's role in emotional healing and recovering.* Berkeley, CA: North Atlantic Books.

Foucault, M. (1977). *Discipline and punishment: The birth of the prison.* London, England: Penguin.

Foucault, M. (1980). Truth and power. In C. Gordon (Ed.), *Power/knowledge: Selected interviews and other writings 1972–1977* (pp. 109–133). Hemel Hempstead, England: Harvester Wheatsheaf.

Freedberg, D., & Gallese, V. (2007). Motion, emotion and empathy in esthetic experience. *Trends in Cognitive Sciences, 11*(5), 197–203.

Freedman, J., & Combs, G. (1993). Invitations to new stories: Using questions to explore alternative possibilities. In S. Gilligan & R. Price (Eds.), *Therapeutic conversations* (pp. 291–303). New York, NY: W. W. Norton.

Freedman, J., & Combs, G. (2002). *Narrative therapy with couples ... and a whole lot more! A collection of papers, essays and exercises.* Adelaide, Australia: Dulwich Centre Publications.

Frese, L. (2002, November 10). *Learning for sustainable living: Swaying.* Workshop held as part of Experiential training program: Adding a body focus to counselling practice, Gosford, New South Wales, Australia.

Gallese, V. (2007). Before and below 'theory of mind': Embodied simulation and the neural correlates of social cognition. *Philosophical transactions of the Royal Society of London. Series B, Biological sciences, 362*(1480), 659–669.

Gillet, G., & Franz, E. (2013). John Hughlings Jackson: Bridging theory and clinical observation. *The Lancet, 16*(381), 528–529.

Hanson, R. (2017). Commentary on B. A. van der Kolk (webinar), *How to target treatment to help patients reclaim their lives after trauma. Part 1: How to help clients break the cycle of traumatic memory.* Retrieved from **http://www.nicabm.com/vdk-trauma/confirmed/?/0**

REFERENCES

Hatfield, E. & Rapson, R. (1993). Love and attachment processes. In M. Lewis and J.M. Haviland (Eds.), *Handbook of Emotions* (pp.595-605), New York: The Guildford Press.

Heller, M. (2012). *Body psychotherapy: History, concepts, and methods*. New York, NY: W.W. Norton.

James, W. (1890/1950). The principles of psychology. Mineola, NY: Dover Publications.

Keleman, S. (1975). *Your body speaks its mind*. Berkeley, CA: Center Press.

Kelly, C. (2010). Development of mental health first aid guidelines on how a member of the public can support a person affected by a traumatic event: A Delphi study. *BMC Psychiatry, 10*(49).

Kezelman, C., & Stavropoulos, P. (2012). *The last frontier: Practice guidelines for treatment of complex trauma and trauma-informed care and service delivery*. Sydney, Australia: BLUE KNOT FOUNDATION. Formerly Adults Surviving Child Abuse (ASCA). See **https://www.blueknot.org.au/Portals/2/Practice%20Guidelines/ Blue%20Knot%20Foundation%20Guidelines_WEB_Final.pdf**

Kihlstrom, J. F. (2005). *Trauma and memory revisited*. Paper presented at the 6th Tsukuba International Conference on Memory: Memory and Emotion, March 15, 2005, University of California, Berkeley, USA.

LaCombe, P. (2014). *Stress response cycle* (video). Retrieved from **https://prezi.com/bvymx5la8lap/stress-response-cycle/**

Lagattuta, K. H., & Wellman, H. M. (2001). Thinking about the past: Early knowledge about links between prior experience, thinking, and emotion. *Child Development, 72*(1), 82–100.

Laub, D., & Auerhahn, N. (1993). Knowing and not knowing massive psychic trauma: Forms of traumatic memory. *International Journal of Psychoanalysis, 74*, 287–302.

LeDoux, J. E., & Gorman, J. M. (2001). A call to action: Overcoming anxiety through active coping. *The American Journal of Psychiatry, 12*, 1953–1955.

Levine, P. (with A. Frederick). (1997). *Waking the tiger: Healing trauma*. Berkeley, CA California: North Atlantic Books.

Madigan, S. (1996). The politics of identity: Considering community discourse in the externalizing of internalized problem conversations. *Journal of Systemic Therapies, 15*, 47–62.

Madigan, S. (2010). *Narrative therapy*. Washington, DC: American Psychological Association.

Masarik-Williams, E., Polizzi, T., & Punshon, S. (2016*). Sensory modulation and trauma informed care with adults*. Workshop presented at Washington Occupational Therapy Association Conference, Washington DC, USA.

Mason, P. (2014). *Understanding the brain: The neurobiology of everyday life*. University of Chicago. Course available at **https://www.coursera.org/learn/neurobiology**

Meares, R. (2016). *The poet's voice in the making of mind*. New York, NY: Routledge.

Miller, C., & Boe, J. (1990). Tears into diamonds: Transformation of child psychic trauma through sandplay and storytelling. *The Arts in Psychotherapy, 17*(3), 247–257.

Morgan, A. (2000). *What is narrative therapy? An easy-to-read introduction*. Adelaide, Australia: Dulwich Centre Publications.

Morgan, A., & White, M. (2006). *Narrative therapy with children and their families*. Adelaide, Australia: Dulwich Centre Publications.

Myerhoff, B. (1986). Life not death in Venice: Its second life. In Turner, V. W. & Bruner, E. M. (Eds.), *The anthropology of experience* (pp.261–285). Chicago: IL: University of Illinois Press.

Newman, D. (2010). Using narrative practices with anxiety and depression: Elevating context, joining people, and collecting insider-knowledges. *The International Journal of Narrative Therapy and Community Work 2*, 22–29.

Ogden, P. (2015). *Sensorimotor psychotherapy: Interventions for trauma and attachment.* New York, NY: W. W. Norton.

Ogden, P. (2016, June 9). Movement sequences and personality development: A psychology of action. Workshop at the International Child Trauma Conference, Melbourne, Australia.

Ogden, P., & Fisher, J. (2015). *Sensorimotor psychotherapy: Interventions for trauma and attachment.* New York, NY: W. W. Norton.

Ogden, P., & Minton, K. (2000). Sensorimotor psychotherapy: One method for processing traumatic memory. *Traumatology, 6*(3), 149–167.

Perry, B. D. (1999). Memories of Fear: How the brain stores and retrieves traumatic experiences. In J. Goodwin & R. Attias (Eds.), *Splintered reflections: Images of the body in trauma* (pp. 9–38). New York, NY: Basic Books.

Perry, B. (2006). Applying principles of neurodevelopment to clinical work with maltreated and traumatized children: The neurosequential model of therapeutics. In N. B. Webb, (Ed.). *Working with traumatized youth in Child Welfare* (pp. 27–50). New York, NY: Guildford Press.

Porges, S. W. (2004). Neuroception: A subconscious system for detecting threats and safety. *Zero to Three, 24*(5), 19–24.

Porges, S. W. (2011). *Polyvagal theory: Neurophysiological foundations of emotions, attachment, communication, self-regulation.* New York, NY: W. W. Norton.

Richards, K. (2011). Children's exposure to domestic violence in Australia. *Trends & Issues in Crime and Criminal Justice, 419*. Retrieved from **www.aic.gov.au/media_library/publications/tandi_pdf/tandi419.pdf**

Rose, R. (2005). *Life story therapy with traumatized children: A model for practice.* London, England: Jessica Kingsley Publishers.

Rothschild, B. (2000). *The body remembers: The psychophysiology of trauma and trauma treatment.* New York, NY: W. W. Norton.

Rothschild, B. (2004). *The body remembers casebook: Unifying methods and models in the treatment of trauma and PTSD.* New York, NY: W. W. Norton.

Rothschild, B. (2010). *8 keys to safe trauma recovery. Take-charge strategies to empower your healing.* New York, NY: W. W. Norton.

Sacks, O. (1989). *Seeing voices: A journey into the world of the deaf.* Oakland, CA: University of California Press.

Scaer, R. (2014). *The dissociation capsule.* Presentation at Complex Trauma and the Neurophysiology of Healing Conference, Zurich, Switzerland. Retrieved from **www.traumasoma.com/excerpt1.html**

Schore, A. N. (1994). *Affect regulation and the origin of the self.* New York, NY: W.W. Norton.

Schore, A. N. (2003). *Affect regulation and the repair of the self*. New York, NY: W. W. Norton.

Schore, A. N. (2004) *Affect dysregulation and disorders of the self*. New York, NY: W.W. Norton.

Schroeter, V. (*n. d.*). Polyvagal theory: Introduction for somatic psychotherapy. Retrieved from **http://www. earlychildhoodmentalhealth-sandiego.com/wp-content/uploads/2016/09/C-3-Handout_V-Schroeter_Polyvagal-.pdf**

Seikkula, J., & Trimble, D. (2005). Healing elements of therapeutic conversation: Dialogue as an embodiment of love. *Family Process, 44*(4), 461–475.

Shachar, R. (2010). Combining relaxation and guided imagery with narrative practices in therapy with an incest survivor. *International Journal of Narrative Therapy and Community Work, 1*, 33–55.

Siegel, D. J. (2006). Series editor's foreword (p. xv). In P. Ogden & K. Minton K. (Eds.), *Trauma and the body: A sensorimotor approach to psychotherapy*. New York NY: W. W. Norton.

Siegel, D. J. (2010). *Mindsight: Change your brain and your life*. Victoria, Australia: Scribe Publications.

Sotheren, D. (2002). *Experiential training program: Adding a body focus to counselling practice*. Workshops on 21–22 July, 10–11 August, 14–15 September, 12–13 October and 9–10 November at Gosford, New South Wales, Australia.

Streeck-Fischer, A., & van der Kolk, B. A. (2000). Down will come baby, cradle and all: Diagnostic and therapeutic implications of chronic trauma on child development. *Australian and New Zealand Journal of Psychiatry, 34*(6), 903–918.

Stuebe, E. (2009). *A Schore thing*. Australian Institute for Contemporary Somatic Psychotherapy. Retrieved from **www.somaticpsychotherapy.com.au/index.php?option=com_content&task=view&id=43&Itemid=39**

van der Kolk, B. A. (1994). The body keeps the score: Memory and the evolving psychobiology of posttraumatic stress. *Harvard Review of Psychiatry, 1*, 253–265.

van der Kolk, B. A. (2002). Trauma and memory. *Psychiatry and Clinical Neurosciences, 52*(51), S52–S64.

van der Kolk, B. A. (2006). Clinical implications of neuroscience research in PTSD. *Annals of the New York Academy of Sciences, 1071*, 277–293.

van der Kolk, B. A. (2017). *How to target treatment to help patients reclaim their lives after trauma*. Online course accessed at **http://www.nicabm.com/trauma-treatmentwithbesselvanderkolk/info/**

Watson, L. A., & Berntsen, D. (Eds). (2015). *Clinical perspectives on autobiographical memory*. Cambridge, England: Cambridge University Press.

White, M. (1997). *Narratives of therapists' lives*. Adelaide, Australia: Dulwich Centre Publications.

White, M. (2004). *Narrative practice and exotic lives: Resurrecting diversity in everyday life*. Adelaide, Australia: Dulwich Centre Publications.

White, M. (2006). Working with people who are suffering the consequences of multiple trauma: A narrative perspective. In D. Denborough, (Ed.), *Trauma: Narrative responses to traumatic experience* (pp. 25–84). Adelaide, South Australia: Dulwich Centre Publications.

White, M. (2007). *Maps of narrative practice*. Adelaide, Australia: Dulwich Centre Publications.

White, M. (2011). *Narrative practice: Continuing the conversations*. New York, NY: W. W. Norton.

THE MAGIC LOOM

Epigraph Sources

Introduction
Damasio, A. R. (1994). *Descartes' error: Emotion, reason and the human brain*. New York, NY: Putnam (p. 88).

Chapter 1
Madigan, S. (1996). The politics of identity: Considering community discourse in the externalizing of internalized problem conversations. *Journal of Systemic Therapies, 15*, 47–62 (p. 47).

Chapter 2
Ford, C. W. (1993). Compassionate touch: The body's role in emotional healing and recovering. Berkeley, CA: North Atlantic Books (p. 106).

Chapter 3
van der Kolk, B. A. (1996). Trauma and memory. In B. A. van der Kolk, A. C. McFarlane & L. Weisaeth (Eds.), *Traumatic stress: The effects of overwhelming experience on the mind, body, and society*. New York, NY: Guildford Press (p. 296).

Chapter 4
Siegel, D. J. (2010). *Mindsight: Change your brain and your life*. Victoria, Australia: Scribe Publications (p. 148).

Chapter 5
Rothschild, B. (2000). *The body remembers: The psychophysiology of trauma and trauma treatment*. New York, NY: W. W. Norton (p. 160).

Chapter 6
White, M. (2006). Working with people who are suffering the consequences of multiple trauma: A narrative perspective. In D. Denborough, (Ed.), *Trauma: Narrative responses to traumatic experience* (pp. 25–84). Adelaide, South Australia: Dulwich Centre Publications (p. 74).

Chapter 7
Morgan, A. (2000). *What is narrative therapy? An easy-to-read introduction*. Adelaide, Australia: Dulwich Centre Publications (p. 119).

Chapter 8
Damasio, A. R. (1999). *The feeling of what happens: Body and emotion in the making of consciousness*. London, England: Vintage Books (p. 285).

Chapter 9
White, M. (2007). *Maps of narrative practice*. Adelaide, Australia: Dulwich Centre Publications (p. 28).

Chapter 10
Keleman, S. (1975). *Your body speaks its mind*. Berkeley, CA: Center Press (p. 115).

Chapter 11
Van Nuys, D. (2015). Brain, mind, and body in the healing of trauma: Dr David Van Nuys interviews Bessel van der Kolk, MD. *The Neuropsychotherapist, 12* (p. 28).

Chapter 12
Keleman, S. (1975). *Your body speaks its mind*. Berkeley, CA: Center Press (p. 55).

Conclusion
Bruner, J. (1986). *Actual minds, possible worlds*. Cambridge, MA: Harvard University Press (p. 13).

About the Author

Heather McClelland, (BA Dip Ed. Dip PS, Dip Soc Health), is a native of Australia who has lived and worked in New Guinea and Bangladesh, as well as in major cities and regional areas in her home country. She loves her varied roles as therapist, writer, long-term partner, mother and grandmother. Heather now resides in a village in the north of NSW and as well as continuing her private therapy practice she enjoys her community and developing her art, supporting refugees and being able to work directly with Bangladeshi women finding their way out of poverty.

Heather has had a varied career, beginning as a secondary school teacher, becoming ordained in the church when that was a difficult path for women and functioning as a therapist for thirty years in disparate settings including among homeless men and street sex-workers. Her post graduate studies equipped her as a practitioner of narrative approaches to therapy and experiential somatic training enabled her to make her practice more holistic.

Heather's clinical work has taught her that survivors of early trauma move forward in their lives when their awareness of body and mind can be woven together in collegial conversations. In her writing she prioritises the voices of those for whom these therapy approaches has made a difference. She has discovered amazing synchronicity between the findings of science with regard to recovery from the long-term consequences of early trauma and what participants in her therapy conversations have shared with her.

Heather has previously given prominence to stories written by survivors of early trauma by creating and publishing two books: *The Almond Tree: Child sexual abuse and the church* (1988) and *Holy Topsy-Turvydom: Australian Stories of Trauma* (2003).

CPSIA information can be obtained
at www.ICGtesting.com
Printed in the USA
LVHW102201110121
676251LV00041B/697